Phil Bennett

THE AUTOBIOGRAPHY

Phil Bennett

THE AUTOBIOGRAPHY

with Graham Thomas

Best Wishes

Phil Bennett

CollinsWillow

An Imprint of HarperCollinsPublishers

First published in Great Britain in 2003 by
CollinsWillow
an imprint of HarperCollins*Publishers*
London

Copyright © Phil Bennett 2003

9 8 7 6 5 4 3 2 1

A CIP catalogue record for this book is
available from the British Library

The HarperCollins website address is:
www.fireandwater.com

ISBN 0-00-715063-6

Set in Linotype Sabon by Rowland Phototypesetting Ltd,
Bury St Edmunds, Suffolk

Printed and bound by Clays Ltd, St Ives plc

PICTURE ACKNOWLEDGEMENTS

AUTHORS PRIVATE COLLECTION: 1, 2, 7(tl), 8(cr).
ALLSPORT/GETTY IMAGES: 3(b), 4, 5(br), 6(t & cr),
7(b), 9(tr), 10(cr & b), 11(t & cl), 12(cr), 13(tr), 14(t).
CLIVE ROWLANDS/GOMER PRESS: 8(bl).
EMPICS: 3(cr), 7(tr), 8(tr), 12(tl), 15(tr), 16.
HUW EVANS PICTURE AGENCY: 3(cl), 6(cl & br),
8(cl), 9(cl), 11(cr), 12(bl), 12(tl), 14(tr & b), 15(c & br).
POPPERFOTO: 5(cl), 9(br), 10(t), 11(bl), 13(br).
WESTERN MAIL & ECHO: 3(t), 5(t).

Statistics by Stuart Farmer at Media Services

To my wife, Pat, and my sons, Steven and James.

Contents

Acknowledgements   viii

1   A Grand Day Out   1
2   The Lost Years   12
3   The Impossible Job   29
4   Guided by the Great Redeemer   52
5   Brown Envelopes, Whites Lies   68
6   The World in Union   84
7   In to Africa   107
8   Leading the Lions   126
9   Australia Rules   144
10   Vive L'Europe!   156
11   Scarlet Fever   172
12   Scarlet Thread   193
13   The Top Ten   208
14   Legends   232
15   My Favourite Fifteen   252
16   Day Jobs and Night Terrors   269
17   A Final Plea   284

Career Statistics   297
Index   307

Acknowledgements

Phil and Graham would like to thank the following people for their help, support and encouragement along the way:
John Williams and Felinfoel Primary School staff, Mervyn Bowen and Coleshill Secondary Modern School staff, Llanelli Schoolboys coaches and teachers, Felinfoel RFC, Felinfoel Cricket Club, Llanelli RFC players, coaches, committee members and supporters, and everyone else who helped me live the dream of beating the All Blacks: Bob and Mary Bennett, Les and Myrtle Jones, Pat, James and Steven, Terry and Mary Jones, Wendy and Keith John, Tracey and Leigh Francis, Oliver Bennett, Thomas John and Esther Guy, John, Carol and Dave Lloyd, Huw and Carol Owen, Wynford and Pat Thomas, Maldwyn Griffith, Malcolm Hamer, Ian Jones and staff at the recreation and sports department of Carmarthenshire County Council, Leon and Vanessa Lyons, Veris and Geoff 'The Barber' Sherlock, Nigel Walker and everyone at BBC Wales, the sports desk staff of *The Sunday Mirror*, David Evans and staff at the *South Wales Evening Post*, Tarda Davison-Aitkins and all at HarperCollins, Nick Fawcett, Stuart Farmer, Huw Evans, Margaret Haggerty, Catherine Thomas, Ted, Martha and Isabelle Thomas, Dewi and Shirley Thomas.

CHAPTER 1

A Grand Day Out

There were no tears, no long, lingering, last looks back down the tunnel. There were no laps of honour, not even a trophy. Neither were there any emotional farewell speeches in the dressing room. I paused for a moment as I walked towards the dressing-room door, but that was just to catch my breath. I was exhausted. But I was also the happiest and most relieved I had ever felt in a Welsh jersey. We had beaten France and I had led my country to a Grand Slam.

I'd run off the field. Not because it was my last game for Wales, but because I always ran off the field when I was captain to make sure I could shake hands with the opposition skipper. The noise was deafening. There were supporters running every-where with wild faces, trying to grab players as they made their way to the dressing rooms. I found Jean-Pierre Bastiat, shook his hand, and he congratulated us before I rushed towards the tunnel. We had done it, I thought. I was tired, my body ached and my head was pounding. But I felt no real pain – just pleasure and huge, huge relief.

I walked into our dressing room and the players I had been alongside for the best part of a decade followed after me – JPR Williams, Gareth Edwards, JJ Williams, Ray Gravell, Bobby Windsor, Derek Quinnell and Terry Cobner. They all looked as I felt, utterly exhausted but content. I walked over to Gareth and told him quietly, 'That's it. That's my last game. It's been a privilege and a pleasure to play with you, Gar.' He smiled. 'Bloody hell,' he said. 'You're getting out, too. That's my lot as well.' Typical Edwards, he always produced the unexpected whenever anyone else threatened to steal the headlines. Both of us had spent the week reaching the same conclusion. It was time to go. But we thought we were alone in those decisions; neither of us suspected the other had resolved to do the same.

I had come to my decision after our previous game, in Dublin where we had beaten Ireland at Lansdowne Road to win the Triple Crown. It was the triple Triple. Three times in a row we had claimed the Triple Crown, but this was by far the hardest, the most demanding.

I had started the 1977–78 season too soon, but that was all the fault of Prince Charles. In the summer of 1977 I had captained the Lions to New Zealand and returned home feeling physically and emotionally shattered. I needed a break and the tradition then was for Lions to sit out the first month of a season after a tour. But Prince Charles was coming to Llanelli for a commemorative match and I had been persuaded to play. It was a mistake as it meant I began the season without a real break and by the time of the 1978 Five Nations I was feeling the strain. We had beaten England and Scotland but deep in my heart I could hear a voice telling me it might be time to get out. The commitments of an international rugby player seemed to be increasing every year. But I was playing quite well, so I was still uncertain.

Ireland helped make up my mind. The build-up had been incredible. The triple Triple Crown had never been achieved before but to read the papers beforehand you would have thought the result was a foregone conclusion. This would be the crowning glory for the team of Gareth, Gerald and JPR, they said, without much thought given to Ireland. But I knew where Ireland would want to stick our triple Triple Crown, especially on their own patch.

My worries were not misplaced. Ireland thundered into us for the whole game. There was a lot of blood spilt and it was one of the dirtiest Five Nations matches I ever played in. JPR late-tackled Mike Gibson and maybe should have been sent off. Either way, the crowd went ballistic but we somehow managed to keep our heads and win, 20–16, after JJ scored a late try in the corner. But what struck me more deeply than anything was not our achievement but the way it was received by the men who had delivered it. There was no elation or hysteria in the dressing room; the players were almost out on their feet. I looked around the room at the faces. Gareth looked worn out, but Gerald was ashen. I think he had been stunned by the physical ferocity of the game, the number of boots going in on the ground, especially from fellow Lions. That was one of the unwritten laws in those days. You didn't stamp on another Lion. But that afternoon Gerald had witnessed a nasty physical edge to the game which he wasn't familiar with, and which he didn't appreciate. As a grammar-school boy and Cambridge graduate, Gerald had firm ideas on how rugby should be played. After coming through this match he looked ruffled,

3

bemused and very weary. It hadn't been pretty and if it had not been for the strength of body and character of our forwards – especially Bobby Windsor and Terry Cobner – then we would not have withstood the Irish ferocity and would have lost. Gerald was one of a number of Lions who took a good booting on the floor.

Later, at the Shelbourne Hotel in the centre of Dublin, we were greeted by hundreds of Wales supporters as we got off our team bus. They were cheering and singing but amid all the noise and congratulations I was stopped by one fan who looked me straight in the eye and said, 'Great, Phil. Well done. But just you make sure you beat those French bastards in two weeks' time.' The prospect of another brutal battle after a long week of training seemed to wash over me in a wave of fatigue. I had just spent about half an hour enjoying winning the Triple Crown. Now I would spend two weeks worrying about France and the Grand Slam. That was the way of things as a Welsh international in those days. The success was intoxicating and made you feel during matches that some kind of force was sweeping you off your feet and allowing you to perform to the most incredible standards. But in between games the expectations of the whole country were sometimes hard to bear. They were there when you played or trained with your club, when you went shopping or down the pub. It felt like a heavy burden, sometimes too heavy. After each victory we would celebrate like any other rugby team, but as soon as some supporter mentioned the next match, and how important it was that we beat the English/French/Scots/Irish, I would feel a tightening in my stomach.

On the Sunday before the match against France we had our normal training session at Port Talbot. It meant another weekend away from my wife Pat and our two-year-old son Steven. For the first time since I got into the squad in 1969, I resented having to go and train with Wales. I hated every mile of that M4 journey between Llanelli and Port Talbot. To make matters worse, the training session was a disaster. We were awful, so bad that our coach, John Dawes, abandoned things and told us all to go home and have a rest.

The week dragged and I felt jaded. Whatever spark I had that kept me going felt as though it was starting to burn itself out. I told Pat I'd had enough and that the match against France would be my last international. I was 29 years old. As a keen boxing fan I'd seen enough fighters go on for one fight too many and I didn't want to end up like that.

But this was a match for the Grand Slam. In the days before World Cups, the Slam was the ultimate and I didn't want anything to distract us from our goal. So I told no one else apart from Pat about by retirement plans and I took my secret with me on to the field at the Arms Park. There was also one other feeling that kept nagging away. Maybe, just maybe, this team had reached its peak. We had gone through most of the seventies together and now a number of players were coming towards the tail end of their careers. If the team was going to be dismantled then I felt we, the players, should be the ones who removed the first bricks.

I was concerned that my own emotions in the build-up to the match might get in the way, but as it turned out I had more then enough to worry about. We lost Gerald Davies through injury and Gareth Evans of Newport came in to take his place. France were a very impressive side. They had Bastiat, Jean-Pierre Rives, Robert Paparemborde, Jean-Claude Skrela and a fine young scrum-half in his first season called Jerome Gallion.

My own feelings and emotions got buried under tactical considerations and the sense of expectancy that surrounded our bid for another Grand Slam.

I always tried to pick out one flag during the anthems and I went through the same routine this time. I didn't shed any tears, even though I knew this, my 29th appearance, was going to be my last match for Wales. Of course, there was an enormous amount of emotion. I felt it deeply. But I was so wrapped up in wanting to win the game that I kept all those emotions firmly in check. I wanted to savour my last match, but much more than anything I simply wanted to win. We had worked hard that season and 80 more minutes of effort seemed a small price to pay for the biggest prize on offer. If I needed reassurance then it was there in the shape of the players alongside me. I looked at Edwards, JPR, JJ and Fenwick. They were too good to lose this opportunity, I thought.

France scored first, though: a try for Jean-Claude Skrela. They looked good and Gallion was making breaks all over the place. But then Edwards took over and showed Gallion who was boss. It was Gareth's experience versus Gallion's youthful energy and the old master started to win the day. I scored our first try from a solid scrum. Quick heel, Allan Martin . . . pass, sidestep, easy. I'd scored near the corner, though, and as I lined up the conversion I knew I had to concentrate if I was going to level the scores. In those days, we didn't practise our goal-kicking. Neil Jenkins would have been considered a bit odd for having more than a couple of shots at the end of a training session. It was all a bit hit-and-miss. Sometimes you were hot. Sometimes you weren't. That one went over, though, and I felt elated.

Edwards dropped a goal and then JJ finished off a move by

passing inside to me as he was forced out of play and I scored my second try. In the second half Steve Fenwick dropped a goal late on and that was it. Most of that second 40 minutes was just a case of hanging on. We weren't playing well. We were clinging on, but we had the character to do it. We were staggering our way to the finish line and the crowd seemed to be aware we needed a gentle push to finally get there. Edwards, as always, kept urging the players on – 'chopsing', as we say in Wales. I was hoarse trying to do the same. The noise of the crowd's singing seemed to intensify, and somehow we held on. I never normally noticed the crowd when I played for Wales. I blotted them out and kept my mind on the game. But that day, they refused to be blotted out. It was as if their noise, their desire, came on to the field as an extra force. They became part of our weaponry, part of us as a team. I'd never known anything like it.

We won, 16–7. It was a victory based on guts, spirit and a formidable support. Playing ability was way down the list that day, but it was enough to give Wales the Grand Slam – our third in eight seasons.

The night that followed wasn't bad either. I'd taken a bit of good-natured abuse in the dressing room when my conversation with Gareth had been overheard by some other members of the team. Someone shouted, 'Hey, those two bastards are getting out!' Someone else chipped in that we should have to buy all the drinks that night, but even our celebrations could not have gone better. I was presented with a jeroboam of champagne to mark our achievement and we drank most of it even before they had finished the speeches. Then, Rives and Skrela brought more bottles of wine over from the French players' table and joined the party. When those ran out I ordered more myself and told the waiters to put it on the bill of the Welsh Rugby Union. I knew it would mean an inquest on Monday to find the offender, but I didn't care. By Monday I'd be a former international.

There was some talk of convincing me to stay on, but I knew it was the right time to go. Wales were off to tour Australia and the thought of another summer spent away from my family was not very enticing. But there was also that nagging feeling again. This was it. Our time was up. I had been in the squad since 1969, so had JPR, while some of the boys like Gareth and Gerald had been there since 1966–67. I realised that if we were a soccer side then any manager worth his salt would now start clearing a few of us out. It was best to leave through the front door, I thought, than be pushed through the back.

Besides, there was young talent coming through. Gareth Davies and Terry Holmes were the ready-made half-backs, and there were other good youngsters like David Richards pushing for a place. Other countries were learning from our success and I could see that Wales might not have it all their own way for a while until a new team was established. It might take a couple of years – in actual fact Wales won the Triple Crown again in 1979 – but the baton would be smoothly handed on. Now was the time to stand aside and let the youngsters take the reins. The talent was there. Wales was flooded with talent. Once a new posse had found their feet then I had no doubts whatsoever that the Triple Crowns and Grand Slams would continue to be the Welsh currency. The economy may have been heading into a deep recession, but rugby was our business and business was booming.

*

Fast forward 20 years. It's 5 April 1998. Wales have just played France in another Grand-Slam decider. I am walking down Wembley Way on a Sunday afternoon and the weather is glorious. But all I notice is the litter and the debris on the ground – crushed paper cups and ripped flags. I also feel crushed because Wales, too, have just been ripped to pieces. France are champions and Grand-Slam winners, having beaten Wales 51–0 in what was supposedly a home game for Wales. And as the old gag goes, Wales were lucky to get nil.

That afternoon marked 20 years since Wales last won the Grand Slam. Five more years have passed since. If someone had said to me as I left the field in 1978 that Wales would spend the next quarter of a century looking for their next Grand Slam then I would have told them to lie down in a darkened room while I fetched the doctor.

I hated Wembley. I loved it as a football venue, as the home of the FA Cup Final and England's internationals, but as a temporary home for Welsh rugby while they built the Millennium Stadium it was a pain in the arse. The first time I watched Wales play there it took me three hours in the car to crawl the final five miles and the same on the way back. By the time of the home match with France I had learnt my lesson. Pat and I drove up from Llanelli the night before, ready for my day's work with BBC Wales and the *Sunday Mirror*. On the morning of the game we called in at a teashop in Gerrard's Cross and then caught the train into Wembley. The sight of Welsh fans, who had come from all over Wales and England for the game, taking over the carriages with their colours and their singing, filled me with optimism. I spotted one young kid with a scarf and rosette who was almost climbing the walls with excitement as he sat next to his grandfather. Watching him made me feel good about Welsh rugby. It could still excite and inspire, convince a young boy and his grandfather it was worth getting up at the crack of dawn on a Sunday for an expensive 500-mile round trip to see what was meant to be a home game.

Then came the match itself. Wales 0, France 51. I just couldn't believe what I was seeing. France were so superior to Wales it was like watching a training exercise where one set of players practise their attacking and the others half-heartedly pretend to try and stop them. The only difference was that Wales *were* actually trying to stop them. They just couldn't. The gulf in class was a chasm.

Thomas Castaignede was simply magical for France that day at outside-half. He gave poor Neil Jenkins the worst runaround of his life and ran the show from beginning to end. It was one of the best displays I had ever seen from a No. 10 in a championship match. But France weren't just better in one position. They were streets ahead all over the field. The body language of some of the Welsh players summed it all up. They were dragging themselves around the field with their shoulders slumped and their heads bowed, especially Jenkins who looked as though he was living out a nightmare. The pain of their humiliation at being so outclassed was agony to watch. They looked totally devastated. So did the crowd. I know that's how I felt. France scored seven tries and should have had ten. Jean-Luc Sadourny, their classy runner at full-back, scored two, so did Xavier Garbajosa, one of their new boys. Stephane Glas, Thomas Lievremont and Fabien Galthie were their other try-scorers and Christophe Lamaison kicked five conversions and two penalties. Wales looked as if they wouldn't get near the try-line if they stayed at it until the following Sunday and the final insult was when the French put on all seven of their replacements to reinforce the feeling that they were in a training session. The final whistle went and all I wanted to do was get out of there, get away from the shame and indignity of it all.

We walked down Wembley Way among hundreds of Welsh supporters, but in complete silence. No complaints or excuses, no rancour or accusations – not even any of the dark humour that had often followed some of the worst Welsh defeats in the previous years. They were all stunned at the awful magnitude of the defeat. There were no saving graces – absolutely none.

We waited on the platform, among hundreds of Welsh fans and this deathly hush. Incredibly, I spotted the same young kid I had seen before the match with his grandfather. All the bounce and energy had left him long ago. It struck me then how this kid had gone to the game so expressive and come away looking numbed and bored. If he was going to be hooked by rugby then he needed heroes, but Wales had nothing to offer when it came to heroics that afternoon. It hadn't been a surrender, but the resistance had been brushed aside.

Pat and I were meant to meet friends for dinner that evening, but I couldn't face them. I couldn't even face food. I just wanted to get home and forget all about it. It was one of the emptiest feelings I've ever felt after watching Wales and I couldn't even be bothered to fill my empty stomach. If 1978 provided bread of heaven, this was starvation rations for every Welshman there.

Kevin Bowring quit as Wales coach within a few weeks and I thought, 'This is it. Welsh rugby cannot go any lower.' I was wrong. Two months later Wales went to South Africa and lost 96–13.

CHAPTER 2

The Lost Years

Rugby used to be the undisputed national sport within Wales. But in the 20 years between the Welsh Grand Slam of 1978 and that awful day at Wembley, a rival pastime has emerged – talking about what went wrong. The pub chat used to be arguments about rival players. Now the arguments are over rival arguments. Who has the best theory to explain our descent has replaced talk over who has the best players. It's the question I am asked all over the world. What went wrong?

Go into any rugby club bar in Wales and you'll hear all the various theories over what went wrong, usually discussed in the same evening. It was the decline of the grammar schools; it was the decline of the heavy industries such as coal and steel; it was the teachers' strike; it was poor coaching, it was hard-up players unable to resist the tempting offers from rugby league; it's the fault of amateur administrators, the fault of professional players, the fault of the English; it was Western Samoa – the whole of Samoa!

In reality, it was probably all those things and more, but I can only talk from the vantage point provided by my own experiences. When I left the field in 1978, I walked into a dressing room bursting to the seams with enormously talented rugby people. It was a deep reservoir of skills and experience. But the game in Wales, in all spheres, so rarely turned on the tap.

It's often suggested by some that the players from the seventies, those who provided the so-called Golden Era, turned their back on the game and walked away. They didn't have the inclination or the generosity of spirit to put something back. Believe me, it was never like that. Some of us who had written books or newspaper columns after our retirement were simply banned by the Welsh Rugby Union from having anything to do with the game. We had committed the crime of professionalism, even though we had been paid for our efforts off the field rather than on it. We were not allowed to play, to coach, to hold any positions whatsoever. We had never taken a penny for playing, but the moment we opted to give something back to our families for all the time we had been away, we were branded as unworthy of staying within rugby union. And even those who had not sold their souls to the devil of professionalism were never encouraged to take up prominent positions within the game, either in coaching or administration.

After I played my last match for Wales I spent three more years with Llanelli, during which time I came back from a serious knee injury to play one last full season. I trained with track and field athletes to get myself fully fit and discovered a level of fitness I had never known before. I was quicker, stronger, more flexible and had more stamina at the age of 31 than I'd ever had before. But once I had put pen to paper for payment in 1981, that was it. I had to retire. Not only that, I had to cut myself off from any sort of role at the club I had loved and served for 14 years.

Just after I had retired I was asked to play in a charity match for a young man who had been injured in a car accident. It was against an international XV and I was desperately keen to play, but I had to turn down the offer. Because of the regulations at that time, if I had played not only would I have broken the rules myself but I would also through sharing the same pitch have 'professionalised' every other player on the field. I felt like a leper.

The consequence of this rule was to cast adrift so much knowledge. The 1978 team was full of genuine world-class talent, but within two years it had almost all disappeared, not just from the team but from the game as a whole. Even those players who were not deemed professional were never encouraged to have a role. In the three years between 1978 and 1981, I was never contacted by anyone at the WRU, never invited to coach or advise, or even simply to show my face around younger players or kids just starting to make their way in the game. The same went for all the other players. Between 1978 and 1980 the Wales team had lost JPR Williams, JJ Williams, Gerald Davies, myself, Gareth Edwards, Charlie Faulkner, Bobby Windsor, Derek Quinnell and Terry Cobner. Steve Fenwick, Ray Gravell, Allan Martin and Geoff Wheel all followed within a year or so. Not only did the WRU fail to make use of that expertise once we had retired, but over the next few years it became painfully apparent that nothing had been done to make sure there was a regular flow of talent behind us. Apart from one or two whose talent had ripened, the cupboard was bare.

Well-managed soccer sides don't get wiped out overnight. The clubs integrate new players with experienced ones and the next generation is developed until their time has arrived. But there was no planning in the seventies. Within the heart of the WRU – and it was they who ran the game with absolute authority – there was a shameful complacency.

In the eighties, players were thrust into the Wales team and expected to sink or swim. The trouble was, the tide had turned and the momentum was now flowing with other countries that had got their acts together. A lot of those players sank without trace. But these were players who had never been watched and monitored through their developing years, and never been brought along to Wales training sessions to get a feel for international rugby. They were just chucked in and then fished out. I can remember going to watch a Wales training session in 1982, conducted by the coach Terry Cobner, and not recognising half the squad. They were strangers; boys plucked from the obscurity of club rugby and expected to succeed. It was a shock to many when Wales began to lose matches, but it should really have surprised no one.

One or two high-quality players tried to hold things together – guys like Terry Holmes and Gareth Davies – but results started to slide. Scotland scored five tries and thrashed Wales 34–18 in Cardiff in 1982 and then won at the Arms Park again two years later when France also won. It was the first time for 21 years that Wales had lost both their championship games in Cardiff. But even then, I didn't really see a continuous downward trend. The Wales team of 1988, captained by Bleddyn

Bowen, won the Triple Crown. It was an excellent side, inspired by the genius of Jonathan Davies, with solid forwards like Bob Norster, Rowland Phillips and Paul Moriarty, and great finishers in Ieuan Evans and Adrian Hadley. I thought, 'This is it. We've gone through our sticky patch, but these boys are class. We're on our way back.' It was ten years on from my last game for Wales and I thought the decade had been a journey down a wrong turning. Now we were back on the right road and normal service was going to be resumed.

Of course, it didn't quite work out like that. Within a couple of years that side had been ripped apart by defections to rugby League. Jonathan went. So did Hadley, Phillips and Moriarty. Dai Young, Stuart Evans, John Devereux, Allan Bateman and Mark Jones went and others followed in later years like Scott Gibbs and Scott Quinnell. The game was changing, more demands were being made of players and those running the show in Wales should have responded. But the attitude at the end of the eighties was the same as it had been at the end of the seventies. They just believed that Wales had a God-given right to succeed and that if one bunch of players disappeared then another gang would simply carry on the success. At the end of the seventies a generation disappeared because they retired. At the end of the eighties it was even worse in many ways, because the players who went off to play rugby league had not even reached their peak. But the outcome was the same. Welsh rugby was exposed for not having the foresight to look farther ahead than the next payday from a full house. The WRU has often tried to fend off the blame and point the finger at the clubs in Wales. But from my experience, the club scene had not changed. Playing in Welsh club rugby in 1974 was no different to playing in 1981. It was still hard, physical, intensely tribal, but with skilful players who were committed to the game and to the success of their clubs. So the breeding ground was there. It was the development and organisation of that talent that went awry.

When Wales began losing, a kind of panic set in. In the years between 1974 and 1978 the team picked itself. The coaches only had to deal with minor adjustments because of form or injuries and the changes were minimal. But when Wales started to lose consistently a frantic search began for the new saviours. There would be six or seven changes after a defeat with a handful of new caps. It was as if the selectors thought that the winning team was there, it was just that they hadn't stumbled across the right combinations of players yet. There was never any appreciation that the problems ran much deeper.

Instead of clutching at straws by picking ordinary club players and expecting miracles, Wales should have been looking at the fundamentals. Why were fewer kids playing the game at weekends? Why were teachers turning their backs on running sides? Why were some clubs no longer running youth teams? Such problems were never addressed. There was no one within the WRU with the vision of someone like Carwyn James. Carwyn had proved his greatness with Llanelli and with the Lions. Had he been given a role by the Union then he would have seen the bigger picture. He would have identified the problems that were being stored up – the fact that there was nothing to fall back on at the start of the eighties once the top layer had been removed. Ray Williams was doing sterling work in the seventies with players at the top level. But beneath that, nothing was being nurtured. There was no continuity, no process, just blind hope.

The 1988 Triple Crown, far from being the start of a new

dawn, was just a temporary flash in a long winter of darkness. In 1999 Wales went on a ten-match winning run under the coaching of Graham Henry. Again, though, it was a blip, a temporary recovery that eventually faded out, to be followed by more grim results and a further decline in our status around the world. Everyone remembers the highs, but they have been fleeting moments over the past 20 years. Every Welshman remembers the horrific defeats, such as the 1998 thrashings by France, England and South Africa, the shameful tour of Australia in 1991 where Wales lost 63–6 and then brawled among themselves at the post-match dinner. But so many games between 1980 and 1987, and then between 1989 and 1998, have not lingered long in my memory. These were un-remarkable years filled with unremarkable matches. They are the lost years in more ways than one.

'Ladies and Gentlemen, here to represent Wales as we look forward to that country hosting the 1999 World Cup . . . Mr Vernon Pugh.' I remember hearing those words over the tannoy at a Test match in South Africa in the build-up to the 1999 tournament. Looking a little embarrassed, Vernon Pugh, one-time chairman of the Welsh Rugby Union, now chairman of the International Rugby Board, crept on to the field for the presentation intended to launch the countdown to the finals. I have a great deal of respect for Vernon. He is a very able administrator, a bright, intelligent and likeable man, and it reflects well on Wales that he has the top job in world rugby. He also played a key role in making Wales the primary host nation for the last World Cup and I hope that he makes a full and speedy recovery from the illness that struck him during the autumn of 2002. But as he made his way to the centre of the field, I could hear hundreds of South Africans around me asking, 'Who's he?' It was a fair question.

Vernon was a leading QC who had made his name within Wales by writing a report on the Welsh involvement in an unofficial tour to South Africa in the 1980s. He had then gone on to become WRU chairman after the grass-roots 'coup' that had swept former secretary Denis Evans out of office. From that position, he had strode on to become chairman of the IRB, the world game's governing body. It was Pugh who had declared the sport professional following the 1995 World Cup, bringing to an end the 'shamateurism' that had been the prevailing status of the game in so many countries.

So Vernon was a Bigwig with a capital B. But to the crowds of South Africans that day, for a presentation that was holding up a Test match, he was, understandably, Vernon 'Who?' rather than Vernon Pugh. They didn't know him from Adam.

Then it struck me: this was the state Welsh rugby now found itself in. We had no world-famous players, so we had to make do with our administrators. This is what we now gave the world – law craft rather than rugby brains. Of course, it would have made far more sense to have had Gareth Edwards represent Wales and I'm sure Vernon would have much preferred it. He needn't have looked so sheepish. But Welsh rugby had spent 20 years ignoring the seventies generation, so there was not much chance of their rediscovering it in time for the 1999 World Cup. To be fair, Edwards and a lot of other Welsh greats did indeed show their faces at the opening ceremony. But it perhaps sums up the past 25 years in Welsh rugby that a lawyer should have represented Wales that afternoon in South Africa. Legal wrangling and verbal dust-ups have certainly dominated over the rugby out on the pitch.

Vernon manfully did a difficult job heading up Welsh rugby in the 1990s. There often wasn't much to be proud of, but he showed great negotiating skills and, unlike some of the men in suits in the game, I always felt he had a good understanding of the sport and the people who played and followed it. It was certainty a loss to Welsh rugby when he decided to step down as WRU chairman.

That left the way open for Glanmor Griffiths. Glanmor had been treasurer of the Union for a while and seemed to do the job just as you would expect any former bank manager. Nothing too flashy, nothing very imaginative, but he seemed to keep the small clubs happy and balance the books. Suddenly, though, this bloke was both chairman and treasurer of the WRU, and chairman of the Millennium Stadium plc. He has clung on to all those areas of influence for a long time, which I've always felt was wrong. He has seems unwilling to delegate, but you cannot give all that power to one person. It creates suspicion and grounds for resentment and mistrust. Glanmor has had too many conflicts of interest for a long time and I know of many other ex-internationals who feel the same way. Gerald Davies and Gwyn Jones were part of a Working Party that said as much in their report of 2001, but unfortunately not enough of the clubs in Wales backed that conclusion.

Had Pugh stayed on in Welsh rugby then I think he could have steadied the ship more successfully than has been the case in recent years. He was certainly far more of a forward-thinker than Glanmor. But I think he got fed up with the endless back-biting and low-level politics the game seems to attract in Wales. The committee men on the WRU have not changed. They are the same type of people who were running the game when I was playing 20 years ago. Wales were successful then and some have used that as a defence. If amateur committee men were in control in the 1970s, when Wales were successful, then their argument is that they can help Wales be successful again. But the sport has changed. Professionalism altered everything, and professionals now should run rugby as well as play it.

Glanmor likes to blow the trumpet for the Millennium Stadium and his own part in ensuring its construction. Hats off to him, for that one. It's a great arena and the problems that have beset the Wembley project make the construction of such a landmark in the centre of Cardiff something all Welsh people should be proud of. Recently, however, the extent of the debts owed on the stadium and their impact on funding the rest of Welsh rugby have become apparent. I don't profess to be a businessman, but there are deals tied up with the Millennium Stadium that worry me greatly. For instance, it's great for Welsh prestige and self-esteem that the FA Cup Finals are being staged in Cardiff. The hotels, restaurants and shops in the city are also delighted, no doubt. But what is Welsh rugby making out of the deal? Not a lot, it seems. The FA was desperate for somewhere to go while Wembley was being rebuilt, but the stadium was handed over for virtually nothing. In fact, Welsh rugby had to offer up many of its existing deals to the FA! Advertising and sponsorship was handed over to the FA, along with the hospitality income and all the merchandising and other top-ups from normal match-day activity. It's all very well having the richest customers come into your shop, but if they don't spend anything and you end up paying them to come in off the street, then you're soon going to go out of business.

The FA deal sums up a lot of what is wrong with the way the WRU has run its affairs. It was way behind the times when I

21

finished playing and it has stayed there. Friends of mine who run successful businesses have given up trying to deal with the WRU. They are slow to react, complacent, and their marketing of the game is about 100 years out of date. There have been no sponsors for the domestic league for years, the Celtic League hasn't had one either and companies are trying to disassociate themselves from the national team rather than be linked with it. When the RFU launch their competitions in England it's done with some razzamatazz and a fanfare. In Wales there is hardly a whimper. Rather than turning people on to rugby, the WRU are constantly bickering with our top clubs and turning people off. They fail to applaud success stories at the top level – such as Newport's wonderful reawakening of their community's passion for rugby or Dunvant's work with young kids – and arrogantly believe that they know best. The truth is that what general committee members know most about is ensuring their own survival. In short, the Union that Glanmor has presided over for the past few years has been a complete and utter shambles, a total disgrace.

In 2002 there was an opportunity for change within the WRU. A Working Party had been set up, chaired by Sir Tasker Watkins, the Union's own president. Other respected figures were drafted on and they had spent two years considering the future of rugby in Wales, both on and off the field. Men like Gerald Davies, one of the greatest players the game has ever seen, worked hard at examining what had gone wrong and how they could fix it.

The report called loudly for root-and-branch reform, but after initially ignoring it Glanmor Griffiths and the rest of the WRU general committee then set about coming up with their own counter-proposals. Not only that, but they toured all the clubs in Wales in a peculiar sort of roadshow aimed at promoting their own plans and undermining Sir Tasker's.

Just before all the clubs came to vote on both sets of proposals I flew to Scotland for the funeral of my great friend Gordon Brown and sat alongside Gerald on the flight. He was worried. He felt it was a last chance for Welsh rugby – that unless a small executive of professional people ran the game then top-level rugby in Wales would virtually die out. It was in the hands of every club in Wales to vote for radical reform and a fresh start. In fact, they voted against change and gave another chance to those who had failed them so often in the past. Glanmor's blueprint, which called for cosmetic changes, was voted through and the Working Party was left to reflect on two years wasted.

The news of that vote came through to me on the day I was at Oxford watching Pontypridd lose to Sale in the final of the Parker Pen Shield. Ponty had defied the odds to make the final but they had enjoyed a magnificent run and proved that a modern approach, harnessed to young talent and expertise in the right areas, could bring rewards. Unfortunately, the rank-and-file clubs in Wales couldn't see that the governing body was crying out for similar fresh thinking and new faces. They put their own self-interest first, which essentially boiled down to how much money they could guarantee themselves from the Union. In turn, that cash is put in the pockets of substandard players. The process is that which the Working Party was trying to get rid of. Instead of spending cash on players, most small clubs should be funding academies to bring through their youngsters. The Working Party debate was a massive opportunity for change, but it was scandalously rejected. The clubs should have seized it, but they dropped the pass.

On one level I can understand the clubs' dilemma. They are ambitious and want to progress. That often means paying a guy a few quid more than they can really afford to stop him moving down the road. If a club tries to buck the trend then the consequences can be grim. Dunvant are a fantastic little club in the suburbs of Swansea. They reached the top division, built themselves a lovely little ground at Broadacre, and everything was going to plan. But instead of paying the top-level wages they chose to invest in their own youth and junior teams. Their mini-rugby sections are thriving and they are doing a fantastic job for the future of the game. But they recently lost a planeload of players to a rival team because they would not pay the going rate. As a result they are now dropping down the divisions like a skydiver in freefall.

It's a terrible message that is being sent out; it encourages short-term thinking and reduces opportunities to develop the next generation of international players. Anyone who can't see the destructive effect of all this obviously has no care for the future of our game. It saddens me, appals me and leaves me very pessimistic about what is in store for Welsh rugby.

At the other end of the scale are Newport, who have speculated to accumulate. Thanks to their financial backer, Tony Brown, the club were able to bring in big-money signings such as Gary Teichmann, the former Springboks captain and Shane Howarth who played for New Zealand and then Wales. It was a sound policy because it was backed up by a real drive for new young supporters throughout their area. They used their star names, like Teichmann, to sell the club to the kids and they wisely underpinned the strategy with clever marketing approaches to involve the whole family.

As a result, Newport have been the great success story of

Welsh club rugby over recent seasons – certainly when it comes to attendances. They have tapped into something huge. The WRU could learn so much from Newport. If they had half the energy and enthusiasm of the staff at Rodney Parade then maybe Six Nations games would still be sell-outs and every kid in Wales on match day would be walking around in a replica jersey with a red dragon painted proudly on his face. But instead of encouraging Newport, the Union always appears eager to confront them. Instead of learning from their expertise they seem more keen to criticise guys like Brown and their chief executive Keith Grainger. Yet Newport were in exactly the same position as Wales find themselves in now – falling gates, falling interest, and a losing team. They responded in a dynamic way by getting youngsters hooked on Newport and hooked on rugby.

Without young kids coming through at every club in the country, there will be fewer and fewer players to choose our national team from. Without decent facilities for those young-sters to improve, the quality of our senior players will diminish. If the big clubs are also going broke because the marketing and administration of the game are so poor, then they will like-wise go on a downward spiral – able to spend less on youth development, less on elite coaching and modern advances in sports science. English clubs are starting to move so far ahead of Welsh clubs in such areas that they are almost out of sight.

All these problems feed into a growing chasm between Eng-land and Wales on the international field – it being this widen-ing gap that now concerns me most. England moved past Wales more than a decade ago and have been getting farther ahead of us ever since. In the last 13 matches between the sides, Wales have won just twice and on both occasions it was by a single point. More worrying still is that England's winning margins have been getting bigger and bigger. The fixture is becoming seriously one-sided, a foregone conclusion. Perhaps it was a foregone conclusion in Wales's favour in the seventies, but the implications for what was then the Five Nations were less serious. Back then, alternatives to the championship in terms of rival tournaments were simply not on offer. Now, big business, more air links and the growth in broadcasting and sponsorship mean things can no longer be taken for granted.

If England keep thrashing Wales, as they have thrashed us in recent seasons, then I worry seriously for the future of the Six Nations. Scotland's decline has been as bad as Wales's, and Italy continue to struggle. Ireland are just about holding on, but even they struggle away from home to either England or France. The tournament has not yet become a two-horse race, but it is going that way. The more predictable it becomes, the less it is going to appeal to sponsors and broadcasters. Who wants to watch mismatches and foregone conclusions? We have seen Lloyds TSB end their sponsorship of the Six Nations and when the TV contract was up for grabs in 2002 the BBC was the only bidder at the table.

The 2002 victory by England over Wales at Twickenham was one of the most depressing matches I have ever witnessed. It wasn't just the defeat – I expected that – it was the complete lack of atmosphere either before the game, during, or afterwards. Everyone inside Twickenham knew what the result would be. The only question was the size of the winning margin. In the end it finished 50–10 but it could have been a whole lot more. I felt relieved it wasn't 80 points, but the reaction of the English fans left me dumbstruck. There were no noisy celebrations, no goading or even much satisfaction. It was as if they had beaten Italy or Tonga – a job had been completed but that was about it.

I know England have failed to pick up the Grand Slam by losing to Wales, Scotland, Ireland and France in successive seasons, but the Celtic countries cannot sustain their challenge at present. They can rise to the occasion once every few years, but that's not really good enough. My big worry is that England will soon get a better offer to go off and play the Tri-Nations countries. For TV companies an annual tournament featuring New Zealand, Australia, South Africa and England would be very appealing. The French might then have their loyalties tested and it would not surprise me if they went, too. That would leave Wales, Ireland and Scotland on their own and in a real mess. I can't think of too many companies who would break the bank to sponsor a Celtic Tri-Nations featuring three also-rans. Income for Wales would plummet and it could be the end of any hopes of ever getting back among rugby's world elite.

I had a frightening vision of that kind of future when Wales lost at home to Scotland in the final match of the 2002 Six Nations. It was an awful match between two poor sides. There were empty spaces in the Millennium Stadium at the start and thousands more were streaming out before the end. Steve Hansen, who took over from Graham Henry as coach midway through the season, looked a deeply troubled man and he had every reason to be.

Wales, and Hansen, finished the 2002 championship with just one victory, at home to Italy. We were dreadful at Twickenham, plucky in defeat against the French, but awful against Scotland and simply pathetic in losing heavily to Ireland in Dublin. I hesitate to say that record defeats to England and

Ireland represented a new low, because there have been so many other low points to choose from, but it certainly felt as though we were bumping along the bottom.

It's been a painful ride and I have more bruises than I care to count. But for those men in charge of the Welsh teams over 20 years of decline it's been absolute agony.

CHAPTER 3

The Impossible Job

Some time after Kevin Keegan had quit as England soccer manager in 2000, most of the London-based newspapers were having trouble speculating as to who his successor might be. No sooner were they building up the credentials of some particular candidate than the poor bloke would have a panic attack and declare he had no interest in the job. The popular opinion seemed to be that it just wasn't worth the hassle, the aggravation, the heart failure and the inevitable damning criticism when things went wrong. It was, most of the papers decided, not something any sane person would accept and they dubbed it, 'The Impossible Job'.

Then along came this very academic-looking Swedish man called Sven-Goran Eriksson who not only wanted the job but also seemed to thrive in it. Against the odds, he took England to the World Cup Finals and became a national hero. Not even defeat to Brazil in the quarter-finals appears to have dented his reputation.

No, for a real 'mission impossible' try coaching the Welsh rugby team. Graham Henry did it for a while and for a time he became a bigger national hero in Wales than even Sven was in England after England had beaten Germany 5–1. Like his footballing counterpart, Henry took his team to the quarter-finals of the World Cup; but that was when the rot set in. Results nose-dived and so did Henry's reputation. In the end he quit, joining a long line of former Welsh coaches who shone brightly, but briefly, and then hit the ground with a bump.

The comparison with English football is a useful one. Both Welsh rugby and English soccer have a rich history always looming large and threateningly over whoever happens to be in charge. The sports are national obsessions – except when there is any planning for the future to be done – and the respective coaches are forever carrying around unrealistic public expectations, fuelled by an intense and demanding media. The spotlight is very bright and not everyone can cope with the glare. For a time, Henry seemed to revel in it. But in the end, even he was burnt.

Just like the job of England soccer manager, the profile of the Welsh rugby coach has mushroomed over the years. Walter Winterbottom could have gone into most pubs in England in the sixties and very few people would have recognised him. Even Sir Alf Ramsey managed to continue to live a very private and humble existence after England had won the World Cup in 1966.

It was the same in Welsh rugby. David Nash was the first Welsh rugby coach in 1967 and his profile was even more modest than his record of one victory in five matches. Wales then entered the golden years of Grand Slams and Triple Crowns but most fans would have been hard-pressed to name the coach, never mind recognise him in the street. Gareth Edwards, Barry John, JPR and Gerald Davies were the names on everybody's lips but Clive Rowlands and John Dawes were very much men who stayed in the shadows even though they had both been very prominent players themselves. Part of the reason was the structure of what passed for management of the national team. In those days the coach did not pick the side. That was left to a gang of selectors, in Wales the so-called Big Five. These were the men with the power. The coach was there merely to train the players who were given to him and offer them tactical advice and a passionate pre-match speech.

I first got into the Welsh squad in 1968, as understudy to Barry, when David Nash was in charge. David was a decent chap, a quiet man, but a thinker. He deserved a longer crack at the job but no one even knew in those days whether or not coaching was going to be accepted. A school of thought still existed then that viewed coaches as rather eccentric meddlers who should really leave things to the captain and the committee.

Clive Rowlands changed all that. He did the job for six seasons and lost just seven matches. By the time he stepped down in 1974, Wales were leading the way on the field and the coaching revolution was attracting many admirers off it.

Clive was the complete opposite of David Nash. He was loud and ebullient, with a cocky self-confidence and a fiercely proud view of what Wales and Welsh rugby should be all about. I was fortunate in that I knew Clive because our playing careers had crossed during his final days. I knew what a magnificent motivator he was and what effect those powers might have on me. I'd been part of the squad for a West Wales side against the touring New Zealanders in 1967 when Clive was coach. He was presented with a mixed bunch of young kids and old-timers who were all considered not good enough for the Welsh squad. But he used that fact as his trump card when it came to motivation and a fired-up West Wales came very close to beating the mighty All Blacks.

A year later I toured Argentina under Clive with a squad that had been stripped of its Lions players. We were raw and inexperienced but we drew the Test series 1–1 and it was more valuable know-how stored away in the bank for Clive. He was young enough still to have a strong connection with the players, but he was also very ambitious in this new field of coaching and that gave him a little distance from those who were playing under him.

As a player Clive would spend entire matches talking to referees, winding up opponents, doing anything to gain the initiative. He carried that shrewdness into his coaching career, too. He was crafty. He knew how to get the best out of players. He didn't have the analytical brain of Carwyn James but he recognised what made most players tick and usually found a way of winding them up. Sometimes it wasn't subtle, but it was generally successful.

A typical Clive Rowlands team talk before a Wales international match would go like this. There were no team rooms provided in the hotels in those days, so the whole squad would have to pile into the captain's own bedroom. There would be players sitting on the bed, on the dressing table, on the floor, even perched on the wardrobe – anywhere they could find a seat in a small hotel room. It would be stuffy and overwhelming.

Wearing his Wales tie and pullover, Clive would pace the room, fag in hand, ranting and raving. He would demand you performed not just for yourself, but for your father, your mother, your long-lost aunt, the miners, the steelworkers, the teachers, the schoolchildren – in effect, the whole Welsh nation. You were their representatives and you owed it to them to deliver. By the end of this sermon, some boys would be head-butting the walls and others would be crying their eyes out. Then he would briefly mention one or two dangermen in the opposition before ending the whole performance by telling everyone that we were the best team in the world.

The players would then squeeze out of the room and head for the ground. Anyone caught chatting, or worse still smiling, would suffer Clive's wrath. It was a very Welsh, very emotional build-up and it produced a very emotional display on the field. It flowed out of Clive. Then it flowed out of the players during the match.

The problem, of course, was that players could only work themselves into this kind of frenzy so many times. After a while the words become just that ... words. Both Gareth and Barry became a little bored by all the nationalistic stuff and I'd notice they would be yawning or looking at their watch while other players, perhaps less secure of their places in the team, would be lapping it up.

But Top Cat, as Clive came to be known, was a remarkable coach with a fabulous record of success. He learned from his early experiences, especially the tour to New Zealand in 1969 where Wales travelled with confidence but came back on the wrong end of two heavy Test defeats. Clive noted what needed to be done and then put it into practice.

On an emotional level, Clive always made his players aware

of the responsibilities they carried and nine times out of ten they responded. His training sessions could be great fun – full of banter and stirring up the friendly rivalries within the squad. Everything Clive did was on a grand scale and the fans who watched us train were encouraged to feel very much part of the group.

Clive had a good rapport with the players as individuals, too. He would take me aside for a chat, perhaps because he felt I was drifting too far across the field. But rather than criticise players, he would make subtle suggestions to make you feel that it was in your hands. When you made the changes he was seeking he would be delighted and offer plenty of praise.

It was a time of plenty on the field, too, and Clive will always deserve huge credit for his role in helping shape the early successes of the seventies. But after six years in charge, which included a couple of Triple Crowns and a Grand Slam, it was time for a change. Clive made way for John Dawes, but it was still the selectors who called the shots. John was a very different character to Clive, more sombre and measured. He was already a hero for captaining the 1971 Lions to a glorious triumph in New Zealand and his step up into coaching was a natural one. He slipped into the role quite effortlessly, but there was still no huge public interest in the coach. The attention was still very much on the players. That was probably a blessing, as John liked the quiet life.

The only other realistic choice to take over from Clive would have been Carwyn James, my coach at Llanelli, who had masterminded that 1971 Lions success. But Carwyn was too much of a maverick, too outspoken for the conservative tastes within the WRU. Any hopes Carwyn had of getting the job probably disappeared when he spoke before a large audience at

Llanelli's centenary dinner in 1972. A homage to his own club turned into a scathing attack on the Union and the men who ran it. The home truths hit home but rather than concede that Carwyn was right the Union closed ranks and put a black mark against his name. Carwyn could see that any Welsh coach should have the power and authority to do things his own way and pick who he wanted to pick. This was viewed as an all-out attack on the WRU and any possibility that the greatest coach of his generation might have had the top job probably went down the plughole that evening.

We will never know what Carwyn, possessor of the sharpest rugby brain I ever came across, might have done had he become national coach. He would have been hard pressed to have matched the record of Dawesy, who won 75 per cent of his matches in charge between 1974 and 1979, but I think Carwyn would have been there or thereabouts. One thing would have been certain, though. Carwyn would have demanded a role in shaping the next generation of Welsh rugby players, not merely the ones under his direct influence. He would have possessed the vision to see past the next game and to shape the future development of the sport in Wales. He would have seen the lean times coming long before anyone else and taken the decisive and necessary steps to put things right. Sadly, he was never given the opportunity. That Carwyn was denied any influence at that level is one of the great tragedies of Welsh rugby.

Having captained the Lions under James, at least John Dawes had learnt well from the master and he was able to put much of that sound knowledge into practice. Dawesy was quieter than Carwyn. There was no grand oratory, none of the lyrical coaxing that characterised Carwyn's dressing-room patter. John was more into sound common sense, although he had a very secure grasp of tactics and he knew how to persuade players to mix their flair with pragmatism.

I had great respect for John from our own playing days together. My own career with Wales was just starting to get off the ground while John's was finishing, and I benefited greatly from his experience. In 1970 I came into the side for a match against France in Cardiff after Barry John had dropped out through injury. It was a good French side, with a lot of pace behind, while our own back line had been badly hit by injuries and looked rather slow by comparison. John, as captain, turned to me in the dressing room just before we ran out and said, 'Phil, I don't want to see you pass the ball today. Just kick for position and let our forwards do the rest.' I'd never been ordered to play like that before, but I did as I was told. It wasn't much of a match but they were exactly the right tactics in the wet weather and we won 11–6.

That advice sticks in my mind because it went against John's natural inclinations. He had been brought up on good football with London Welsh and he always wanted to put skill, flair and attacking intent at the top of his list of priorities. Luckily for him, and for the rest of the Welsh nation, he was to have a team well blessed to win games in that style for the five years he spent as Wales coach. But the Welsh team of that time never chucked the ball about for the sake of it. We got the basics right and did the groundwork before we constructed anything fancy.

John was fortunate in having his coaching underpinned by the influence of Ray Williams. Ray was responsible for the development of coaches as a coaching organiser and did the job superbly. He was ahead of his time, introducing the weekend sessions for the national squad and formulating drills and skills programmes which the rest of the world came to learn from. Though they seem long ago now, those were the days when the Aussies came over to Wales to learn the latest techniques and ideas on how to coach rugby. John took those training days at weekends, but it was Ray whose vision had brought about their introduction.

Looking back, those Sunday sessions seem so simple and straightforward compared to later years. We would try to run off the aches and pains of the previous day's game and go through the rudiments of a couple of very uncomplicated moves. When JPR Williams caught the ball and counter-attacked, the plan would always be for him to run towards the nearest touchline. Either Gerald Davies or JJ Williams would then offer themselves on the switch and either take the pass or act as a decoy. It wasn't rocket science but it depended on good players making good decisions out on the field. John was our guide. He had a vision for the way he wanted us to play, but this was only a framework. It was up to the players to provide all the detail. We were constructing something and John was the one who surveyed the land, suggested the best materials and provided the boundaries. But the style, the shape, and especially the fine detail was left to the players. For me, that is what rugby is still all about. When I heard of Graham Henry's infamous 'pod system' with the Lions in 2001, I could hardly believe it. Martin Johnson admitted after the tour he found it difficult to know whether or not he should be at a ruck or hanging back waiting for the next one. It wasn't that he couldn't decide; it was that he couldn't remember. This was rugby by numbers, by rote instead of thought or expression. If it could really be played like Henry seemed to suggest then coaches and players could work it all out with the opposition beforehand and no one would need to set foot on the pitch.

On Sunday evening, we would break up and not reassemble until the Thursday for another hour-long training session. The players would be allowed to return home again that evening, following which we would meet up at The Angel Hotel in Cardiff on Friday afternoon and head for the cinema. We would get back at about 11pm, have a quick chat, and then go to bed. In the morning, there would be a team meeting after breakfast. John was fanatical about rugby, but he was wise enough not to let it show. Team meetings would normally begin with a chat about his beloved Manchester United before we talked rugby and if there were any small problems or griev-ances on the part of the players then John would act quickly to sort them out. He was always a players' man.

Ours was a simple, basic, commonsense rugby. Dawesy approved because he shared that philosophy and knew that we had the players to get it right. For the most part the Wales coach at this time was exerting a greater influence over the Big Five when it came to selecting the team, but so many other aspects were still extremely amateurish. When I was dropped by Wales for the game against England in 1975, I learnt the news in a phone call from Peter Jackson of the *Daily Mail*. Jacko was on the ball, just as he still is these days, but I doubt that he'll be the one telling Jonny Wilkinson that he's dropped when the time comes. Things are done far more professionally these days, in that respect at least. I learnt the news from Peter because none of the selectors had the courage to call me. I never even knew why I'd been left out of the squad, but I suspect it had something to do with my decision to play a club game for Llanelli within days of pulling out of a Wales match against Australia because of injury. The fact that I had recovered sufficiently didn't matter. Even so, I could have handled being dropped if the selectors had told me they were doing it. But to be told by a press man left a nasty taste in my mouth. Many things in rugby have changed for the worse in the past quarter of a century, but at least coaches have recognised their responsibilities when it comes to selection. When Woodward axes Wilkinson, or Steve Hansen tells Stephen Jones or Neil Jenkins they are being edged out, then at least those players can expect to hear it from the horse's mouth.

It hurt being dropped, but as Pat and I had suffered the death of our first child only a year previously I was hardly going to lose perspective. As things turned out I was soon back in the side because John Bevan dislocated his shoulder playing against Scotland. My relationship with John Dawes had not suffered from my non-selection. I accepted the decision, if not the manner in which I learnt about it. In fact, within two seasons I had been made Wales captain after the magnificent career of Mervyn Davies was brought to a shockingly premature halt by a brain haemorrhage.

I thought Gareth Edwards would have become captain, but John and his selectors felt Gareth suffered as a player when he carried the responsibility of leadership. I can't say I shared their view. Neither did Gareth and he still can't see it to this day. Still, I became captain and will always be grateful to John Dawes. Our relationship survived me being dropped and we both thrived. We won the 1977 Triple Crown – the second of four in a row – and at the end of that season we went off with the Lions to New Zealand together. I was captain. John was coach. We lost the series but that should not detract in any way from John's coaching achievements. He was a deep thinker about the game, a high achiever, but capable of celebrating

Grand Slams with a handshake and pat on the back rather than anything more openly emotional. He will surely go down in history as one of the best coaches, and certainly the most successful, the country has ever known.

If Clive Rowlands had been a tough act to follow, then coming in to the job after Clive and John Dawes in succession made things extremely difficult. Add in the vital factor of a team that was starting to break up, and this is truly the point where the job did indeed start to become impossible. Wales won another Triple Crown in 1979, just for good measure, and then John stood down. He left behind a team that needed to be rebuilt with careful nurturing, but he also left behind public expectations that were enormous and that demanded instant satisfaction. What a mix. The man left holding the restless baby was John Lloyd.

The 1970s had brought three Grand Slams and five Triple Crowns. In the 11 seasons stretching from 1969 to 1979 Wales either won the Five Nations championship or finished runners-up. Looking back, it was an amazing period of consistent success. Now came 1980 – a new decade, a new Welsh team, but the same level of expectancy. John Lloyd had been a very solid prop with Bridgend, but even his shoulders were not broad enough to carry such hopes and responsibility. Whoever eventually takes over from Alex Ferguson at Manchester United will quickly know the feeling. It wasn't that Wales suddenly became a bad side overnight; they didn't. It was just that winning only 50 per cent of Tests and losing to teams Wales had previously brushed aside was an unpalatable change of diet for supporters used to heaven's bread. The big names had gone and the difference they made could be seen clearly. Tight matches now started to go in the opposition's favour rather than to Wales and the coach began to take hostile criticism in the media, which had also grown accustomed to reporting success. John Lloyd spent two seasons in charge as Wales coach, and although he had some bright ideas he was replaced in 1982 by John Bevan and his assistant Terry Cobner.

Bevan and Cobner were a good mix. John, who sadly died in 1986 after an illness, had coached Aberavon, while Terry had been virtually a player-coach during his time with Pontypool. Both had played for Wales during the golden era of the seventies, both had toured with the Lions, and both knew what they were expected to live up to. They worked hard, were respected and shrewd in their handling of players and began to lay the foundations for what proved a brief period of recovery for Wales at the end of the 1980s. But Cobs and John, like John Lloyd before them, were operating in the toughest times for a Wales coach. They had so much to live up to and yet a quickly diminishing supply of talent from which to choose. Without anyone in the senior circles of the game in Wales able to identify a real shift in power, rather than just a blip, the cards were stacked against all three of them.

If someone had said to me in 1970 that Tony Gray would one day be a Wales coach then I would have thought they were either mad or had been drinking. Tony was a guy who I had toured Argentina with. He was a quiet, diffident North Walian who didn't seem to have the size of personality to take on such a big job. But, helped by Derek Quinnell, a man everyone respected, Tony became Wales coach in 1985. In some ways they were an unusual pair. Derek had no first-class coaching experience, while Tony had cut his teeth outside of Wales with London Welsh. Neither, then, were at the top of the coaching tree but they went about their job with a quiet determination to get things back on track – and for a while they managed it.

I had a lot of time for Tony Gray. He recognised good players and got them to express themselves and play somewhere towards their potential. He had the vision and bravery to make bold selection decisions – such as picking two other fly-halves, Mark Ring and Bleddyn Bowen, alongside Jonathan Davies in 1988 when Wales won at Twickenham. With a strong pack and the finishing power of Ieuan Evans and Adrian Hadley outside the flair of the three fly-halves, the 1988 side was a strong one. It deserved the Triple Crown success and came close to a Grand Slam. They were a very good team and I think they would have given any of the sides from the seventies a real run for their money.

I can remember being in the BBC Wales TV studios a few days before Wales played France in the final game of the 1988 championship. A Grand Slam beckoned but I felt Wales had looked tired against Ireland while France were a strong-looking side who had caught my eye despite losing to Scotland. I felt very guilty tipping France to win before the match and my fellow studio guests, Ray Gravell and Allan Martin, were appalled at my lack of belief. Unfortunately, I was proved right. But that defeat was a narrow one, just 10–9, and there was real, hard evidence that Gray and Quinnell were making progress. Unfortunately, they then had to tour New Zealand in the summer of 1988 and they happened to run into one of the finest and most ruthless All Black sides ever produced. Wales lost the first Test 52–3 and the second 54–9. All of the European teams would have gone the same way. This was the period when the gap between northern and southern hemisphere rugby suddenly widened to a gulf.

Of course, instead of realising that, the WRU pushed the panic button. It was completely unfair and ridiculous but the decision was made to sack both Tony and Derek. Everyone in Wales was shocked by the scorelines, but not half as shocked as seeing the coaches dismissed in the same year as they had won the Triple Crown. Talk about overreaction! Wales had lost heavily, but to the best team in the world. Real progress had been made in the two years leading into that Triple Crown, but it counted for nothing in the minds of the incompetents on the WRU.

What was really needed was a thorough examination of why the New Zealand players were so much better than our own. What had they done to move so far ahead? But that might have pointed a few too many fingers at those running the game, so they pointed a loaded shotgun at the coaches, instead. Clive Rowlands had been given a similar bloody nose by the All Blacks in 1969, but Clive was given time to get things right and he did it. Gray and Quinnell were not given that time – despite their successes – they were just given the boot.

Jonathan Davies pleaded the case for sticking with Tony and Derek. He urged the Union to consult the players who were eager to become more professional, more organised and more skilled. Bleddyn Bowen said the same thing. But the WRU ignored Jonathan. They wouldn't even let him address them on the subject at their own AGM. Disillusioned and demoralised by it all, Jonathan left for rugby league in the autumn of 1988. Others followed his path and Welsh rugby went from flying high with a Triple Crown into a destructive tailspin.

I felt very sorry for Tony and Derek. It was such a waste of their talent. It was also confirmation that the WRU were now reacting to defeat like the very worst kinds of soccer club chairmen. There were huge, fundamental problems with Welsh rugby in the 1980s, but the reaction to defeat now involved the forming of a lynch mob to go after the national coach, even though merely being paid to play and coach was still seven years away.

John Ryan succeeded Tony Gray in the autumn of 1988 and the bottom line for John is that he didn't have a hope in hell. This was now the time of the mass exodus to rugby league and Ryan had to try to make silk purses from cauliflower ears. His record of just two victories in his nine matches in charge shows he didn't make many purses.

John had not entered the job on the back of a long playing career with Wales or a sparkling record as a club coach. He was a decent man, but out of his depth when it came to rescuing Wales from the tidal wave of destructive neglect that was now starting to gather a rapid momentum. Instead of treading on solid ground established by steady progress under Tony Gray, poor old John was up to his knees in a mess that he had no chance of sorting out. Somehow, Wales managed to narrowly beat England in 1989 but by the following year the pattern of the next decade was being firmly established. Wales were well-beaten 34–6 at Twickenham and England scored four tries to one. These days no one would bat an eyelid, but back then this was viewed as a national humiliation of epic proportions and there were few dissenters when Ryan decided to stand down. I rarely get to attend post-match press conferences, as they normally take place when I am still on air for Radio Wales, but that day's was late starting and I shuffled into the back of a crowded room. I'll never forget John Ryan's face that afternoon. He looked wretched – a broken man. The responsibility was obviously too much for him and when the hacks started their grilling he seemed to melt away in his own misery. At one point I felt he was on the verge of tears. Had his captain, Robert Jones, not done well in deflecting some of the blame away from the coach then John could have suffered even more torment. It was a sad, sad sight. The nature of the Welsh job was changing because the identity of the man in charge was so much stronger than it had been before. John's misfortune was to walk into this brighter spotlight at a time when the players in Wales were simply not up to it, and so all that focus was thrust upon failings rather than success. John wasn't cut out for such intense scrutiny and I was hardly surprised when he threw in the towel.

The WRU needed a saviour, primarily to save their own disintegrating reputation, and they looked around for suitable candidates. The outstanding team in Wales at that time, and arguably in the whole of Britain, was Neath. So Ron Waldron, their respected coach, who had a slightly maverick reputation, was asked to step into the breach and he accepted. Ron did what anyone else in his position would have done; he relied on those he felt he could trust. In his case it was players he knew well at Neath. Suddenly, the team was half-full of Neath players, but still half-cocked when it came to shooting down anyone that mattered.

Wales lost at home to Scotland and then away to Ireland. Following the defeats to France and England, which had triggered Ryan's resignation, it meant Wales suffered their first ever championship whitewash. I can remember bumping into Ron that evening in Lansdowne Road. He was forlorn. 'It will always stick with me,' he said, shaking his head. 'The man who led Wales to a whitewash.' It was a harsh self-judgement, considering he had only been in charge for half the tournament, but

45

things weren't about to get much better. In fact, they simply got a whole lot worse.

Wales lost three of their 1991 championship matches as well and drew the other, against Ireland. It meant that for the third season in a row we were left holding the wooden spoon – a staggering reversal of the fortunes of the past.

Wales went on to tour Australia that summer and suffered record defeats, conceding 63 points in the Test and 71 points in a provincial match. The defeat to the Aussies was the cue for a fight to break out among the Welsh players attending the official post-match dinner.

Wales left Australia with their reputation in tatters, their dignity stripped away and poor old Ron nursing a heart complaint that soon forced him to step down. Much of the personal bitterness that had been directed Ron's way could hardly have improved his health. It's true he gave away cheap caps to certain Neath players who were of dubious inter-national quality, but that was not the real reason why Wales were declining. If Wales had been winning, no one would have noticed. Nobody complained that there were too many players from London Welsh during the 1970s. Ron was a good coach. He had proved that by shaping Neath into a very formidable team and bringing through players the rugby league clubs were eager to snap up. His emphasis on physical fitness may have been overdone but he was on the right lines, as other national coaches were to discover. It was the situation Ron found himself in that was all wrong. Chucked in at the deepest of ends it was little wonder that the waves engulfed him. The 1988 Triple Crown had been firm evidence of a revival in Welsh rugby, but the WRU pulled the rug away with their clumsy sackings, and confidence ebbed away from players, coaches and everyone else involved for the next three years.

I have no doubts that Ron's health problems were related to the stress of the job. It had become impossible to deliver success and impossible to live with the consequences of failure. By the end, I was glad to see Ron get out. Once your health and family life are put at risk then no job is worth it.

With Ron gone, there was more panic among the general committee of the WRU. I can recall a lot of daft names were being muttered by people who should have known better, but someone with a bit of vision and common sense must have won the day because the Union wisely asked Alan Davies, the Welsh-born Nottingham coach, to take charge on a temporary basis for the 1991 World Cup. His temporary stint became permanent and he eventually coached Wales right through to 1995. You might have thought that would have included the World Cup of that year, but thanks to their own methods of madness the WRU sacked Alan just a few weeks before the tournament – creating exactly the same situation before that World Cup as when he had come in four years before. Most countries change their coach a month *after* a World Cup, but Wales like to be different.

Alan was different. He was a bit eccentric although I have to say I didn't really take to his bow ties and braces. Neither did most of Wales. He had a plummy English accent and the red bow ties just made him look even more of an outsider. But he was a very sound coach and he should always be acknowledged for applying a brake to halt the speed at which Wales were careering downhill.

Alan took over at a terrible time following that shameful trip to Australia and although he brought some stability to the squad the 1991 World Cup was still a complete disaster. Wales lost to Western Samoa long before anyone took them seriously – the Samoans, of course, would later leave their mark on others – and although we scraped past Argentina we were thrashed by Australia, again, and found ourselves turfed out with the rest of the also-rans before the knockout stages. Once again, we were in desperate straits.

The results gradually began to improve, though, and even if Wales were still losing too often for most people's liking, Alan at least lifted the spirit and confidence within the squad. It wasn't a time of great achievements, but throughout 1992 and 1993 the team began to regain a bit of self-respect. We were no longer quite the laughing stock we had been in the summer of 1991. One of Alan's best decisions was to take on Gareth Jenkins of Llanelli as his assistant and I still firmly believe the time will come when Gareth will gain another crack at Test rugby. He and Mike Ruddock have clearly been the best Welsh coaches at club level over the past decade.

Although Alan and Gareth stopped the rot, they found it hard to convince the public that they were entirely on the right lines. A blame game had set in, fostered by a sense of parochialism that had spun out of control. I was used to petty village jealousies, but even though the rest of the world had moved on Welsh supporters appeared trapped by their own narrow-mindedness. Just as Ron Waldron was continually castigated for picking too many Neath players, so Alan found himself sniped at by those who felt he was leaning too far towards Llanelli, Gareth's club. When Wales played against France in Paris in 1993, there were eight Llanelli players in the side. The scoreline, 26–10, was certainly no disgrace but there was a lot of flak directed towards Alan by the anti-Llanelli brigade.

It all became too personal and I found it ridiculous. Among the most unpleasant and unappealing attributes of some Welsh supporters is their willingness to heap blame on some small band of folk for the failings of a nation.

The level of bitterness shocked me the night Wales lost at home to Canada in 1993 a few months after the French defeat. It was certainly a humiliating loss, our first ever against the Canadians, but there was a hostility towards Alan that was unjustified. Certain people in the game, including former Welsh internationals, questioned Alan's credentials simply because he hadn't played for Wales. I'd never felt that was a necessity for the job. After all, Carwyn James only played twice for Wales and yet he was the greatest coach I ever came across. In my mind it didn't matter. It was never a factor for me when Graham Henry became Wales coach and it didn't matter with regard to Alan.

As it turned out, Alan had the best possible answer to his critics: Wales won the 1994 Five Nations championship, the last occasion Wales have won the tournament. They beat Scotland, Ireland and France and lost a respectable match to England at Twickenham when they were going for a Grand Slam and Triple Crown. The team was well organised, efficient, difficult to unsettle and occasionally unpredictable – much like the coach. But within a year Wales were whitewashed in the championship just a few weeks before the 1995 World Cup. Alan, Gareth and Bob Norster, the team manager, were all forced out and the Australian Alex Evans was asked to take Wales to the tournament with just a few weeks to prepare and pick a squad. Deep down he probably knew he was on a hiding to nothing, but coaching at international level must have an appeal that temporarily blinds people to the blindingly obvious.

Alan Davies won 18 out of 36 matches in charge. Not a bad return when you consider the situation in which he found himself when asked to take over the reins. He introduced a level of professional back-up for players that hadn't been seen before and through careful attention to detail he transformed the team from an organisational shambles in 1991 to a team that lost only 15–8 to England at Twickenham when chasing that Grand Slam. If Nigel Walker had been given a few more passes earlier on in that match, then who knows what might have happened. But the problems of Welsh rugby, the real structural and especially the administrative weaknesses, couldn't be disguised by simply tightening up the national side's defence. The foundations of the game were still unstable and one grisly night in Johannesburg the roof fell in when a poor Irish team beat Wales to knock us out of the 1995 World Cup, once again before the knockout stages had even begun. Alex Evans was at the helm, a caretaker who found that not enough care had been taken on innumerable areas of the sport.

Typically, Alex was slated for packing the Wales team with too many Cardiff players, the club he had enjoyed great success with. It's become a knee-jerk reaction in Wales, even though it makes about as much sense as a car driver blaming engine problems on where his passengers are from.

Alex sounded off with a few home truths about the state of Welsh rugby, and was rewarded not with a full-time job offer but with the suggestion it was time he went home to Australia. He left in the winter of 1995, the tenth man to try the impossible job and the owner of the briefest record in it – just four games, which included only one victory. What has been striking about all the appointments is the complete lack of consistency and continuity. No coach was ever brought through the system. There hasn't been a system – just a succession of stabs in the dark, and it's been pretty dark for much of the time since the end of the 1970s. Two World Cups – 1991 and 1995 – were completely wasted because of this policy of chop and change and a pitiful lack of foresight. But at the start of 1996, the WRU promised that things would be different. For the first time they appointed a coach who had come through some kind of process by coaching Wales at U19, U21 and A-team level. Kevin Bowring, it was said by the Welsh Rugby Union, would take Wales through to the 1999 World Cup. He was also the first paid, full-time Wales coach after the move to professionalism. However, given the deep-rooted problems in Welsh rugby, I didn't think the money would save him. And I was right.

CHAPTER 4

Guided by the Great Redeemer

The catastrophic 51–0 defeat to France at Wembley in 1998 didn't turn Kevin Bowring grey. He was lucky on that front because he was completely grey when he came in. But the look on his face that Sunday night in London was the familiar expression of a man who knew his time was up. If the Welsh players hadn't forced him to that conclusion with the abject nature of their pitiful performance then the supporters must have convinced him through the silence that lasted the entire second half. It only pointed in one direction for Kevin and if he hadn't fallen on his sword a few days later then someone on the Welsh Rugby Union would have knifed him, if only to put him out of his misery.

It was all far removed from the optimism that had developed during the early stages of Kevin's reign. He wasn't pulling up trees in terms of results, but there was progress and more importantly his teams began to play with a style and verve that enabled every supporter to feel proud of the side again. Young players – like Leigh Davies, Arwel Thomas and Rob Howley – were given their opportunity and responded by playing with great flair and imagination. The future looked bright and even a defeat at Twickenham to England in 1996 was well received because Wales showed style and adventure before going down by just one score, 21–15. There was a three-year build-up period to the 1999 World Cup and after shamefully wasting the opportunities of the previous two tournaments there seemed a genuine determination to make this one count.

I liked Kevin Bowring. He was enthusiastic and energetic and had plenty of bright ideas on how rugby should be played and how rugby players should be developed. He had come from a background with London Welsh, so the usual accusation of bias towards one Welsh club or another wouldn't fit. The critics would have to dig a little deeper to find their dirt. I had played against Kevin and remembered him as a good, solid back-row forward who might have won caps for Wales in other eras when the competition wasn't so strong. I knew he could do well in the job and for a while that's exactly what he did do.

The sad thing for Kevin is that he knew that his own ability, and that of his players, was not going to be enough. He could see there needed to be change in both the running of the game and the attitude of the newly professional players – fewer easy matches, greater time spent on physical training and conditioning, a back-up of staff on the management – but the WRU turned a deaf ear. It must be very galling for Kevin to know that many of the things he asked for were given to his successor Graham Henry on a plate. Or perhaps it isn't, because Kevin now works for English rugby and the RFU.

Judged purely on results, the Bowring era was nothing special. In three Five Nations championships he won four matches out of 12. But Wales beat France 16–15 in 1996 and lost narrowly 27–22 in an exciting match in Paris the following season when the French won the Grand Slam. It seemed we weren't that far behind. He freshened up the team, and youngsters were given their opportunity. Wales were easy on the eye, even if the win–loss column still didn't make such easy reading.

Things started to go wrong sometime during 1997. Wales finished the Five Nations by losing 34–13 at home to England in the last match at the old Arms Park before they tore the old stadium down. The scoreline wasn't a demolition, but it was very one-sided and Wales seemed to lack confidence against a side much stronger physically and quicker, with the honourable exception of Rob Howley. In the autumn, Wales had to play New Zealand at Wembley. Bowring had become very taken with the southern hemisphere approach to the game and wanted Wales to try to play a similar ball-in-hand game to the Australians, having taken Wales on tour the year before and suffered two big defeats to the Wallabies. The trouble was that Wales didn't really have the players to adopt those kinds of tactics. It wasn't Bowring's fault. The Welsh club game at this time was slow and ponderous. Players would trundle from one set piece to another and then the referee would blow at the first breakdown in open play. It was all too static compared to the Aussies and the All Blacks.

Rather naïvely, however, Bowring believed that Wales could take the All Blacks on at their own game at Wembley and run them off the park. It backfired. Instead of running in the tries, the only thing that flowed was Welsh mistakes whenever we tried to counter-attack. Ironically, New Zealand showed the way with a much more pragmatic approach. They ran it when it was on, but Andrew Mehrtens kicked for position on the rare occasions his side were under pressure. The result was a comprehensive New Zealand victory by 42–7.

Things started to slip after that defeat. It's often the way and it's up to a coach to try and switch track, to offer something different in approach. Bowring wasn't able to, or maybe he simply didn't have the resources. Wales were slaughtered at Twickenham, 60–26, and it was obvious that the players had lost faith in what they were meant to be doing. Wales were okay as an attacking force, but defensively we were flimsy. The breeze, itself, could have blown us away. The Wembley defeat to the French was the last straw and Bowring decided it was time to go. Another decent man had bitten the dust.

Kevin was a capable man, though, and should have been retained somewhere along the line within Welsh rugby. For instance, he could have gone back to looking after one of the age-group sides, where he had proved very successful. Instead, he was thrown on the scrap heap, leaving it to England to re-habilitate him as a coach. He's firmly in the English system, helping to advise and guide other coaches, and he's obviously highly regarded by Clive Woodward. That's a credit to Wood-ward and England, and an embarrassing loss to our own game. It's yet another example of waste by Welsh rugby, which can ill afford such flagrant inefficiency. Wales were to pay a heavy price – literally – because the next national coach would cost £250,000 a year, about five times what the WRU were paying Bowring.

Graham Henry was a brilliant coach, a master media manipulator, and an impressive illusionist. He did wonderful things for Welsh rugby, but there was a sense of the illusionist's routine about Henry because when he went back home to New Zealand in 2002 Welsh rugby was in pretty much the same state as when he was appointed in 1998. For a couple of years he seemed to sprinkle magic wherever he intervened, but by the end people had had enough of the smoke and mirrors show because most of the tricks were no longer paying off.

When the WRU appointed Henry in the summer of 1998, I felt it was a good decision. I'll clarify that, because I knew they had already offered the position to Mike Ruddock and I had felt for a while that Mike had all the attributes for the job. The Union had asked their director of rugby, my old Wales team mate Terry Cobner, to trawl the world for the right man to replace Kevin Bowring. Cobner got as far as Dublin where Mike was coaching Leinster. He was in no rush to return to Wales, but when your country calls and offers you the top job then it's hard to resist. Mike said yes and Terry told the WRU general committee he'd found the right man. It was a good appointment as Mike was a very talented young coach who had enjoyed massive success with Swansea. I also felt his decision to coach in Dublin had widened his perspective and would protect him from the accusations that he was too closely identified with one Welsh club. The memory of how people had undermined Ron Waldron because of his Neath associations was still fresh in my mind.

But Mike was never to get his backside in the national coach's seat. The WRU general committee did an amazing U-turn. Having told Cobner they would back his judgement they then told him to keep looking for candidates because they had heard through a few murky sources that a New Zealander, currently coaching Auckland, might be interested in coming to Wales. His name was Graham Henry.

It was a despicable way to treat Mike and it's to his enormous credit that he shrugged his shoulders and went back to coaching Leinster. He later became the Wales A-team coach, and although he's finding it tough going at Ebbw Vale at present, where there are major financial problems, I've no doubt he would still make a very good Wales coach if given a crack after the 2003 World Cup.

If Ruddock would have got around his Swansea connection because of his experience in Ireland, Henry was a complete outsider. He was coming from the other side of the world and in that sense the slate had been wiped clean. But he has always been a man who could negotiate a good deal and since Wales were desperate, and he had just led the Auckland Blues to two Super 12 titles, he didn't come cheap. England had wanted him the year before but he had turned them down because he wanted to coach the All Blacks. But in the summer of 1998 the politics of New Zealand rugby seemed to be making that a less likely proposition. Henry was in his mid-fifties and knew the clock was ticking. If he was going to complete the transition from school headmaster to top coach then Wales was his big chance. So he took it. In countries where rugby matters, there is always a political agenda, and Wales were fortunate in that the politics of New Zealand rugby suddenly helped them sidestep the political problems at home of appointing another Welsh club coach. I was amazed when the press revealed Henry would earn £250,000 a year, making him by far the highest-paid rugby coach in the world. After all, Henry was hardly a name that conjured many memories within our rugby culture. It wasn't as if Colin Meads was coming over. But if that was the price of success, then, like most Welshmen, I was prepared to pay it.

There was a huge sense of expectancy before Henry's arrival and the character of the man was the perfect foundation on which to build a myth. He was very charismatic, clever, and hugely entertaining. He delivered great one-liners, normally deadpan but always followed with a twinkle in his eye and a knowing half-smile. Because he was an outsider he said things that no Welsh coach could have got away with. He challenged the way our rugby was organised, made observations that were brutally honest, and, most importantly of all, the results were spectacular.

In June 1998 Wales lost 96–13 to South Africa in Pretoria. It was the time before Henry's arrival and following the U-turn over Ruddock. Dennis John was the caretaker coach put in charge for the tour and a busload of players had dropped out before they had even left Cardiff. A few more injuries while they were out there left Wales threadbare and the Springboks simply tore us to shreds. It was so one-sided and utterly contemptuous that the crowd booed when the Boks spilled the ball near the Welsh line in the final seconds because it denied them 100 points. After the game the South African coach Nick Mallett described Wales as the worst international team he had ever seen. We had reached the bottom of the barrel and the only sound I could hear was the scraping and splintering of wood.

Into this mess strode Henry, a hired gun from out of town. It was a fresh start; a new era was about to begin. Those players who had cried off the summer tour now all claimed their various aches and pains had healed. So it was a full-strength team that took on the Springboks again at Wembley in November. Henry had told them they could beat South Africa and they very nearly did. Only a lack of concentration in the final few minutes saw Wales throw away the lead and eventually go down 28–20. After the game, people were euphoric, including the media and even some of the Welsh players. The only man who kept perspective and seemed mildly irritated was Graham Henry. 'We lost when we should have won,' he said. I realised then that his standards were much higher than ours. He wanted to be a winner and he wanted Wales to be winners again. I liked his style.

Things started quite slowly after that initial jolt. Wales were beaten by Scotland in the opening match of the 1999 Five Nations and then lost at Wembley to Ireland in a rather shabby and disorganised display. With France and England to come there seemed every possibility we were going to be white-washed again in the championship.

But then something quite extraordinary happened. Whatever message had temporarily lifted the players against South Africa, suddenly returned. Henry's claim that Wales could play a fast, open, expansive style was gloriously proved right with a thrilling 34–33 victory over France in Paris. The first half of that match was rugby of the highest standard and Wales were simply magnificent. Scott and Craig Quinnell tore into the French pack, Colin Charvis was everywhere, and Neil Jenkins controlled things from outside-half. The French darling, Thomas Castaignede, had a chance to win the game for the home side with the last kick of the match but struck it wide. Wales had won in Paris for the first time since 1975 and the scenes inside the Stade de France, and in Paris that evening, were wonderful. So many people had waited so long for that victory that they were ecstatic.

Who knows what might have happened if Castaignede had put that ball between the posts? Wales would have lost and may then have been beaten by England in the final match of the championship. Sometimes matches, reputations, whole careers can turn on such small margins. But Castaignede missed and a newly confident Wales beat Italy in a non-championship match a fortnight later. Then came the unforgettable 32–31 victory over England at Wembley and that astonishing last-gasp try by Scott Gibbs. Wales had turned a corner and the players believed Henry was the man responsible. Whether it was he or not doesn't matter. It mattered only that the players thought he was the reason for their change of fortune. They believed in the Henry factor.

After beating France, Italy and England, Argentina were beaten twice in their own country – the first time any team had whitewashed the Pumas on their own soil. The Henry band-wagon rolled on. In June of that year, Wales beat South Africa for the first time in 93 years of trying. Then Canada and the USA were brushed aside before Wales proved the Paris result was no fluke by beating France again just prior to the World Cup. At this point, a month out from Wales hosting the tour-nament, Henry was undoubtedly the most popular man in Wales and probably the most instantly recognisable. He was mobbed wherever he went. He was a guru, a national hero, a huge celebrity, and a prophet all rolled into one. People out-side of Wales were unable to realise just how overblown this profile became. Henry didn't ask for it. It just happened. He actually called for some realism and perspective. But the more he growled and grumbled like a dour Kiwi, the more praise would be heaped on him from every corner of Welsh society. It was the natural overreaction of a nation starved of success suddenly gorging on victory after victory.

I met Henry a few times during this period of heady

optimism. He had a presence about him, and a nice line in dry wit. He was impressive and yet there were odd moments when glaring gaps in his rugby knowledge would suddenly emerge. But he had some very good ideas and his drive, energy and sense of purpose made you feel you wanted to be alongside him on this incredible journey.

He was shrewd, too. All Welsh coaches take it as read that they will suffer a lot of stick from former internationals. It goes with the territory. It's not simply the regular voices in the media; there are always plenty of ex-internationals who will gladly be stirred by a poor performance into saying that the current coach has got it all wrong and things were so much better in their day. It's not that all ex-Wales players have a mean, vindictive streak. It's just that we care enough to want the team to do well.

Henry was obviously aware that this could present a problem for him and as he was an outsider the criticism might become harsher than normal if things went badly.

His solution was to invite a whole host of former internationals to attend a series of trial matches at Swansea one Saturday afternoon and then ask them to sit in on selection. Glad to be of service – or perhaps flattered – we all trooped along. There must have been around thirty of us. We enjoyed a pleasant lunch in the clubhouse before the action and then took our seats.

Henry had asked us all to concentrate on our own particular positions. I sat alone in the stand, with David Watkins sitting not far from me, and we watched the four guys vying for the Wales No.10 shirt. It was hard work as we were required to watch one player constantly whatever action was taking place. But I also felt it was a useful exercise in establishing how we

61

regarded the players in our positions. They were under real scrutiny. Afterwards, everyone was invited to join Henry for a selection meeting at which all the positions and various candidates were discussed in detail. JPR Williams gave his view on the four full-backs, JJ Williams and Ieuan Evans chatted about the wings, and so on right through from 1 to 15. Henry listened to all shades of opinion and made occasional notes. Finally, he thanked everyone for coming and every ex-international in that room went home thinking they were now part of the inner sanctum.

They weren't, of course. I don't think for a minute that Henry pored over our opinions. He probably folded his notes, put them into his pocket, and promptly forgot all about them. I don't imagine our musings made the slightest difference to the Wales team he eventually picked. But the point is that he had charmed us, won us over, and made everyone feel part of the action. There was an element of an elaborate con trick to try to muzzle his potential critics and for a time it probably worked. Yet even then there were certain things about that afternoon that made me suspicious. He wanted to charm us, but he also wanted to put a few of us in our place. Henry asked me which outside-half had impressed me. I told him Neil Jenkins should be his first choice but that Shaun Connor had caught my eye and explained why. Henry stroked his chin and said, 'That's interesting.' Then he turned to Leigh Jones, one of his advisors at the time and now coach of Newport, and asked, 'What do you think of Connor, Leigh?' 'Not up to it,' said Jones, without looking up. Henry glanced back at me, with a smile on his lips and then moved the discussion on.

I felt hurt by that. Henry appeared to be trying to de-value my opinion in front of a large and illustrious gathering. I thought, 'Who the hell does this guy think he is?' But I bit my tongue as I genuinely felt there was a useful point to the whole meeting and I didn't want to be seen as someone who was trying to undermine things. Within a week or two, Henry had developed his elaborate trick a little farther. He invited the same bunch of ex-internationals to the Vale of Glamorgan Country Club and Hotel just outside Cardiff, which had become headquarters for the Wales management and the team. A grand title had been given to the project now. I think they called it 'The Mentors' Scheme'. Basically, this involved making every former Welsh international present a personal advisor to the man who currently played in their position. In theory, this was a perfectly good idea. I've always felt that current players could benefit a great deal by talking to some of the older ones. For instance, young Welsh props like Iestyn Thomas, Ben Evans and Darren Morris could learn so much from informal conversations with a legend of the front row like Graham Price, someone who has not only achieved great things but recognises the finer points of that area more deeply than anyone else and commands such complete respect.

Henry, however, wanted to formalise that kind of relationship and guide it himself. Again, there was plenty of good food on offer and the wine flowed freely amongst the invited guests. Gareth Edwards sat and chatted to Rob Howley, while I enjoyed the company of Neil Jenkins and Stephen Jones. I knew Stephen well as I had followed his career closely since he was a young boy in Carmarthen. I had met Neil on a couple of occasions and found him a likeable bloke. Quite what I was meant to teach Neil, who had done pretty much everything in the game, I wasn't sure, but he asked me for my phone number and I gladly gave it to him. I joked that if every he wanted a good tip on the horses he should give me a call. It was all very relaxed and light-hearted, just exactly how that kind of relationship should be if it's going to work.

But Henry wanted something more structured, with reports and assessments. He talked about how they did this kind of thing in New Zealand and what a good system they had in place. I had an entirely open mind and was willing to be part of anything Henry wanted to do, but three months down the line it was as if that evening had never taken place. There were no follow-up conversations with me, or any of the other mentors as far as I could gather; no one from the Welsh management ever asked for a single word or opinion on how the boys were performing or what feedback we had given them. There were no files or paperwork. The system that Henry had trumpeted simply didn't exist.

Looking back on it now, perhaps it was just that Henry and his large back-up team simply had too many other things on their plate to concern themselves with the mentors' scheme. Or maybe they had second thoughts. It would have been nice to know, because the nagging thought is there in my mind that perhaps it was just a cynical exercise in silencing potential critics. Former internationals were hardly going to slate Henry if they were supposed to be in partnership with him. But the reality was that none of us were briefed by Henry or by his team manager David Pickering, any more than we were briefed by Tony Blair. It was a sham.

In professional sport, however, the real judgements are not of a person's sincerity. You are judged on your record. And Henry's record throughout 1999 was incredible as he took Wales on an amazing ten-match winning streak. He restored pride and dignity to the team after the depths of a year before and I, for one, will always be grateful. Suddenly, during that summer of 1999, everyone in Wales was talking about the rugby team again and was proud of their efforts. Even the fact that two of his players – Shane Howarth and Brett Sinkinson – were New Zealanders who had no right to be in a Welsh shirt didn't seem to matter. I felt uneasy about their presence, but like most of the Welsh media I was swept along with the euphoria of success and it took newspapers from outside Wales to expose their bogus credentials in early 2000. Looking back, I feel a certain sense of shame that I did not voice my concerns and discomfort about the two Kiwis before the Kiwigate scandal had broken and it was discovered that their grandparents had no Welsh connections after all. I admire guys like Byron Hayward who spoke up and was critical of their selection. At the time Byron's complaints were dismissed as sour grapes because he wasn't in the team, but he was completely right to be concerned about the tarnishing of our heritage.

Whether Henry knew he was breaking the rules we shall perhaps never know. The International Rugby Board cleared him of misconduct and found the WRU guilty of administrative incompetence rather than cheating, but it was certainly a stain on his reputation. He misjudged the mood of a nation when he expected the public would be as flippant about the issue of Welsh qualification as he and his management team had been. The team had begun to lose its sparkle and now one of the great magician's tricks had been exposed.

Strangely, that summer of 1999 when Wales beat the Springboks for the first time, was the pinnacle of Henry's achievements and influence. The World Cup of that year showed the team had already begun the descent that would finally end with that humiliating defeat to Ireland in the Six Nations of 2002.

Part of the problem at the World Cup seemed to be that players began to believe their own publicity. They thought they were better than they were and the hard work that had led to such huge improvements was obviously on the wane. Almost every individual Welsh player at that time began to let his own standards slip. Wales lost to Samoa in the pool stages and were bundled out of the tournament in the quarter-finals by the eventual winners Australia. I noticed, for the first time, that Henry had begun to criticise his own players for their mistakes and shortcomings. Cracks were beginning to appear.

In 1999 Wales had beaten England at Wembley, but 12 months later, just as the eligibility scandal was about to break, we were thrashed 46–12 at Twickenham and it could have been a lot more. To Henry's credit, Wales recovered to beat both Scotland and Ireland that year but the coach had already fallen out with some of his key players, like Rob Howley. Things were starting to spin out of Henry's control. When he was interviewed on TV the sparkle had gone, the self-confidence was draining away. The defeats mounted up and although there were a couple more highlights, such as another victory in Paris in 2001, these were temporary blips on the graph, which was now heading steadily downwards. The autumn of 2001 was awful, with a shocking home defeat to Argentina and a pathetic thrashing at the hands of Ireland in a match that had been post-poned due to the foot-and-mouth crisis. Ireland were first up at the start of the 2002 Six Nations and the 54–10 defeat at Lansdowne Road must rank as one of the most passionless Welsh displays of all time. There was nowhere for Henry to go after that disgraceful performance and he knew it. Within a few days he had resigned.

On reflection, Henry should not have accepted the offer to coach the Lions to Australia in 2001. The invitation was made in the summer of 2000 when things had already taken a turn for the worse with Wales. He should have realised what a massive job he had on his hands and told them to appoint someone else. But he was human, fallible like the rest of us, and I don't hold it against him for allowing ego and ambition to get the better of him. After all, I accepted the offer to captain the 1977 Lions when I should have turned it down. Henry's employers at the WRU should have been stronger and persuaded him to concentrate on the job in hand. As things turned out, the Lions tour took a massive toll on Graham, both physically and emotionally. He came straight back home to the Wales job and it was plain to everyone he was never going to be the same again.

After the 2002 Dublin defeat, Henry was interviewed for BBC Wales's *Scrum V* programme on the Sunday morning at the team hotel. He looked physically diminished, weary, his voice quiet and apologetic, and there was a haunted look in his eyes. I had seen that look before . . . in Kevin Bowring, Alan Davies, Ron Waldron and John Ryan. Now there was another name to add to the list. An impossible burden had again resulted in the only possible outcome. When Henry was made Wales coach in 1998, Glanmor Griffiths, chairman of the WRU, had used the phrase 'last-chance saloon' when discussing the future of the international game in Wales. Only three-and-half years into his five-year contract and Henry was pushing through the saloon-bar door, while Griffiths and others continue to sit comfortably at the table.

CHAPTER 5

Brown Envelopes, Whites Lies

Rugby union went professional in 1995, but Phil Bennett had beaten them to it by around 19 years. I'm not talking about illicit payments or even rugby league; after much consideration I eventually rejected the two big offers I received to go north. This particular foray into the ranks of paid sportsmen was something even more secretive, more unsuspected and more alien to my own world than the other code. This was pro-celebrity darts!

My agent, Malcolm Hamer, and a pal of mine, John Lloyd, had arranged for me to take part in a tournament in Leeds. A number of celebs from various fields had been invited to pair up with some of the big names in darts at the time, a sport that was just starting to attract major publicity and lots of cash. There was the Crafty Cockney Eric Bristow, the ice-cool Englishman John Lowe and two Welshmen – the big man Leighton Rees and the larger-than-life Alan Evans. I had been drawn to play with a very friendly guy called Cliff Lazarenko, although I'll admit the main attraction was the £200 I was told I could pocket for taking part. For a steelworker from South Wales, even someone playing rugby for Wales and the Lions, 200 quid was not to be sniffed at.

There was a packed hall and the beer had already begun to flow when I met Cliff backstage and explained that I was to darts what Leighton Rees was to downhill skiing. 'Don't worry,' he said. 'Just try and hit the board rather than the wall.' His humour must have calmed my nerves because we won our first round without too much trouble. Cliff was throwing really well and we won our second-round match, too. The quarter-final was also safely negotiated and by now Cliff was on fire. Our semi-final was against Eric Bristow and Fred Trueman. Fred was a bit of a star when it came to pub games and he actually presented a lunchtime TV show at the time that featured darts, skittles, bar-football and arm-wrestling. It was obvious he'd played a lot of darts and it was also apparent that the local audience wanted Fred to win, to defend the honour of Yorkshire.

But Cliff hadn't read the script and in a moment of inspiration, the Lazarenko–Bennett dream team put Fiery Fred and the Crafty Cockney firmly in their place. There was uproar. Punters were screaming and booing the place down. Fred and Bristow were at each other's throats, each blaming the other for the catastrophic defeat. 'You're bloody hopeless, Truman,' said Bristow. 'I'm the celebrity. Cricket's my game, lad. You're supposed to be the expert darts man,' argued Fred.

The storm had hardly died down by the time we had beaten John Lowe and the actress Liz Fraser in the final. A few more drinks had been consumed by this stage. If I missed the board and hit the wall, then Liz's darts weren't even finding the wall. Cliff threw the winning darts and punched the air in celebration before giving me a huge handshake. I assumed that Cliff's joy owed much to the fact that as well as a nice trophy, he was soon handed a big cheque for his night's work. I was given a smaller trophy and an envelope, as well as the dartboard, which Cliff had kindly autographed.

Once I was sitting in my car I opened the envelope. Inside was a cheque for £1,000. I was stunned. I'd never seen so much money. I put the envelope on the dashboard and drove out of Leeds before anyone had a chance to change their minds.

For the next few weeks after I had banked the cheque I walked around the house in fear. My anxiety had me breaking out into a sweat every time the phone rang. Surely, it was only a matter of time before the WRU got wind of my crime, I thought. They had their spies everywhere. They never missed a trick. My winnings would reach the ears of WRU secretary Bill Clement and I would be summoned to hand over the cash before being branded 'a professional' – a term of abuse in rugby union in those days – and kicked out of the game for good. But a miracle came to pass and I never heard anything from Bill or anyone else at the Union.

If you think I was overreacting then you obviously have no idea of the level of paranoia and pompous hypocrisy that ran through the administration of rugby union in those days when it came to the notion of payment. International rugby was booming and matches were played in front of huge crowds with millions more watching on television. But if you were paid a penny for playing you were 'professionalised' and banned. If you were paid to coach, scout, talk or write about rugby while you were still playing then the same applied. Not only that, but being in the mere presence of professionals, such as attending a rugby league trial game and gaining no payment, could taint you and again lead to a ban. You had been professionalised. If you then came back and played rugby union then you could professionalise others.

Professionalism was like a disease. And the four Home Unions of Wales, England, Scotland and Ireland saw it as their job to prevent you from being infected. I don't know how Bill Clement used to spend his day, but it must have involved reading a lot of newspapers and watching a good deal of television. Any signs, however small, of the corrupting influence of professionalism, and Bill would be on the phone. In those days a few of us would sometimes be asked by the BBC to make a guest appearance on the show *A Question of Sport*. It was always nice to be recognised as successful in your particular sport, it was good fun to go up to Manchester for the filming, and you might have thought the WRU would have welcomed the publicity. Instead, the Union used to send out dire warnings that any money earned must be handed over immediately to the WRU to be put into its charitable trust.

The boys at the Beeb knew this and were sympathetic to our cause. We used to be given a cheque for £150 and £100 in cash. The cheque was sent on to the Union. The cash was put in your pocket. The show got its rugby players, the Union got their cheque, and the players kept a little cash. Everyone was happy. Well, everyone it seemed except Bill Clement. Bill was a nice man but he was as tight as a duck's backside. He phoned me three days after one appearance and reminded me to send him a cheque. I did. About six months later, the programme happened to be shown again. Within a couple of days he was on the phone. 'Phil, I noticed you did another *A Question of*

Sport, this week. I trust you'll be sending us the appearance fee.' I lost my cool and shouted, 'Bill, mun, it was a bloody repeat!' 'Well, don't they pay you for those, too?' he asked.

If ever a man was well named it was Bill. Even getting legitimate expenses out the Union's coffers could still leave you out of pocket. Early on in my international career, I had yet to come to a generous arrangement with my bosses about time off from the steelworks and spending a weekend in Dublin to play for my country was leaving me around £40 out of pocket. Delme Thomas, Norman Gale and I travelled from Llanelli up to Cardiff Airport together in one car in order to fly out for the game. But since the mileage rate entitled us to about £3.50 each we all decided to put in individual claims. Almost as soon as we had checked into our hotel in Dublin, we were summoned to see Bill for the Spanish inquisition. 'I know you all shared the same car, so why are there three claims? Either you rip up this claim, or else this will be the last Wales match any of you are involved in.' I was young and prepared to let them put the cuffs on me there and then, but Norman had been around a bit. 'Listen, here,' said Norman. He then listed how in debt he was to friends, family, work colleagues, the bank manager and a few others who had helped in different ways to allow him to play for Wales. Grudgingly, Bill backed down.

The best Bill Clement story, though, was told to me by my old mate Bobby Windsor. He insists it's true. Having given sterling service for Wales and the Lions all over the world in the furnace of the front row, Bobby decided that the WRU should at least help him with the hire fees for the dinner suit he was obliged to wear at official dinners. So he went to see Bill Clement. Bobby explained how times were hard in the steel industry in Gwent, and, like many others, he had been put on short time. His wife and family were feeling the pinch and every bit of extra cash could help. 'So, if maybe the Union could help me out by hiring the dinner suits then that would be appreciated,' said Bob.

'I'm sorry,' said Bill. 'That's against the rules.'

'Well what about my shoes?' said Bobby, getting a bit desperate. 'Surely, you could help me out and allow me to buy a decent pair of shoes to look smart in? These ones are falling apart.' At this point, according to Bobby, to emphasise the point he took off his shoe and showed Clement across the desk how the sole was flapping at the toes. Bill thought about it for a few seconds and then quietly opened a drawer on his desk marked 'Ticket Money'. He took out a huge bundle of notes and untied them from their tightly wound rubber band. As Bobby was waiting for him to count out the cash, Clement chucked the rubber band over to Bobby and said, 'Here, that should sort out the problem with your shoes.'

I never had to wear rubber bands to hold my shoes together, but neither was I was ever paid to play rugby. I had 16 years of first-class rugby – 10 of those were spent at the very top level. But until I decided to write a book near the end of my playing days in 1981 it was all done without reward. I'm not bitter and I don't begrudge current players the money they earn nowadays. In fact, professionalism should have been accepted years before it was and good luck to those who can make a career out of rugby union. I loved the opportunities rugby gave me and I would hardly change a thing. The sport had its own freemasonry. It gave me respect, and meant I travelled the world for nothing. Thousands of boys who grew up near me never saw anything of the world, but rugby gave me a passport to explore. I met the emperor of Japan and the king of Fiji.

73

I saw wonderful countries like Australia, New Zealand, South Africa and Canada. And, as an amateur, I had the freedom to take a week off from the game on the very rare occasions when I felt tired.

We kept ourselves as fit as work commitments allowed, but when there was a chance to celebrate our successes we got stuck in – even if we hadn't the money to afford it. Take, for example, the time I ended up drunk in Paris, and insulted Sacha Distel. That was in 1977 after Wales had lost 16–9 to France. Jean-Pierre Rives had become the pin-up glamour boy of French rugby, a rugged back-row forward but with striking blond hair and a talent for self-publicity that almost matched his talent on the pitch. Rives worked as a public relations man in Paris for Pernod-Ricard. So, you might say he knew of a few bars and clubs where he and a bunch of Welsh players looking for a good night out would be assured of a warm welcome. Gareth Edwards, JPR Williams, JJ Williams and myself tagged along with Rives after the official post-match dinner as we went on a tour of the Paris nightlife. Everywhere we called, Jean-Pierre was greeted like a national hero and if the bar-owners had to fetch champagne for him and his new Welsh drinking partners then it seemed they regarded it as a small price to pay. We ended up in a nightclub where Sacha Distel was singing on stage. He may have been an international superstar, but I'm afraid to say I didn't recognise him in the state I was in. Suddenly, he had come off stage and joined our group. The drinks continued to flow and then Jean-Pierre was introducing me to him. 'Did you enjoy the set?' asked Sacha. Unaware who he was, I told him it was okay, and that 'Raindrops Keep Falling on My Head' was all very well, but did he know any Tom Jones? There was a puzzled look and a silence, which I decided to break by teaching my new pal Sacha how to sing Delilah. My performance must have relied more on volume than much vocal ability because it wasn't long before the bouncers were moving in on our group and Gareth was dragging me out through the doors just as I was halfway through the second chorus. Strangely, I was never asked back for an encore.

Those kinds of nights kept us entertained well enough, and so long as we didn't have to fork out for the expensive bottles of champagne we were happy. But there was one thing that Bobby Windsor, Gareth, JPR, Gerald, Steve Fenwick and the rest of us used to discuss and that was the pettiness of official-dom. They took us for granted and took us for fools. We would be playing matches in Cardiff or at Twickenham in front of 70,000 people, so it was only natural that we would often reflect on the fact that everyone made from the deal except us. It might not have been so bad if there had been some concessions shown, some gratitude and common sense. But in the seventies we used to have to pay for our wives' train fares to come to Cardiff for an international match and then pay for a hotel room if they wanted to spend the night with their husbands. None of us asked to be paid. It was never discussed. But we deserved better treatment when it came to the small issues like expenses, meals and accommodation.

The only money I did gain from playing rugby – and it was not a direct payment from playing – came from a very primi-tive and naïve form of sponsorship. The sports manufacturers adidas® used to pay us a couple of bob for wearing their boots – and it virtually was just a couple of bob. Gareth Edwards was at the top of the tree and there was a sliding scale. It was peanuts really, no more than a couple of hundred quid for the year, but it still had to be handed across in a brown envelope at the back of a car park on a selected day near the end of the season. Poor adidas® never knew this, but I wore their boots mainly because I liked them, not because they were paying me. If they hadn't given me them, I'd have bought my own. But I think they might have just been given the better half of the deal. After all, it must have been a very cheap form of advertising for them. When I kicked at goal for Wales, then the TV cameras could be on me for a minute and a half as I prepared to take it. How much would that have cost them if they had booked an advert? We knew we were being short-changed, but no one actually did the sums. After all, the Union always said that if you really wanted to get paid for playing then you could always go and play rugby league. Twice, I seriously thought about it.

I've always been a big rugby league fan and I still am. I watch a lot of live games on TV and have enjoyed the atmosphere and the quality of the rugby when I've been to the grounds. Rugby league folk are humorous, friendly, open and honest. They have always had a frank attitude towards money and the paying of players, and I've admired that over the years. My first offer was an open and simple one. Come and play for us and we'll pay you £8,000 said Halifax. I was 18 years old and in 1967 a sum of £8,000 could have bought half the terrace houses in my street in Felinfoel. I remember coming home one night and there was a big black car parked outside our house. A group of small boys were standing admiring it while their mothers and fathers were looking out from behind their curtains to see whom the people with the posh car had come to visit. It was me.

Two men in suits with northern accents introduced themselves and explained why they were there. My mother gave them cups of tea and sandwiches and they left me to think about it. All I could think of was whether someone might have told the WRU and whether I'd be banned for allowing them into the house. But I did think long and hard about it because it seemed like a fortune. I knew it would take me years to earn that kind of sum if I stayed. They were also going to find me a day job in Halifax and buy me a car. It was a tempting prospect, but the truth is that it was also terrifying because I was just a kid. I looked on a map and Halifax seemed like the other end of the earth. I think my mother was also worried about her son leaving home to go far away and play in such a rough, tough sport as rugby league. So I stayed.

There were plenty of other enquiries after that over the years. Not concrete offers, just strangers who'd come up to me and other players after a game and tell us they were the Welsh representative of so-and-so rugby league club and was I interested in going up for a trial. I wasn't. But the next serious offer came in 1975 when an agent acting for St Helens approached me in the lounge at Stradey Park one evening, long after everybody else had drifted away. He told me Saints had liked what they'd heard about my performances on the Lions tour to South Africa the year before. They wanted me to come and play the same way for Saints and they offered me £35,000. More agonising followed. Again, it looked like a major sum of money. But I was older and maybe a little bit wiser. I took advice from a few people and the feeling was that if I was going to go to rugby league I should wait two or three years until I was later into my twenties and had achieved everything I wanted to with Wales. But I have to confess that the money was very tempting. I didn't court any more offers when I eventually reached the later stage of my career, and even if there had been more I don't think I would have gone. I loved playing for Llanelli, representing Wales, and, more important than anything, I had a wife and two children whom I didn't want to uproot.

Looking back now, even in the early eighties, rugby union had ceased to be an amateur game, especially in the southern hemisphere. The All Blacks were starting to enjoy time off from work to train and before long the fruits of their labours on the field were also swelling their bank balances through sponsorship deals put into trust funds. We in the north were lagging behind and the rugby world was dividing. Not only were they getting away from us in terms of quality, but their preparation also was so much more thorough. That, of course, fed their improvements as players and increased the gap in quality. So I don't regret the change to an openly professional sport in 1995. It had to happen. Vernon Pugh, the chairman of the International Rugby Board, was right. The game was living a lie.

The transition, however, was badly handled. In effect, there was no transition. It happened overnight and in the UK it seemed to catch everyone out. What we should have had was 6 or 12 months to get everything planned in a uniform way across the world. The people with the business acumen and the rugby knowledge to make it work could then have been brought in.

What actually happened was a power struggle. Those who had a rugby background wanted to protect their own positions, while those with some financial expertise often seemed to be out to make a quick buck. Small club committee men couldn't cope. They got the shock of their lives when players started making demands, and no one really knew what the right wage levels should be. It was chaos and clubs such as Neath, Richmond and London Scottish went bankrupt. As for the players, a lot of them thought the gravy train had just pulled into their station. Overnight, they imagined they would have a status and wealth like soccer stars. There seemed to be an assumption everywhere in rugby at that time that the game was incredibly attractive to sponsors and TV companies. There was talk of breakaway leagues, of massive TV deals, with companies falling over themselves to televise club rugby. It was all a pipe dream, of course. The only real market was the one to televise international rugby. It's only very recently that I detect a willingness among broadcasters and sponsors to believe that club rugby could have a mass appeal through a tournament like the Heineken Cup.

As for the modern-day players, a lot of them are pampered and spoilt. Even more of them are just plainly overpaid. But I don't blame them for wanting to cash in, because this climate will not last forever and we have already seen a lot more realism come into the sport in the last couple of seasons.

I've no axe to grind with the very best players. Just as Ryan Giggs can justify his wages through his box-office appeal, so can a handful of rugby players. Jason Robinson, Jonny Wilkinson, Scott Quinnell, Brian O'Driscoll, Martin Johnson – these are high-profile sportsmen whom the public will pay to see. They put bums on seats and they should make hay while the sun shines because it's a short and demanding career at the very top. I would have loved to be able to make my own family financially secure through playing rugby in Wales. It's a great way to thank your nearest and dearest for the sacrifices they have made to allow you to play rugby. But where the game has gone mad is in the payments to run-of-the-mill club players by employers who are continually pleading poverty.

I don't blame the players. They have families to support and if someone's daft enough to pay £100,000 a year to someone who may not even be a current international, then good luck to him. But it's generally not money supported by real income. It's only there thanks to some rich benefactor. We've seen it over and over again in both Wales and England. We've even seen it in Scotland and Ireland where you would think the Unions, who fund the provincial system, would have more sense than to provide generous retirement homes for blokes from the southern hemisphere. I know of a lot of ex-players who are bitter at some of the rewards earned nowadays. They see the cash on offer for Welsh players and they can't understand why failure and underachievement should be rewarded when they were not rewarded for success. They have a point.

I would have loved to be a professional rugby union player, with the ability to pursue that career and remain in Wales. I would have relished the extra preparation time, the chance to get as fit as I possibly could have been. I'll admit I would have found a lot of what the boys do nowadays – the meetings and video sessions, for instance – a bit of a bore, but if that was the flipside of the coin then I'd have taken it.

So it does annoy me when I see some current players take that privilege for granted. A leading international player can set himself up with a nice little nest egg after six or eight years, so they should be extremely grateful. For instance, when Colin Charvis refused to make himself available for Wales's extra training sessions during the 2002 Six Nations and missed the opening match against Ireland, I was stunned. Colin's point was that the sessions had been rearranged by Graham Henry and clashed with a week when he had promised to take his younger sister on holiday to visit relatives in Jamaica. But two things struck me. First, what was he doing booking a holiday so close to the championship, anyway? It smacked of an amateurish attitude towards a career that has provided him with a very good standard of living. Second, the pride of playing for Wales should still mean so much that you are willing to make certain sacrifices – including risking the disappointment of your sister. The likes of Bobby Windsor, Graham Price and Charlie Faulkner were so desperate to form the Welsh front row in the seventies that they would have done anything to pull on that shirt. The very idea that there could be a clash with something as mundane as a week's holiday would have been inconceivable. In my opinion, Colin made a big mistake. On the field I don't doubt that Colin gives his all and is just as committed as all the players before him. Since taking over the Wales captaincy from Scott Quinnell there has been an impressive maturity about him and he has displayed previously hidden leadership qualities. He's also a very fine international back-row forward. But when I see a lot of these players nowadays strutting around with their headsets on, listening to music as if they haven't a care in the world, I do wonder whether it's all too easy for them. Maybe a lack of alternatives when it comes to selection has created a comfort zone.

It does anger me when I hear current players say to me, 'I'm disappointed I'm not in the Wales squad, Phil. But then again, I've still got a nice club contract and if Wales don't want me then that's their problem.' When was I dropped I felt devastated. There wasn't any loss of income, but there was a massive loss of pride, honour, prestige and self-respect. All I wanted was for the next game to come around so I could prove to

81

them I deserved to be back in the side. Bobby Windsor won 28 caps, while our reserve hooker at the time, Roy Thomas, sat on the bench for most of those games. Roy was Bobby's mate but Bobby was damned if he was ever going to come off the field just to give Roy a cap. They would have had to shoot him first. I'm sad to say that attitude seems to have gone. Too many players in Wales have become indifferent about whether they play for their country or not.

There are some exceptions. I know playing for his country still means everything to Robin McBryde, the Wales and Llanelli hooker. He has taken his fair share of stick for some performances, but Robin just wants to hang on to his place for as long as he can because he takes huge pride in wearing the jersey. But Robin seems to be one of the last of a dying breed.

It's sad to say it but England players have adapted to professionalism far better in so many ways than we have in Wales. Some Welsh players have responded recently, but generally we are miles behind – light years. The competition for places in Clive Woodward's squad is more intense and it appears to have galvanised a more ruthless attitude. When you look at men like Martin Johnson, Danny Grewcock and Ben Kay you realise what a fantastic work ethic is being created by the whole English set-up. The three of them are pushing each other so hard. First, it was Johnson who was world class in the England second row, then along came Grewcock. Now Kay has been right up there among the very best and suddenly the pressure is on the other two to respond. Perhaps that is what professionalism is all about – pride in your performance. If that is the gauge then you strive to make sure all your preparation, your fitness regimes, your diet, and everything else allows you to produce your best performance. The English clubs, and the

RFU, have provided a much better environment for their players to do all that than we have in Wales. The competitiveness of English rugby has focused players' minds and they have reacted by making the most of all the facilities and the back-up that is provided.

Unsurprisingly, we have all seen the consequences of this difference expressed on the field in recent seasons. For Welshmen, it hasn't been a pretty sight. We need a new attitude to professionalism in Wales. Instead of thinking they have made it when they gain a contract with their clubs and with the WRU, the players must realise they have only just started out, that the hard work is only beginning. Attitudes are changing, but it will take time. I was pleased to see at first hand the superb attitude of the young players who toured South Africa with the Welsh squad in 2002. They were enthusiastic and determined to do well and improve. They were also proud to play for Wales.

Back in the seventies the WRU believed that if you were paid it made you a professional. It wasn't true then and it's not true now. Gareth Edwards was the ultimate pro in terms of his attitude, although he played for Wales for nothing. Likewise, too many current-day players bank the cash but prepare like amateurs.

CHAPTER 6

The World in Union

Professionalism has changed rugby union beyond all recognition in many respects. It has altered the way we view players, teams and their achievements. Clive Woodward coached England to the Triple Crown in 2002. Did anybody notice? Did anyone care? Winning a Triple Crown was once a badge of honour, but now it's barely acknowledged and seems to carry all the impact and significance of finishing runner-up in the Boat Race.

It wasn't always like that. Wales won four Triple Crowns on the trot back in the seventies, two of which were wrapped up neatly inside a Grand Slam. The big prize back then was the Grand Slam and if Woodward had managed to nail down one of those in the years they slipped through his grasp, then it would still count for a great deal as far as his judgement by the media was concerned. But it would not be the ultimate performance indicator. Nowadays, that has become the World

Cup – and Woodward recognised as much when he asked to be judged on his performance at the 1999 tournament.

Unfortunately for Clive, England could not get past the quarter-final, but at least Woodward knew the score. The World Cup has come along and dwarfed everything else in world rugby, except, maybe, Lions tours. For any coach, in the northern or southern hemisphere, it's the acid test; what the coaches of Australia, New Zealand and South Africa are working towards each year when they harness their players' talents for the Tri-Nations and what the Six Nations coaches have in mind when they talk about progress from one Six Nations to another.

The Six Nations used to be it; for everyone it was the final destination, the end of the line. Now it's part of a great four-year cycle, which the whole of rugby rides from one tournament to the next. National coaches have become like national prime ministers. The only difference is that while one job carries a term of office stretching between general elections, the other spans the four years between one World Cup and the next.

It took Wales a while to catch on to this development. Like much else that passed Welsh rugby by in the eighties and nineties, the World Cup sailed past without the people that matter really noticing its significance. So Wales changed their coach weeks *before* the 1991 World Cup, did the same again in 1995, and changed jockey again just 12 months out from the 1999 tournament.

There were no World Cups for rugby players like myself who played in the era prior to 1987. That was a pity because although the sport was amateur there was always sufficient interest in the Tests against the major touring nations to

85

suggest that a tournament where they could all come together at the same time would be a fantastic step forward for the game.

South Africa would have provided a problem had there been a tournament in the 1970s because of the political situation there. But who knows? Perhaps a World Cup at that time, without an invitation extended to rugby-obsessed South Africa, might have nudged the country towards an end to apartheid a little sooner. When the tournament was eventually hosted by South Africa in 1995 it certainly made me feel the country had been forced to change because it knew the world was coming through its doors and the world would judge it.

The final of that tournament in Johannesburg still stands as my best sporting memory since I gave up playing rugby in 1982. It was the only time since I retired that I have felt such a charge of pure emotion run though my body. When Nelson Mandela walked out to meet the Springbok players before the final there was an energy and a tension in the air that you usually only feel so sharply when you are actually playing yourself. But that afternoon 70,000 people felt it. It was electric and as soon as the great man greeted François Pienaar in the centre of the field, both wearing Springbok jerseys, you could sense there was no way South Africa were going to lose that final.

I think the 1995 tournament has been the best World Cup that rugby has seen and it will take some beating. Not that it was particularly memorable for the right reasons if you were a Welshman.

Wales opened their group games with a convincing and comfortable victory over Japan, but then they had to play New Zealand at Ellis Park. The All Blacks are not normally lacking in motivation to do well for their country, but just in case they were not quite at their maximum levels of single-mindedness Geoff Evans, the Wales team manager at the time, topped them up nicely. In the press conference before the game, he said Wales were bigger, faster and stronger than the All Blacks and therefore had nothing to fear. Nice one, Geoff, I thought when I heard his remarks. Almost before the words had finished coming out of his mouth I could visualise them being repeated by Sean Fitzpatrick in the All Black dressing room.

It was a nonsensical thing to say – especially when you consider this was uttered at a World Cup when the eyes and ears of the world's media were present. What was he thinking? Did he really think it would inspire his own players or somehow strike fear into the hearts of the All Blacks? Had he not looked at the Welsh playing record against New Zealand? I don't think I was alone in cringing with embarrassment when I heard him say it. It served only to heap more pressure on his own players and wind up the All Blacks. For dull remarks made on the eve of Tests, it takes some beating. It was the utterance of an amateur just as the rest of the game was moving speedily towards professionalism.

Jonah Lomu had taken the tournament by storm and it was to their huge credit that Wales stopped Lomu from scoring that night. But the All Blacks still won 34–9, could easily have scored more if they had not slackened off, and Wales were lucky to get nine. It meant Wales had to beat Ireland to make the quarter-finals, but it was a task that proved beyond them and they lost 24–23.

Alex Evans, the Australian, was the Wales coach at the time and although he had done a very good job with Cardiff I felt he made some very poor decisions before the tournament. The biggest was to take the captaincy off Ieuan Evans and give it to

Mike Hall. On the surface it probably made sense to Alex because Hally knew Alex's methods and demands from their time together at Cardiff. But Ieuan was the one world-class player Wales had at the time and Alex should have realised the detrimental affect it would have on him. Worse still was the effect it had on the whole Welsh squad. The decision immediately divided them into the Cardiff camp, who had strong previous loyalties to Alex, and the rest who were equally as loyal to Ieuan. Alex had been in Wales for a good while and he knew the tribal nature of Welsh rugby. He should have been striving to unite the players, not split them.

In the week leading up to the Ireland game there were plenty of stories flying about of unrest and unhappiness in the Welsh camp. Most of them centred around Alex, Mike, Derwyn Jones, Hemi Taylor, Jonathan Humphreys and what was perceived as a Cardiff mafia that had taken over the squad. It may have been true. It may have been complete rubbish. But the fact was that some inside the squad believed it to be true and for that Alex has to shoulder a large part of the blame. The result was a passionless and insipid display against Ireland and exit from the World Cup before the knockout stages.

I was leading a Gullivers' tour party of Welsh supporters who now found themselves with tickets to see Ireland take on France, while the Welsh team got ready to fly home. With a couple of jars of Guinness inside us we all became Ireland fans, but they were not good enough to beat France and so the French were left to take on the host nation for a place in the final.

Everyone present that day will remember the Durban semi-final match for mostly one reason – the rain. It poured down all day. Seven inches fell inside twenty-four hours. Before the

At home in Felinfoel aged 4, my toes were just starting to twinkle and I was perfecting my sidestep in order to stay out of trouble.

My first cap for Welsh schoolboys aged 15 against England in 1963–64. It was my first trip to Twickenham and we won 11–3.

My best match. My wedding day with Pat on 21 March 1970. She was my biggest supporter at the time and she has remained so in the years since.

With my mother, Mary, after beating France in 1978 to win the Grand Slam. I had decided in the week leading up to the game that it was to be my last match for Wales.

Three sons of Felinfoel: In the clubhouse with James (left) and Steven who both followed me in playing for our village club.

Time to relax. Enjoying South Africa with Pat and my pal John Lloyd in 1997, 23 years after I had toured the same country under apartheid with the Lions. The 1974 tour was a trip I came to regret.

A pint with the boys. Celebrating on New Year's Eve 1988 with friends Wynford Thomas (left) and Huw Owen. Two years later, New Year's Eve would be memorable for very different reasons following my car crash.

Captain Fantastic: Watching the inspirational Delme Thomas lift the WRU Cup in 1973 after yet another victory in the final for Llanelli.

Attacking the old enemy: Timing a pass to Ray Gravell as we look to open up England again during a Six Nations battle at Twickenham in 1976.

Dawesy: John Dawes inside the old Cardiff Arms Park – as successful a Wales coach in the second half of the seventies, as he had been a player in the first half.

The Invincible Lions: The squad that toured South Africa in 1974 and didn't lose a match. I'm sat to the left of our mascot.

Gone fishing: Fellow Lions JPR Williams (left), Gareth Edwards (centre) and England's Tony Neary use a fishing trip as an excuse to relax with a drink and try out their shades.

Big man, big appetite: Fran Cotton, who tucked into opposition front row forwards on three Lions tours and was a colossus of English rugby.

Broon of Troon: The late, great Gordon Brown of Scotland. As ever he sees the funny side during a break in training on the 1974 Lions tour of South Africa.

That winning feeling: Lifting the WRU Cup as captain at Cardiff Arms Park after Llanelli had beaten Swansea in the final. It was our fourth consecutive win.

One for the road: Fellow Lions tourists enjoy a final farewell drink before we fly off to New Zealand in 1977. From left to right: Willie Duggan, John Dawes, Derek Quinnell, Doug Morgan and Phil Orr.

Hard nut: The toughest, bravest and funniest hooker I ever played with – the one and only Bobby Windsor – considers his options during a game of pool on the 1977 Lions tour of New Zealand.

Sign here: Gordon Brown obliges for a young fan during a break on the 1977 Lions tour in New Zealand as JJ Williams looks on.

Breakfast in bed: The speedy JJ Williams re-fuels for another day of touring in New Zealand in 1977, but Steve Fenwick is not so quick off the mark.

Perfect day: Scoring the first of two tries for Wales against France in 1978. We won, clinched the Grand Slam, and I retired a happy man. Team-mate Gareth Evans starts to celebrate.

Perfect ending: My second try in the same match at Cardiff Arms Park. France scrum half Jerome Gallion got his tackle in, but I scored and captained Wales to the Grand Slam.

Steady hands: Receiving the 1977 Welsh Sports Personality of the Year award in the year I captained the Lions.

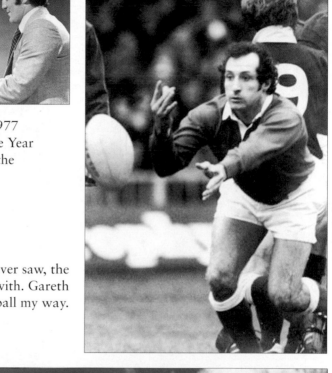

The greatest: The best I ever saw, the best I ever played with. Gareth Edwards passes the ball my way.

One last shove: The feared and famed Pontypool front row of Graham Price (left), Bobby Windsor (middle) and Charlie Faulkner pull on a Welsh shirt for old time's sake to remind Wales of what we've been missing.

Sidestep and sideburns: JPR Williams, socks around his ankles, was the most ferociously competitive player of his generation and a reassuring presence at full back.

Hero: Gareth Edwards walks back towards his team-mates after scoring his legendary try against Scotland at Cardiff Arms Park in 1972. Spike Milligan argued for a church to be built on the spot where he slid over.

Baa Baa black: Looking for a way out of the mud, playing for the Barbarians – the amateur rugby club which has refused to die in the professional era. Scotland's Jim Renwick is in support.

Life under Clive: Posing for pictures at a Wales training session, which were always enjoyable and well-attended by fans, during Clive Rowlands' time as coach. (Back row, third from left).

match could start there was an unforgettable contest between the heavens and what looked like a bunch of black washer-women who carried their mops, brushes and buckets on to the King's Park pitch in an attempt to defeat the rain. I suppose they did defeat it in a sense because the match went ahead but I could not have been alone in the stadium in thinking the pitch was barely playable. All that planning and preparation before the tournament, all the modern technology that is now used by groundsmen at major stadiums, and yet the semi-final of the World Cup hinged on whether or not a bunch of women could sweep the surface water away with a few long-handled brooms.

At least there was some Welsh interest in the game that day. Derek Bevan was referee. Derek's first big decision was to declare the pitch playable and the game duly went ahead after an hour-and-a-half's delay. He had some other big decisions to make during the match, as well, the most crucial of which was to deny France a try that would have put them in the final in the dying minutes. Abdel Benazzi went very close and then there were strong grounds for feeling that France should have been awarded a penalty try. But destiny appeared to be with South Africa that day, as it would be again in the final, and they edged through 19–15. The second semi-final was in Cape Town the following day. The two teams were England and New Zealand, but the match belonged to one man – Jonah Lomu. The talk before the match was how Lomu might struggle against the experience and pace of Tony Underwood and the expert tactical kicking of Rob Andrew. But all the talk was proved worthless two minutes into the game when Lomu scored his first try. He scored a second and then a third and stopped at four. It was quite possibly the most devastating individual performance that I had ever witnessed on an international rugby field. Of course he was powerful, but Lomu also had startling acceleration and for such a big man he had incredibly nimble feet, which allowed him to run narrow channels down the touchline. New Zealand eventually scored six and England had been destroyed.

After the match, which England did well to lose only 45–29, Will Carling described Lomu as 'a freak'. I thought that was a bit ungracious and almost insulting. Anyone who had seen Lomu's growing impact on the tournament would not have been surprised by what he achieved against England. It was no way freakish. In many ways you could see it coming. England were a very good side, but they played by numbers and in zones. They were predictable. The All Blacks attacked whenever they felt England might be vulnerable. It didn't matter where they were on the field or how many phases had been gone through from the set piece. All that mattered was their attitude and intention. It has taken England a long time to play with the same freedom and variety, but even if Clive Woodward fails to bring home the World Cup in 2003 he has at least taken England along a path whereby they cannot be worked out as easily as they were in 1995.

After the game, I found myself in a bar alongside Welshmen, Irishmen, Scotsmen and Japanese supporters who all celebrated as if their team had actually won the World Cup. There is nothing quite like sharing in the celebrations of an England defeat to bind other nations together. To be perfectly honest, I had wanted England to win that day and part of me would love to see England win the World Cup. They are Wales's nearest neighbours and it would do a power of good for rugby in the entire northern hemisphere. But there is also a part of me, deep inside, that smiles with satisfaction and relief every time England fail to make the grade. Before the Cape Town match I had watched England fans singing 'Swing Low, Sweet Chariot' as they did the Conga outside a bar. I winced a little when I thought what they might be like if they actually beat the All Blacks. It is the same feeling I have when I walk through the Twickenham car park and watch the Home Counties set enjoying their Harrods' hampers. Maybe it's just a gut cultural instinct, or a class thing, but when England lose there is always this small sigh of relief. At least Henry will not be hooraying at my expense.

Don't misunderstand me. It's not as if I think Wales were the most generous and gracious winners when we were successful. We weren't. Sometimes in the seventies I know our supporters could be as unbearable in victory as anyone. It's just that, unlike those from other countries, English fans always seem to behave in victory as if success is somehow the natural order of things.

After raising a glass or two to New Zealand, along with my group of Welsh supporters, I can remember the bar manager turning to me near the end of the evening and telling me they had broken all records for bar takings. 'If only England could lose every night,' he said. I smiled and someone else ordered another round.

It got better because England then had to play France in the third-place play-off in Pretoria. If England thought the stadium would be empty then they must have been shocked at the packed stands for what is always, in soccer and rugby, a fairly meaningless exercise. The large attendance can be easily explained. The tour companies are always on the look-out for an uncomplicated, easy-to-arrange night out in midweek, and what better way of entertaining crowds of Welshmen, Scots and Irish than bussing them into a stadium where there was a chance of witnessing another England defeat. France had never had so many neutrals on their side.

England played poorly and lost 19–9. Later that evening I met Will Carling's father, Bill, a very decent bloke but who was obviously a bit down. What he must have made of a bunch of Welshmen singing and slapping each other's backs when their own team had flown home two weeks ago, I can only imagine.

At least, most of them had flown home. Some of them couldn't quite face it. In Durban, Pat and I were having a meal in a pub one night when I was aware of this looming presence behind me. I turned around and there was the big Wales second row Derwyn Jones, all 6 foot, 10 inches of him, with a worried look on his face. Behind him were Jonathan Humphreys, the Wales hooker, and their Cardiff clubmate Adrian Davies. All three looked rather anxious.

'What are the papers saying at home, Phil?' asked Derwyn with a nervousness not normally associated with someone of his size.

I looked back down at my plate and grimaced. 'Well, it's not great by all accounts,' I said.

'I knew it,' said Derwyn in a rising panic. 'We can't go home yet, boys. We're going to have stay a bit longer until it all dies down.' The others nodded and stared hard at the floor.

I think I must have spoilt their evening, which was a bit harsh on poor old Jonathan who had enjoyed a decent World Cup. The three of them must have arrived home at some stage that summer, but by then they couldn't even say they had been beaten by the tournament winners. South Africa saw to that in the most astonishing final. It may not have been the most spectacular rugby match but the 1995 World Cup Final at Ellis Park will live in my memory as the most extraordinary sporting occasion I have attended. The buzz in Johannesburg on the day of the final was amazing. There was colour and noise and bustle on every street corner. What struck me immediately that morning was how the black population felt involved and interested in the result. They wore Springbok colours on the streets, they chanted for the Boks, they even sang 'Shosholoza' – the black working-man's song, which had been adopted as a kind of rugby fans' anthem – in the bars and restaurants. If you had suggested to me back in 1974 when I'd been in South Africa with the Lions that kind of response – that kind of unity among the population – then I would said it was impossible. It is inaccurate to say it brought the whole South African nation together, because I know from visiting townships that there were millions of people who couldn't give a fig for the South African rugby team, or for rugby in general, and maybe many more who had more basic concerns to worry about, but it still felt as if there was a fresh spirit of progress in the country that day which I had certainly never experienced before.

Inside Ellis Park itself there was a raw, rowdy atmosphere long before the kick-off. The term 'carnival atmosphere' is a cliché, but this really felt as though you could have taken the supporters out along the streets, and the noise and the music would have carried on all day. I was sat surrounded by a group of Springboks supporters who were on their feet with excitement when the enormous South African Airways jet flew low over the stadium, but the moment when Mandela came out on to the field to greet the teams was the real high point. There was so much pride and dignity about the man. He wore a

Springboks jersey and green cap, and a huge, beaming smile. It was a gesture of reconciliation that spoke volumes for the man, and the emotion of the moment reduced grown men all around me to tears.

In 1974 Mandela had been a prisoner. Now he was the figurehead for a whole nation united behind their team. 'One Nation, One Team' had been the South Africans' marketing slogan for the Springboks and for a few moments before kick-off you could almost believe South Africa was indeed a united nation. They were certainly a united team. New Zealand had been hot favourites to win that final, but something about that reception for Mandela convinced me that the 15 Springbok players would deliver the performance of their lives. I simply couldn't see them losing. There was the prospect of becoming legends for all time if they could win the day.

In many ways it was a poor-quality final, but finals are rarely high quality. Tension inevitably gets the better of players. Lomu looked enormous when he stood by the touchline just in front of me at kick-off. But like every other All Black that day he was cut down to size by the sheer hunger and determination of the Springboks. They oozed defiance and a shared sense of destiny. They needed extra time, but the will of an entire country seemed to drag that drop-goal attempt from Joel Stransky to fall between the posts.

So South Africa were world champions and although they were not the most talented team in the tournament they deserved their triumph for their team spirit and their single-minded dedication. It is also true to say that the South African organisers had used every trick in the book in order to help their side. At every break in play there would be a blast of some or other South African rugby song over the tannoy. Flags would be flashed up on the giant screen, anything to whip up the crowd into another frenzy. My wife, Pat, was most indignant and complained about how unfair it was for the poor New Zealanders. She had a point, but it was to the huge credit of Sean Fitzpatrick, the All Blacks skipper, that no issue was made of it after the final. Fitzpatrick even approved of the extra razzamatazz and said it was just what the sport needed.

We joined the crowds of people celebrating around Ellis Park and it really was a privilege to be there as whites and blacks who didn't even know each other embraced and shared their joy and excitement. It was the most incredible day of sport I have ever experienced. It was a real honour to have attended the 1995 World Cup and the other three tournaments cannot match it for drama and historical significance – but they had their moments.

The 1991 World Cup, staged by the four home unions and France, is painful to reflect upon as a Welshman because we were desperately poor in all three games until we crept out again in the pool stages. The opening defeat, 16–13 to Western Samoa, was a shock from which Wales never recovered and although they scrambled past Argentina there was never a remote chance of beating Australia in the final match. We were completely outclassed, losing 38–3.

Mark Ring was one of my favourite players at that time, a real genius who delighted Cardiff supporters with his brilliance and invention. He had great vision and wonderful ball skills but a few minutes into that opening match against Samoa it was clear that our Welsh fly-half, upon whom so much depended, was playing on one leg. His other was heavily bandaged and he was only operating at about 50 per cent capacity. It was a ridiculous decision by Alan Davies, the coach, and Bob

Norster, the team manager, to even consider playing him. Ringo was also asked to do the goal-kicking, and although he landed a couple some of his other attempts would have been laughable had not the pain he was suffering in having to take them been so obvious

Samoa scored a disputed try, but they were the better side and they roughed Wales up with some ferocious tackling. They had hungry young players who went on to become proven, high-quality internationals such as Brian Lima, Frank Bunce and Pat Lam, and they deserved their victory.

Wales beat Argentina 16–7 in a poor game and although I had seen two games in Cardiff, as well as one at Llanelli and another at Pontypool, I'm sure I wasn't alone in Wales in thinking that the real excitement of the 1991 World Cup was going on elsewhere.

England had run the All Blacks close at Twickenham and so had the Italians in a marvellous display at Leicester. Scotland and Ireland were going well and the Canadians had given France a real scare after beating Fiji. In Wales, though, things seemed pretty muted and I don't think I had ever seen Wales lose in a more one-sided contest than the defeat to the Wallabies that put us out. Australia scored six tries and it was my first view close-up of a young Aussie second row called John Eales. He looked such a fantastic athlete, and his handling, speed and fitness made the Aussies appear as if they had an extra back-row forward on the field. Eales looked every inch a world-class forward and ten years later he was still at it when the Lions lost to Australia. He is modest, approachable and hugely respected around the world and was, without doubt, one of the all-time greats of the game.

Wales were out and the tournament had proved disastrous,

consisting of one narrow victory, one shock defeat and one complete thrashing – all played out at the Arms Parks where opponents used to fear us. It was 13 years since I had been part of a Grand-Slam-winning team but that day it felt like an eternity.

Australia went on to play Ireland in a Dublin quarter-final that provided the tournament with a real shot in the arm. Gordon Hamilton scored a wonderful individual try and with six minutes to go Ireland were leading the Aussies 18–15. But the Wallabies were so professional, so patient. They bided their time, refused to panic, and scored a well-crafted try through the cool-headed Michael Lynagh to win the game 19–18. Truly great teams never believe they are beaten until the last whistle is sounded and this was the emergence of a truly great side.

I was back in Dublin a week later to see Australia beat the All Blacks in the semi-final in which it was the genius of David Campese that this time proved the difference between the sides. I think it was one of Campo's great matches. His critics had always admired his skills and frills but they had claimed he rarely produced when it really mattered. But against New Zealand, with a place in the final at stake, he was head and shoulders above everyone else on the field. He destroyed New Zealand that day and the Wallabies could have won by more than 16–6.

England beat Scotland 9–6 in the other semi-final in a gutsy, hard-fought victory at Murrayfield and the scene was set for a final between northern and southern hemispheres and a wonderful contrast of styles.

England were methodical, single-minded, limited in many ways, but very effective. They relied on a huge pack to win ball and then counted on Rob Andrew to provide most of their points. Paul Ackford and Wade Dooley were their second rows – hard men with a mean streak. Mick Skinner, Mike Teague and Peter Winterbottom formed an aggressive back row with the emphasis on persistence and determination. The front row of Jason Leonard, Brian Moore and Jeff Probyn provided a very steady platform in the set pieces. If you had watched England on the training field then you knew what you were going to get on match day. The pack would win the ball and Andrew would either kick up in the air, into touch, or at the posts. That was it. If the ball ever went out to Will Carling, Jeremy Guscott or Rory Underwood, it was by accident rather than design.

But it had proved very, very effective. England had won the Grand Slam that year and they were the only force in the northern hemisphere which looked capable of taking the World Cup to Europe. For what they wanted to achieve, England had struck upon a near perfect group of players – hard forwards, consistent half-backs, and outside backs who could tackle. They had shown the potential of their side by winning their quarter-final in Paris, 19–10, against a French side that tried to match the English up front and failed totally.

But in the week leading up to the final a strange thing happened. England were suckered. They fell for the oldest trick in the book. They took more notice of their critics than they did of their own instincts. Campo had started the ball rolling. He slaughtered England's style of play and condemned them for being boring and predictable. Then a host of other players weighed in as well and suddenly England felt as if they were having to justify their tactical approach. The best justification would have been to parade the World Cup trophy around Twickenham, but instead the criticism seemed to get under

England's skin and their whole approach in the final against the Aussies changed.

Finals are all about winning. They are not about pleasing neutrals. You please your own fans by lifting the Cup. It was the approach Llanelli had taken to every Welsh Cup final I had ever played in. It was the approach South Africa took against New Zealand four years later at Ellis Park. But England tried to change their spots. Instead of using the physical strength of their forwards, they tried to find holes along the back line and Australia plugged them all.

It was the biggest mistake of Will Carling's career and I am sure he will always regret it. Generally, I always held a huge regard for Carling as a player and as a skipper. But on that afternoon, he allowed the team to deviate from the core of their success. Had England concentrated on their strengths and just tried to grind out a victory then I think they would have become world champions. I doubt they will ever get as good a chance again; it was a final at Twickenham with a crowd that was vastly in favour of England, on an English autumn afternoon, against an opposition that was still some way short of maturing. Take Tim Horan and Jason Little. They were kids just starting out. In short, England held all the aces but they played the wrong card.

England had the power and the men of experience and if I had been Carling I would have told them to keep the ball and grind out the ugliest, most boring and predictable victory they could manage.

The Wallabies tackled superbly and organised their defence very well, but England were never confident when they moved the ball and too many moves lacked any kind of cutting edge. Rob Andrew tried to dance and throw long passes and the

99

Aussies kept knocking England down. Instead of trying for a rapier, with which they were not comfortable, they should have used their bludgeon.

It finished 12–6 to Australia but it was not a classic final – the Wallabies did not function that smoothly – and the bottom line is that England blew it. Their fans were disappointed, but those of them who knew their rugby must also have been hugely frustrated.

The consolation, I suppose, is that at least England were there to contest the final on their own ground. In 1999 Wales were bundled out by the Aussies at the quarter-final stage and we were all forced to watch Australia and France share the big day at the Millennium Stadium.

The 1999 World Cup was not a tournament I ever expected Wales to win, but there was enough of a momentum being gathered in the months beforehand for all Welshmen to harbour a little dream. Under Graham Henry, Wales had won eight games on the trot going into the finals and those victories had included two wins over France, one against England and a first ever over South Africa. Henry-mania was at its high point, there was a hard, streetwise edge about the side which I had not seen for years. The only worry in the months leading up to the competition seemed to be whether or not the stadium would be finished on time.

It was. Just about. It meant I could relax and enjoy the opening ceremony. Some people complained it was 'too Welsh' and yet I don't remember anyone claiming the 1995 event was 'too South African' and I can't imagine the 2003 ceremony will have the Australians modestly hiding themselves away. Stuff them. We were the hosts and it was our party. There was Shirley Bassey in a red-dragon dress, Cerys Matthews in a

Welsh jersey, Bryn Terfel and Max Boyce. When the stadium roof was opened we even had some traditional Welsh drizzle.

Wales had a lot of experience in their side; Shane Howarth, Mark Taylor, Scott Gibbs, Neil Jenkins, Rob Howley, Garin Jenkins, Dai Young, Colin Charvis and Scott Quinnell had all been around for a while. Howarth, together with Peter Rogers and Brett Sinkinson, had given the side a more professional edge gained from their southern hemisphere experience and it was at that time when everything Henry touched appeared to glow with success. Given that background, I really felt Wales could do well. They had their strongest side for years and the team spirit running through the team was matched by a fanatical support that had been given fresh impetus by the building of the new stadium. The stage was set, although nagging at the back of my mind was the thought that our likely quarter-final opponents were going to be Australia.

The opening game didn't match the opening ceremony, but at least Wales had got away to a winning start against tricky opponents in Argentina. It was obvious the players were nervous and I expected much better things against Japan and Samoa.

After Japan had been thrashed 64–15 I began to think Wales could be real contenders for the tournament as it seemed the team were riding a wave of euphoria every time they played in their new home.

Then came the defeat to Samoa. It was the turning point of the Welsh campaign and probably the turning point in the career of Henry as Wales coach. Certainly, things would never be as good as they had been until that run was abruptly ended. Samoa exposed Wales defensively and deserved their 38–31 victory. To beat the Aussies, Wales would have needed to feel brimful of confidence but as soon as Samoa had punctured the momentum of that winning surge I always felt it would prove beyond Henry's side.

Australia duly beat Wales 24–9, squeezed past South Africa in the semi-finals, and went on to beat France to lift the trophy. They were worthy winners and in my view a much better all-round side than the 1991 champions. For Wales, it was a huge improvement on 1991 but once again I felt the team had not fulfilled its potential. Just like England in 1991, the circumstances and environment will never be better for Wales to do well at a World Cup.

Rugby had changed a great deal since 1995 with the introduction of professionalism, but the game's soul remains the same. It is a social occasion, a sport that brings people together. Just as I had cheered on teams in bars in South Africa, I watched England play South Africa in the 1999 quarter-final on a TV screen from a bar in Dublin where I was to cover France against Argentina later that day. Ireland had gone out to the Argentinians and much of Dublin seemed like a morgue that day. Irish supporters wandered around with tickets for a match at which the guests of honour were not going to turn up. But the gloom didn't last long. As soon as Jannie der Beer started kicking the first of his amazing five drop-goals to condemn England to a 44–21 defeat then the Irishmen and one Welshman in that bar had something to cheer. As I have said before, I genuinely want England to do well when they meet the big three Tri Nations teams. Had I been watching this match alone in my hotel room then I would been urging England on. But something about the atmosphere in the bar of the Berkley Court Hotel made me share in the Irish enthusiasm for an English defeat.

It was a staggering performance from der Beer, for which he never really gained the credit he deserved. The most drop-goals I ever managed in a club game was three, but to do five in a Test match, and a World Cup quarter-final at that, was an incredible exhibition of skill.

I was sorry to see Ireland out before the quarter-finals, because I think they would have given the French a real run for their money at Lansdowne Road. But not half as sad as the games I saw at Murrayfield where the stadium was half empty to see Scotland play.

Scottish supporters did not embrace the World Cup. Maybe the ticket prices were too high. Perhaps it was down to poor marketing. But being in Edinburgh during the tournament I felt as though I had taken a wrong turning. There was a party going on somewhere but you couldn't help feeling it wasn't in Edinburgh. Then again, apart from the atmosphere in Cardiff it was difficult to feel at any of the other venues that the tournament had really caught fire. That is the consequence of jointly hosting the tournament in five different countries. It becomes too fragmented. You always have the feeling that something better must be happening elsewhere. I think the 2003 World Cup will benefit from being played only in Australia and not shared with New Zealand. I also feel that when it comes back to Europe next it should be in France or England solely and not shared among the Six Nations. Wales, Scotland and Ireland may not have the stadiums to hold their own World Cup, but a joint Celtic bid spread across three countries would be better than one spread across five.

After the quarter-finals, there was one match at the 1999 World Cup that will stand the test of time. France against New Zealand was an absolute classic. The French were written off as no-hopers and it was true that their form until that match had been fitful at best. Yet it was not just the size of the upset but also the style of the victory that will live with me from that Sunday afternoon at Twickenham. New Zealand had the size, the power and the organisation to make France look small and inhibited. Yet it was France who stood tall. Jonah Lomu may have scored two tries for the All Blacks, but for me the result was a triumph for the smaller players such as Christophe Dominici, Philippe Bernat-Salles and Christophe Lamaison. They proved that skill, speed, courage and imagination can triumph over size and power. I felt that was wonderful because the game had been moving far too much in the direction of power at the expense of skill and cunning.

France played with so much flair and excitement that they inspired themselves as the match wore on. It was a fabulous victory, probably the best performance by any side in any World Cup.

I can remember walking out from Twickenham that day among a crowd of All Blacks supporters. I have been among Welsh fans on plenty of occasions after bad defeats and although the atmosphere is quiet there is normally a spark of Welsh humour here and there to lighten the gloom. Among the All Black fans it was like being at a funeral, especially as they were all dressed in black. I turned and told one guy it was only a game and they would come back from this defeat. But he was completely lost in his own despair. That's New Zealanders, I suppose. They are serious about winning, but they take the business of losing more seriously than most, too.

After that epic semi-final, the final was always going to be a bit of an anti-climax. France were never going to reach those heights again and Australia ran out quite comfortable winners, 35–12. Tim Horan provided a few flashes of magic for the Wallabies and he was unquestionably the best player in the tournament. His strength, his positional sense and his all-round qualities were there for all to admire.

The tournament scaled the heights on occasions, and I'm so glad and very proud that Wales hosted the final and the opening game as well as the Wales group matches. It could have been the chance of a lifetime for Wales, but it didn't quite work out. The best Welsh performance at a tournament, by far, remains the inaugural World Cup in 1987 where Wales finished third. But because it was the first it was the tournament that made the least impact on us all. Nobody really knew how successful it would be and whether the whole concept would take off and flourish.

New Zealand won it and I can remember the huge smile on the face of David Kirk when he lifted the trophy. Wales beat Ireland, Tonga, Canada and then England in the quarter-finals – a sequence of results that would now have the Welsh Assembly declaring a Bank Holiday. But the semi-final against New Zealand was a mismatch and Wales conceded eight tries in a 49–6 defeat.

That left a third-place play-off against Australia. The Aussies had David Codey sent off early on for stamping and Wales won thanks to a fantastic Paul Thorburn conversion from the touchline.

England were pitiful and it was the dross they served up in that tournament which, I feel, prompted the RFU to take their whole coaching, management and selection process seriously. Four years later they reached the final and should have become world champions. Wales went from third to nowhere as they failed to make it past the pool stages in 1991. That sums up the

105

nature of World Cups. They give the sport a natural cycle. Teams grow, mature, flourish and then start to decline and the trick is to make sure the tournament coincides with the top of your own circle rather than the low point. The Wallabies of 1987 were not good enough to beat Wales, but by 1991 they had passed us by and gone out of sight. They were in decline in 1995, but returned to form in 1999.

New Zealand were the best side in the world in 1987, ordinary in 1991 and underachieved in 1995 and 1999. England have looked world-beaters at times between tournaments, but never actually during a World Cup itself.

I would love to have played in a World Cup in 1978, when Wales would have given any country a run for their money. I think we could have beaten France, England and Australia and been a match for the All Blacks and South Africa on neutral turf. We would have certainly fancied our chances and reached a semi-final at least, possibly a final. Who knows? It didn't happen because the sport's administration had not yet grown aware of the commercial appeal.

I can honestly say with my hand on my heart that I never look back on my career and think of the money I could have made had it been a professional era. But from a purely playing point of view, a World Cup in the seventies would have been wonderful. Wales would have boasted a very strong squad, innovative coaches, and genuine giants of the game like Gareth Edwards, who would have been the Lomu of his era. It didn't happen, but there's no harm in thinking what might have been.

CHAPTER 7

In to Africa

As the World Cup grew and its tentacles spread around the rugby world, it became the main money engine for the sport. Tours, which once provided financial windfalls for host countries, appeared to be losing significance. It reached a stage in the mid-nineties when it seemed that many people in influential positions were claiming the Lions would disappear now that the professional era had arrived, with the suggestion made that countries would only be interested in short tours as single teams and not as Britain and Ireland combined.

But for me the Lions has always been something unique and very, very special. It is the greatest rugby club in the world. When I was young I would listen to the radio and collect newspaper cuttings of great Llanelli men like RH Williams, who became a legend in New Zealand in 1959, and the wonderful Terry Davies. I can recall a favourite player of mine, Ken Jones, scoring a fantastic try in South Africa and it was that kind of excitement over events happening in far-off countries that made me completely sold on the Lions.

They had a high profile, but they also had this mystique. To a young kid in South Wales they weren't just rugby players, they were explorers on expeditions to faraway lands. So it was a dream come true for me when I was picked to tour South Africa with the Lions in 1974. You are not told you have been picked. The Lions do things their own way. They write to you and offer you an invitation to tour, but I still couldn't quite believe I was going until we all went to London and were kitted out with the blazers and all the gear.

We went to Lillywhites to collect it all and I felt like a king. We were given two Lions blazers, three pairs of trousers, shirts, ties, socks, a pair of shoes and a huge kit bag. With Wales, you were only given one set of everything if you were touring, so already I was aware that this trip would be something special.

There had been huge hostility towards the idea of a tour to South Africa that year because it was viewed as something else that would be used to prop up apartheid at a time when feelings against South Africa were running higher than ever. I was aware that black leaders like Nelson Mandela were in jail and that the treatment of black people in that country was brutal and unjust. Even if I hadn't known it then I would soon most certainly have been made aware of it by the letters I received from politicians begging me not to go – including one from a young man who sounded very passionate and determined. His name was Neil Kinnock.

I had other letters that were far more sinister, but the bottom line was that I was a young man of 25 who wanted to tour with the Lions. Of course I had doubts, but I made up my mind after a team meeting held that weekend in London.

Willie John McBride was someone I had played against on a number of occasions for Wales against Ireland, but I did not really know the substance of the man. It was his fifth Lions tour and it was he who convinced me to go on my first. There were some demonstrators at our base in London, but Willie John rose to his feet and made a wonderful speech in front of the rest of the players. He understood all the self-doubts and nagging consciences and said if anyone felt those feelings outweighed their ambition to win a Test series in South Africa for the first time in Lions history then they should not go. He would shake their hand and respect their decision.

It was selfish, I suppose. He was asking us to put ourselves first as sportsmen ahead of other considerations. But it convinced me, and I think many others, that we did not want to pass up a rugby opportunity such as this. My Welsh teammates Gerald Davies and John Taylor had decided not to tour, but I fell in behind Willie John at that meeting and there could be no turning back.

I have often considered whether or not I made the right decision. I was naïve and certainly had a somewhat narrow view of the world. Politics, and the problems of other people, seemed a long way detached from my own life. I certainly don't regret going because it was a once-in-a-lifetime chance to achieve something no other touring party had managed. But now, on reflection as a wiser man than I was then, the tour should not have gone ahead because it was to be another 20 years until the apartheid system was done away with and in my subsequent visits since 1974 I have seen at first hand the way in which the country denied so many people their respect and human dignity.

We had four days together in London and then the plan was to fly to South Africa and prepare at altitude. We were met at Jan Smuts Airport in Johannesburg by people who were desperately thankful that we had made the trip – although there were to be times when I realised not everyone was so happy to see us there. But in general, from the time we hit the ground we didn't have time to reflect on the consequences of being there. We were on a rugby crusade and there were plenty of battles to be won on the pitch.

As it turned out we won game after game after game, and then the overriding aim became to stay unbeaten. It was an obsession that left little time for thinking about anything else. In those days, Lions tours did not attract the thousands of travelling supporters we saw in Australia in 2001 or in South Africa in 1997. I don't think our own army of British fans ever numbered more than about two or three hundred. But given the background to the trip there was a huge irony regarding many of the people who were cheering us on. When we won the Third Test at Port Elizabeth and JJ Williams scored a couple of tries, the one stand erupted into cheering and there was hardly a white face among them. Willie John played on this and when he ran out at the start of games, he would wave the Lions soft-toy mascot above his head towards the black sections of the crowd and they would start jumping somersaults. Anything that undermined the white South Africans was okay by them.

All these memories came flooding back to me 21 years later when I was back in South Africa for the 1995 World Cup. In 1974 Nelson Mandela had been locked up as a prisoner in Robben Island while we toured the country. Now he was president.

When Mandela walked out to shake hands with the players of South Africa and New Zealand in the moments before the World Cup Final, it struck me just how powerful sport can be in symbolising friendship and forgiveness on a grand scale. Here was Mandela, a convict in 1974, standing in the middle off Ellis Park Stadium wearing a Springbok jersey and cap, shaking hands with the men who for many had represented the ideas of racial superiority that had excluded so many of his countrymen. It was probably the most moving moment in sport I had ever experienced.

To see him walk out there with such dignity, and shake hands with the black wing Chester Williams and all the white players in the Springbok team, summed up everything about the man and how he had united a nation. It was hard to believe. As Lions tourists in 1974 we knew Mandela was in jail but all we were told was that he was a troublemaker and a terrorist.

In Johannesburg in 1995 I was taken, along with a group of friends, on a trip to Soweto. The poverty and deprivation that the officials had tried so hard to hide us from in 1974 was laid bare. It was a humbling experience and enjoyable as we stopped off for a pint in a bar and chatted about the tournament and the Springboks' chances of winning. But it was a sobering experience to see the extremes of wealth that still existed and then to travel back to Johannesburg and witness the decay in the centre of the city where areas I had remembered as thriving and bustling in 1974 were now no-go crime-ridden places where the old hotels we had stayed in had virtually been reduced to rubble.

I had been back to South Africa on a couple of occasions between 1974 and 1995, but only for brief stays to play in

111

World XV Invitational matches. Again, I was still young, obsessed by rugby, and perhaps blinkered to the real issues involved in visiting a country like South Africa. When I played in 1978 I met a guy called Errol Tobias, a coloured South African who played for the World XV. We went to the cinema together one night before the game and although they took Errol's money and allowed him in, the looks of displeasure on the white faces left me stunned.

I went back to South Africa on one other occasion between 1974 and the 1995 World Cup. It was my last season before retirement in 1981. This time I was very uncertain that I should be playing rugby there, but I felt obliged to honour the family of a player I had squared up to back in 1974. Rompy Stander was a prop for the Springboks who played against the Lions in 1974, but who tragically had died from a heart attack as a very young man, leaving a wife and two kids. I was asked to play in a benefit game for his family and found it difficult to refuse as the request had come from our old liaison officer from the 1974 Lions tour, a true friend called Chute Visser. Bill Beaumont, the Grand-Slam-winning England captain, was due to come with me to play for a World XV side but was forced to pull out when threats were made against his clothing business from their suppliers overseas. The Australian and New Zealand governments had ordered their players not to go as well, so the event collapsed into something of a shambles. The so-called World XV became a mixture of odd individuals like me who wanted to raise money for the family, ageing former Springboks who had been persuaded out of retirement, and a bunch of students.

Again there were demonstrations and on reflection it was selfish of me to have gone. I felt I was doing the right thing for a former opponent's family, but I suppose I was still blind to the much wider picture of the problems within South Africa. The memories of those two trips I had made since 1974 came flooding back as I sat in that bar in Soweto in 1995. To see blacks and whites sharing a drink and chatting about the greatest rugby tournament of all coming to their country was incredible. Of course, there were still awful problems in South Africa in 1995 and they have not gone away. Crime levels are frighteningly high. But at least the country is moving forward and facing those problems with honesty. In 1974 South Africa was also a dangerous place, but the Lions were simply hidden away from the shocking realities of life under apartheid.

As I have admitted, on reflection it was probably the wrong decision for the Lions to tour South Africa in 1974. But you make choices in life and you have to live with them. From a rugby viewpoint in many ways it was the highlight of my career. We played 22 matches and did not lose a single one of them. We drew once, in the fourth and final Test, but only thanks to some very dubious decisions from the referee. We played the Springboks four times and did not lose. We scored ten tries in those Tests and conceded just one and we went through the country, from one end to the other, beating the best provincial sides South Africa could offer and often playing some fantastic rugby.

We handed out some real beatings and had a wonderful time off the field in the company of a squad of players second to none. The leadership shown by Willie John was an inspiration for all of us. We were devoted to him to the extent that although not many players were used in the Test series there was none of the moaning and whingeing that characterised the 2001 Lions tour to Australia. Those who played in the midweek side were proud to represent the Lions and they got on with the job of winning so that the Saturday team was always brimming with confidence and self-belief.

There are other great contrasts with the Lions tours of today. We had a coach, Syd Millar, and Alun Thomas was our tour manager. That was it. Two men. No army of specialist coaches and technical advisors as they have now. Not even a doctor or a physio. When I was injured after the Second Test, and needed stitches to close a wound on my instep, the man who held the needle was Irishman Ken Kennedy, our hooker. Ken was a doctor, but that was incidental. He was on the tour as a player and I remember I had to wait, bleeding, while he finished his shower before stitching me up. I wonder what Jonny Wilkinson would have felt in Melbourne, after the Second Test in Australia in 2001, if the guy treating what was then a suspected broken ankle had been Keith Wood? Don't get me wrong, Ken did a great job and 27 years on the scar is even starting to fade, but looking back it makes you wonder how we all survived for four months.

It was the same before we left for that tour. When we gathered in London someone from the Four Home Unions Committee was obviously something of a modern thinker who had the bright idea of testing our blood before we went and comparing it with tests taken on the tour to make sure we were all still healthy. We lined up in front of our two doctors – Dr Ken Kennedy, our hooker, and Dr JPR Williams, our fullback. To show a bit of loyalty I thought I'd better get into JPR's queue for my sample. John went on to become an orthopaedic surgeon but at that stage, when dealing with fellow rugby players, he didn't have what you might call the bedside manner. The shrieks of pain from the head of the queue confirmed my worst fears – JPR was banging in this needle like a vet taking blood from a horse. Bobby Windsor, one of the hardest, and funniest, men I ever played alongside, vowed never to let JPR loose on him again. Sure enough, when the tests were taken again eight days into the tour, Ken's queue was about five miles long while only three Welshmen with a deep sense of loyalty lined up in front of JPR.

We were amateurs in 1974 and the back-up we enjoyed was strictly of the amateur variety, too. Nowadays, the Lions have every minute of their day planned and detailed with military precision. In 1974, we had to think on our feet – even when it came to trying to get away from the distraction of supporters. The fans probably didn't number more than a couple of hundred but they could be quite vocal and intense – especially if they were from Wales. On the day before the vital Third Test in Port Elizabeth, the match in which we could clinch the series by beating the Springboks for a third time, Willie John decided to try to get all the players in the right frame of mind away from all the supporters. Somehow he commandeered this old bus and we were driven out into the middle of nowhere down a dirt-track to where Willie said he knew of a friendly restaurant. His mission, he admitted, was to get us away from the 'Welsh heavies' as he called them. We were sat there, quietly relaxing as Willie told us to clear our minds before the biggest match of our lives, when suddenly the dust was turned up as an old truck trundled towards us down the approach road. Everyone turned, expecting to see some locals pile out, but instead it turned out to be a bunch of Welsh fans who quickly flocked around Gareth Edwards and started telling him how the Lions should go about winning the game the next day. There was

115

steam coming out of Willie John's ears but the rest of us thought it was hilarious.

I suppose if you had splashed out money to follow the Lions to the southern hemisphere in the seventies, when long-haul travel was certainly not cheap, then you had a right to get up close to those you were cheering. Not that such close attention was necessarily unwelcome. After that thwarted get-away trip with Willie-John on the Friday before the Third Test, I was taken by minibus for a check-up on my injured foot on the Saturday morning. As we left the hotel, I sat back and viewed the scene. There were police and security checks all around the hotel and a large crowd was being held back behind crash barriers. One guy, though, seemed to have negotiated his way through and was strolling down to our hotel entrance with a small case under his arm. As he got nearer I recognised him as Des Harris, a mate of mine from my home village of Felinfoel. He spotted me and quickened his pace, still holding the case.

'Phil!' he said excitedly. 'You said on your postcard that you were missing your pint of Felinfoel, so I've brought you some to stop you getting homesick.' In a flash, the case had been opened and he was thrusting two bottles of beer from the Felinfoel Brewery into my hands. It must then have occurred to him that I had the biggest game of rugby in my life in about three hours' time. 'Tell you what,' he said. 'You don't have to drink it now. Save it for after the game.'

We won that Third Test, 26–9, which was a thrashing in those days, and the Felinfoel bitter tasted as good as it had ever done. Considering we were without both Gerald Davies and Mike Gibson for that tour, two men who are legends of the game but who chose not to go, we set some pretty high stand-ards for touring Lions teams to follow. We were a side full of big names – JPR Williams, Andy Irvine, Ian McGeechan, JJ Williams, Gareth Edwards, Fran Cotton, the late great Gordon Brown, Fergus Slattery, Mervyn Davies and Roger Uttley – but there were no stars. Willie John would not allow it. Everyone was treated the same and shared the load. That included the midweek side.

We played some fantastic rugby and individual players seemed to reach new heights. Uttley had been a good second row with England, but converted to a back-row forward he was a giant. JJ was a very good wing for Wales, but on that tour, with hard ground underfoot, he was as good as any wing I have ever seen – as good as Gerald Davies, Ieuan Evans, David Duckham or any other wing you care to mention. Bobby Windsor played the finest rugby of his life, Mervyn Davies responded to those who felt Andy Ripley might get his No. 8 spot, and Ian 'Mighty Mouse' McLauchlan was a keystone of the pack at loosehead prop.

Players became inspired. We trained hard every day; individuals got as fit as they had ever been in their lives and we had a bond of friendship and respect that bound us together. Small things on the field can often lay the basis for the general mood among players on tour. There was the incredible impact of Scott Gibbs's tackle on Os du Randt in the 1997 series against the Springboks, but for us it was Mervyn Davies who set the tone for the determination we required with a monumental tackle in the opening Test. He hit Morne du Plesis, the star of the Springboks back row, so hard he must have gone back five yards and had all the breath knocked out of him. The crowd gasped. They couldn't believe that this tall, scrawny Welshman had dealt out such punishment to their hero.

One of the litmus tests on any tour of South Africa is the

117

match against Orange Free State; they view their rugby players as walking symbols of their virility and manhood.

To no one's great surprise the match against the Lions became one of the dirtiest I could ever remember. Boots and fists flew from the first minute to the last. There was blood everywhere. Our dressing room resembled a doctor's waiting room on a busy Monday morning but I went to theirs with Chute Visser, our liaison officer, and found it more like a field hospital in a war zone. Free State players were lying around in a daze while doctors worked on their cuts and bruises. We hadn't played that well and it was the closest we came to losing, Free State having been winning with only a couple of minutes to go. But Gareth Edwards eventually created a try for JJ with a moment of brilliance and we won the game 11–9. We had beaten them. But we had also beaten them up.

Before I take too much credit for that performance I should say that I didn't actually play in that match. I was injured with the cut on my foot and a damaged knee. In fact, I played only one match outside the Tests following those injuries in the Second Test.

But even when you were injured you still felt a huge part of what was happening on the field. That was the spirit which ran through the squad. It was the happiest group of players I ever toured with.

Syd Millar did a marvellous job, and Willie John was incomparable. But Alun Thomas from Swansea, together with those two Irishmen, deserves huge credit for the way he did his job as tour manager. We were criticised in South Africa, and back home afterwards, too, in some quarters, for being a violent side that used intimidation. If intimidation means standing up for yourself in order not to be the victim of intimidation then

118

I suppose we must plead guilty. But too much was made of things like the famous 99 call and maybe still is.

The 1974 Lions squad's 99 call has passed into the folklore of the game but like most myths it is part truth and part fantasy. The reality is that I only heard it called perhaps three or four times during the whole tour.

Let me give the background. Gareth Edwards played so well in the second match against South West Africa that it was obvious the South Africans would have to target him. They didn't wait long. By the time we met Eastern Province in the fourth game they had decided to go after Gareth. He took some cheap shots and soon Willie John had all his forwards in a huddle. The next time Gareth was hit late the 99 call went up and about six Lions forwards piled in. Basically, Eastern Province were given a hell of a beating and Gareth was then left alone. It wasn't premeditated in the sense that it was something Willie John dreamt up in his room one night. It was purely a response on the field to something that happened. But the bottom line was the message it sent around South Africa. You might have got away with nice British boys turning the other cheek in years gone by, but these Lions are going to hammer you if you try it on. The call was something rarely discussed in squad meetings. I only remember one occasion where Willie John suggested that if things boiled over he would call 99. 'At that point I want you forwards to hit the nearest Springbok standing next to you,' said Willie. Bobby Windsor piped up, 'Are we allowed to hit two?' Essentially, though, the call belonged to the forwards and the fine details were certainly something they never discussed with the 11-stone weakling playing outside-half.

It needs to be remembered, though, that this was long before the introduction of neutral referees. Some of the refs we had in 1974 could not have been more in favour of the home sides if they had worn home jerseys with a number 16 on their back. So in those circumstances we simply could not afford to leave the protection of a player like Edwards to some biased local official.

The 99 call was used sparingly during the Test series, because apart from a couple of almighty punch-ups in the Third Test the Springboks seemed to get the message. The match against Natal at King's Park was different, though, because we were fighting half the crowd as well as the home side. We had clinched the Test series but there was still no way we were going to let anyone take our unbeaten record. At one point, however, the crowd must have resented our forwards' approach because there were beer cans raining down on us from the stands. Willie John brought us all together in the middle of the field and told us to cool things down. It calmed down until their captain, Tommy Bedford, came round offside at a line-out and Fran Cotton smacked him full in the face. There was a brief silence, which must have been while the crowd reached for their fullest beer cans, then another shower.

I think we played 11 minutes of injury time after the police had cleared the pitch of fans and beer cans and then the match ended with JPR fighting with Bedford again. Tommy was fine about it afterwards but Mrs Bedford wanted to carry on the fight with JPR in the after-match dinner. We survived, some-how, drew the final Test 13–13 in Johannesburg, and then flew home to a wonderful welcome at Heathrow where thousands turned out to meet us.

Not all of them wanted to shake our hands, though. Some would rather have wrung our necks and among the demonstrators was Peter Hain, now MP for Neath and a government minister. Labour MPs, who had tried to stop us going, turned up to be photographed congratulating us and even Ted Heath was there as Leader of the Opposition. A paint pot was hurled at us, someone ducked, and it hit poor old Ted.

Years later I met Peter Hain when he was with some friends at Wembley and I told him he owed me 42 quid for a laundry bill. He looked confused so I pretended that the paint he and his mates had chucked at Heathrow that day had bounced off Ted Heath and ruined my own suit. One of Peter's companions was Eddie George, the Governor of the Bank of England and a man who loves his rugby. Peter quickly changed the subject.

It's strange how life moves on. One minute Peter Hain is part of an angry mob throwing paint at you, the next he is a very senior politician in the Labour Party, which was busy sweeping back into power when the Lions were next out in South Africa in 1997.

The 1997 tour was another great adventure and having been stunned by the changes in the country at the 1995 World Cup I was eager to return. I combined my media commitments with working for Gullivers as a tour guide and Pat and I arrived the week before the First Test.

Some pre-tour assumptions had already bitten the dust. The big English forwards had been left out of the front row where forwards coach Jim Telfer had cleverly used the much smaller but more mobile Tom Smith of Scotland, Keith Wood, and his Irish team-mate Paul Wallace.

Unfortunately, Rob Howley also bit the dust when he dislocated his shoulder against Natal, but the Welsh contingent was strong through Neil Jenkins, Scott Gibbs and Ieuan Evans.

Scott was in the form of his life and deservedly went on to win the man of the series award, but the goal-kicking of Neil Jenkins in the Second Test at King's Park was perhaps the one individual contribution that clinched the series. He scored five penalty goals and never looked like missing.

The Lions clinched an 18–15 victory through Jerry Guscott's drop goal and afterwards I walked across the huge car park areas that surround the ground towards the Gullivers pub. The Springbok fans were completely devastated, while the Lions held an all-night party. I sank one or two beers myself that night and felt extremely happy that boys like Jenks, Ieuan and Scott had been able to savour what I had savoured 23 years earlier – a series victory over South Africa.

Like our group in 1974, the Lions of 1997 were led by a man of huge physical presence and enormous stature in the game. We had Willie John McBride. They had Martin Johnson. Willie John was not given to overcomplication. For him rugby was a simple game. When he popped his head up from a scrum he didn't really care about how many mis-moves and dummy scissors you had performed in the back line, just so long as he was moving forwards. If he had to start running back-wards towards his own line then you knew you were in for a bollocking.

I think Johnson is of the same vein. On the occasions I've met him I've been struck by his honesty and down-to-earth common sense. Like Willie and most second rows, Jonno thinks matches are won up front and the backs simply decide the extent of the winning margin.

Johnson doesn't waste his words and neither did Willie John. I can still remember his team talk before we left the hotel for the decisive Third Test against the Springboks in 1974. You could have written most of it down on the back of a small envelope.

He came into our team room and said almost nothing. Hardly a word. He just sat there with a very calm expression on his face and muttered almost under his breath about families, wives and children. Then, more intense silence as we all sat there captivated by this man's presence. Finally, just as I felt I was going to scream for someone to say something, Willie took a deep breath and said, 'Okay, men. I think you're all in the right frame of mind and you know what we have to do. Let's do it.'

It was the same when we reached the stadium. Nothing else mattered other than entering the arena absolutely convinced that we would win again. Our tour anthem, inspired and invariably led by the late, great Gordon Brown, and sung on the team bus on the way to games, became 'Oh Flower of Scotland'.

Our bus that day arrived at the ground in Port Elizabeth before we had finished our rendition. But no one moved an inch because Willie John had not moved from his seat near the front. *He* was still singing and so *we* all carried on singing. Suddenly, you could feel the bonds between us strengthen as we sang with real feeling and gusto. We were ready to do whatever was required for the collective cause. It was another masterstroke by the skipper.

Johnson has the same ability to gain the utmost respect of those who play under him. He is an outstanding forward who's not afraid to put it about a bit. I like that in a captain. He leads from the front and gives his all. It didn't matter to the Irish, the Scots and the Welsh in 1997 that they were captained by an Englishman. Johnson had the respect of all of them.

123

Comparing players of different eras is, of course, no more than a bit of fun, but in my view Johnson has to bow to Willie John as a skipper. Along with his ever-present pipe, Willie John packed the wisdom and experience of an incredible four previous Lions tours in his luggage for our 1974 trip to South Africa and I don't think any captain will ever command that level of respect and know-how. Perhaps there is more to Johnson as an overall player, but whatever shortcomings Willie John had on the field were compensated by a deep knowledge of what made other players around him perform to their absolute peak. That included the midweek dirt-trackers as well as the Test side – he had a knack of inspiring absolute conviction to the cause.

Mind you, I saw evidence of that quality under Johnson, too, in 1997. Once again a match against Orange Free State sticks in my mind, although the victory this time was far more comfortable than the one we achieved in 1974. The Lions won 52–30, with the England wing John Bentley scoring a hat-trick of tries. It galvanised the Test players and underlined the unity of the whole group. The Lions played sublime rugby with so much pace and skill that they destroyed a Super 12 side at altitude on their own ground.

One last thing about South Africa: the climate is so good that when you wake up every day you cannot wait to get into training. The sessions are in sunshine under blue skies with clear air. You eat well, rest well and generally feel in great nick. It all helps you reach levels of fitness that you never reach at home no matter how hard you train. You could see, for example, that men like John Bentley, Neil Back and Eric Miller – to name but a few – were in the peak of condition and fitness, yet none of them could get into the starting line-up for that 1997 Test.

There were no such problems, however, for Gareth Edwards. A great player whatever country he played in, after three months hard training in South Africa he was unstoppable.

CHAPTER 8

Leading the Lions

When I was offered the captaincy of the 1977 Lions to New Zealand it suddenly presented me with the most difficult dilemma of my career. It is 25 years since that trip, but the memories are still vivid and the scars run deep. Like the 2001 tour to Australia, there were mistakes made along the way by the management as well as by the players. My own big mistake was to agree to be skipper.

It had been a hard season in 1977. Wales had lost to France but we had won the Triple Crown by beating Scotland at Murrayfield and the style and substance of that victory had clinched Lions places for a lot of the players. Mervyn Davies would have been the natural choice to lead the tour, but he had been robbed of that honour after suffering a brain haemorrhage. As a result there were no outstandingly obvious candidates and my name found its way to the top of the list.

Roger Uttley of England and Scotland's Ian McGeechan –

who went on to coach the Lions so superbly – were mentioned but somehow our victory in Edinburgh seemed to have put me in the driving seat. Even so, when the call came through from coach John Dawes to say I was the choice I was stunned. It was the biggest honour in the game for a player from these isles and yet I couldn't see past the sheer size and weight of the responsibility. It was then that I began to have second thoughts – not just about captaining the squad but about going on the tour at all. That may sound strange, but there seemed plenty of reasons for self-doubt at the time. I was tired. I had just gone through a very tough season with Wales and with Llanelli. I was 28 years old, but I had not had a summer at home for ten years and the thought of leaving home to spend three months in New Zealand was something that filled me more with dread than excitement.

The reason for that is clearer now than it was then. I had changed as a person after the birth of my son, Steven, who was not even two years old at the time, and I hated the idea of leaving both Pat and Steven behind for so long. I felt especially protective because our first child, Stuart, had died just three days after being born. To hold and then to lose what looks to be a perfect and healthy newborn child makes you feel as though your whole world has ended. The only thing that mattered to me after that was Pat, our family and close friends. Even two years later, playing rugby seemed a lot less important than it had previously. Yet in a strange kind of way rugby also helped pull me through. It was certainly no longer the be-all and end-all, but it was a distraction able sometimes to take my mind off things.

The doctors at the time were tremendous and had the good sense to suggest to me that the best thing for both Pat and I would be if we tried for another baby as soon as possible. Steven was born in the autumn of 1975, 18 months before the Lions tour to New Zealand. I had been brought up on Welsh Sunday schools, but was no great churchgoer, and yet I can still remember very clearly going into the little chapel at Morriston Hospital on the night Steven was born. It was two o'clock in the morning as I pulled open the door and slipped in. In the quiet of the night I knelt down and prayed to God to keep Steven healthy. I had been very fortunate in rugby. I asked then for all my good fortune to pass to my son.

Thankfully, he was a beautiful, healthy little boy and Pat and I were overjoyed at his arrival. By the time the Lions tour loomed large in the spring of 1977, I was taking Steven for long walks in the countryside around Felinfoel, pushing the pram like the proudest father in the world and feeling that our lives were back on track again. Deep down I didn't want to go to New Zealand and I should have said so, like a few others such as Gareth Edwards, JPR Williams and Gerald Davies. But my friends and family were so thrilled that I had been asked to captain the Lions that I didn't want to disappoint them. Pat was also insistent that I should accept the honour, probably because she knew I would spend the rest of my life wondering about it if I turned it down. Events then took on a momentum of their own. Handshakes and congratulations in the village, telegrams and letters from people all over the world . . . to have suddenly pulled out would have meant an awful lot of disappointed people.

We spent three days in London preparing for the tour and I knew then that I was making a big mistake, but I didn't have the heart to let people down. Instead, I rang Pat every night and finished each call trying to hold a conversation with an 18-month-old toddler.

As I boarded the plane it struck me how this was going to be very different to captaining Wales or Llanelli. Leading those teams was easy. I knew all the players and what made them tick. They knew me. But did I really know how to motivate and inspire Englishmen, Scotsmen and Irishmen? I felt unsure.

When we arrived the weather was awful and the wind and rain lasted for days. We had 15 Welshmen in the squad and a Welsh coach in John Dawes. I knew how to communicate with them well enough, but my ease in their company only made me feel less sure about how I would get on with the other 15. I feared a split and my fears eventually proved well founded. It's strange what self-doubt can do to you. I even thought I wasn't physically big enough to be a Lions captain. Willie John was a big man and loomed large in the minds of the opposition. So did Martin Johnson. I was a little fly-half from West Wales and I felt unsure how some of our huge forwards were going to react to being ordered about in the dressing room by someone they could swat away like a fly.

Size matters. When I was 19, I captained Llanelli against Neath at the Gnoll. Nobody liked to visit Neath. Along with Pontypool they were the hardest bunch in the country. Brian Thomas was an enormous man who knew the effect his presence had on young 11-stone flyweights like myself. He came over to toss the coin before kick-off and stood there almost blocking out the light with a huge black eye, somehow sustained in his own dressing room. He looked down at the Llanelli captain and laughed in my face. 'You! What's wrong, have Llanelli run out of grown men to captain their team these days?' I felt intimidated and not surprisingly we lost the match.

Neither had I bargained for all the additional work a Lions captain has to deal with – or at least had to in those days. With Wales the team was on autopilot. It almost captained itself. But in New Zealand there were management meetings that I had to be part of; selection; complaints from players ranging from being left out of a side to who they had been told to room with, functions to attend; and the dealings with the press corps, which had grown considerably since 1974. The manager, George Burrell, was a nice man, while our coach, John Dawes, had done it all as a player and captain of the Lions himself. But somehow the chemistry among us was never quite right.

Perhaps it was the conditions that caused the friction and sapped morale. It seemed to rain every day for three months, which was something of a contrast to the wonderful sunshine of South Africa three years earlier. The rain itself I could cope with, but in those days we were given one training kit, not the half-dozen sets the Lions players of today are provided with. After each morning session you hung this soaking, muddy heap of clothes on the radiator in your room. Dawesy was a hard taskmaster on that trip and often insisted on afternoon sessions on top of morning training, which meant putting this cold and filthy kit back on before it had dried. Not the best way to prepare your game plan to meet the best team in the world.

But at the end of the day, rugby tours are all about results and specifically results in the Tests. If Martin Johnson's 2001 Lions had won the final Test in Australia then no one would have given two hoots that Austin Healey had mouthed off before the game. In 1977 I could see how critical it was going to be for us to win the First Test in Wellington. If nothing else it might take attention away from the rain. Gordon Brown was not fit and for some reason we had gone for Phil Orr in the front row ahead of Fran Cotton. The All Blacks were not vintage and although they built up a small lead we were still very much in the game. I kicked a penalty to put us 12–10 ahead and suddenly we were breaking out of defence with a huge overlap that must have been six against two. All we needed was smooth hands and calm heads and we would be in under the posts for an 18–10 lead. Instead, poor old Trevor Evans didn't see the All Blacks wing, Grant Batty, lurking and the interception led to a 70-yard sprint and breakaway try for New Zealand even though our prop Graham Price chased him and almost caught him.

So we went in at half-time losing 12–16 when we should have been 18–10 ahead. The wind held sway in the second half and there were no further scores. We were 1–0 down in the series and the inquests began soon after the final whistle. If we had lost the First Test in 1974 I think we could have handled it, but the splits in the camp seemed to intensify after that first defeat to the All Blacks.

The media pack in 1974 numbered around eight and they were all men who had been on the scene for years – the old school like JBG Thomas of *The Western Mail*, Pat Marshall of *The Express*, and Terry O'Connor of the *Daily Mail*. It was a cosy club in some respects, but their lack of numbers meant there was little competition among them and they tended to be very supportive and discreet. If they went into a bar and found a player having a few beers when he should have been tucked up in bed, they were more likely to join him rather than go off and write about it. But in 1977 the press boys had changed. There were far more of them and they wanted to outdo each other for stories, which were not restricted to what happened on the field. Rugby had at last tickled the fancy of the tabloids.

Even though we were still amateurs, rugby players, in the language of the tabloid reporters, were now just footballers with different-shaped balls! I suppose if we had won the First Test then they would have been supportive, but we had lost and a lot of flak was flying our way from the papers back home. On reflection, we should have been able to handle the stick, but we lacked experience on and off the field. Without Gareth, JPR, Gerald, Fergus Slattery and Roger Uttley (who had unfortunately done his back in just before we left) we lacked sufficient strength of character and body.

A huge personal regret was that Ray Gravell, my Llanelli team-mate, had refused to tour. I begged Grav. I pleaded and quarrelled with him at his house and then tried to coax him to change his mind. I did everything but he insisted his shoulder was not right. I couldn't even get him on the field for Llanelli. John Dawes and I wanted Grav to be our big blockbuster down the middle to take on the All Blacks' midfield, but Dawesy told me that unless Ray played just one game before the squad was picked it was going to be difficult for the selectors to choose him. Llanelli were playing Maesteg on a Wednesday night and I told Grav that all he had to do was step on the field. The plan was that I would create an opening early on and put Grav through the hole. One run – that's all he had to make – and the selectors would have picked him. He could then complain he felt a bit stiff and go off soon afterwards, certain of being named in the tour squad. But Grav dropped out before the match and the selectors had to look elsewhere. There was nothing seriously wrong with Grav's shoulder, but there was something seriously wrong with his head. For whatever reason sometimes he just didn't fancy it.

It was the same when I was captain of Llanelli. We would

have a massive match the next day – Swansea or Cardiff – and Ray would have a twinge in his knee. I would be around his house on the Friday night and eventually persuade him to play. The next day, when it came time to board the bus, Grav wouldn't be there. It was an amateur sport and it was his choice, I suppose. When he was on the field, Ray Gravell was as hard and fierce a competitor as they come. But sometimes the hardest part was just to get him on to the park and although he went on to become a Test Lion in 1980 in South Africa we missed him badly in 1977.

After losing the opening Test, it became open season on the Lions back home. I felt shocked that such heroes of Lions rugby as Barry John, Mervyn Davies and Carwyn James could rip into us in print, but that was my mistake, not theirs. As a player you always overreact to criticism. As an ex-player you become aware that every generation has the right to comment and pass judgement on current players. It's all merely personal opinion, but that's what the sport is all about – passion and opinion, such as you find it in every rugby-club bar throughout Britain and Ireland. As Lions captain, however, I had a much narrower focus. I wanted to win, and anything I read or heard that seemed to undermine the cause got under my skin and irritated the hell out of me.

The New Zealand media and public were also quick to try to rubbish us. Six years before our arrival the 1971 Lions had given them the biggest rugby lesson of their history. When the All Blacks had toured Britain in 1972–73 they had faced more problems, both on and off the field. I had beaten them in a Llanelli shirt and they finished the tour losing to the Barbarians in an unforgettable match in Cardiff – the game that included *the* try by Gareth Edwards. If I had banked a pound

133

for every time I've been asked about that try I'd have retired long ago. In any proper Test match I would have booted the ball into Row Z but this was the Baa Baas and the onus was on us to entertain. So I managed a couple of sidesteps and away we went. It's the one moment that everyone of a certain generation seems to remember, but the whole of New Zealand seemed to remember it a little less fondly in 1977. So it would be fair to say that from the moment we stepped off the plane we were probed and examined for any signs of weakness that would allow the All Blacks to gain some revenge.

The omens had not been good when we arrived and I quickly realised that not much would be done to smooth our passage. Our first game of the tour was against Wairarapa-Bush in Masterton on the South Island. The weather had been awful – wind and rain, which turned to sleet. A lot of thought had obviously gone into giving the Lions the 'right' surface to play on, so before our match three exhibition games for different age groups were played on the same pitch. By the time we ran out in the driving rain the mud was ankle deep. Our wingers almost died of hypothermia that afternoon, but we concentrated sufficiently hard to win 41–13, though I was not the only one who must have spent the last five minutes of the match imagining the luxury of a lovely hot shower. I was still imagining it in the dressing rooms afterwards because for some reason, which was never properly explained, the showers were cold. Some of the players started to turn blue and we left the ground wrapped in blankets, huddled in the back seats of taxis bound for our team hotel. As I've said, it was hardly a good omen.

If the showers were not very welcoming that was nothing compared to the attitude of the local media. Like the All Blacks they were also obsessed with the idea that the Lions must be made to suffer after having the cheek to win in 1971. If we weren't taking a good kicking on the field from some provincial headhunters then the blows were coming in from the headlines in the New Zealand newspapers. No Lions tour is a Sunday school outing and there were times when we did not behave like angels, but some of the stuff written about us was incredible. Every few days we would read about our so-called exploits of the night before. Often the story would concern how we had wrecked the lounge of the hotel in which we were staying – the very same lounge in which we were reading this stuff over breakfast. I used to scan the room for damage to try to discover some clue as to where this fiction might have come from.

If our drunkenness hadn't turned us violent then, apparently, it led to wild sex parties involving dozens of local women picked up around the town. Such stories were all a bit unsettling for blokes with families back home, especially when the wives started to call a few days later, the headlines in New Zealand soon being echoed in the newspapers back at home. It also seemed to unsettle Bobby Windsor, our hooker, who demanded to know where these orgies were taking place and why he hadn't been invited!

The hysterical coverage of our trip was obviously increased after we won the Second Test at Christchurch to square the series at 1–1. We had made six changes but the difference in our forwards' performance seemed to stem from a player who had taken it upon himself to become the pack leader – Terry Cobner. Cobs has always been a man I've huge respect for and he has done impressive work at the grass-roots level in Wales as the Welsh Rugby Union's Director of Rugby. Back in 1977

135

he directed our forwards into a single-minded, organised group that took the All Blacks' pack apart. I'll never forget Terry's motivating words to his forwards before the game. He told them to think of the people back home who would be fumbling around in the middle of the night trying to tune in their radios to listen to the match; the people getting up for work in his hometown of Pontypool and so forth. He wasn't going to let those people down, and he didn't expect anyone else to, either.

JJ Williams scored the only try of the game and we won 13–9 in a rough, tough uncompromising match. Some of our players were spat at and had beer thrown over them as we left the field but that didn't dampen our celebrations in the dressing room. It was a great feeling to beat the All Blacks and we were back on even terms. I felt we could now go on and clinch the series, although I was still very frustrated that the First Test had slipped through our fingers, since had we led 2–0 I think we would have been home and dry.

One of the advantages of being captain of the Lions is that you are given the luxury of your own room, while every other player has to share. This meant I wasn't kept awake by any of the tour snorers but the privacy gave me plenty of time to reflect, such that I had as much trouble sleeping as I would have done sharing with Bobby Windsor. Pat was writing to me twice a week and sending photos of little Steven, and my homesickness began to get to me. I looked at the pictures of other people playing with him and realised that it should have been me. As in every other summer, I was an absent husband and father. Little things began to irritate me. We had a policy that the management had decided to adopt to deal with the critics among the press. John Dawes demanded certain press guys were blanked and I can remember passing blokes in the corridor desperately trying to recall whether or not they were those I could say hello to or had to ignore. It was ridiculous.

With the series poised at 1–1 and everything to play for, this period should have been the highlight of my career. Here I was, captain of a Lions team that had fought back against the All Blacks and stood on the brink of achieving something special. But if the management had announced the tour had been cut short and we were all flying home the next day I would have been delighted. I simply wasn't enjoying the whole experience; the hotels were getting to me, the travelling, the terrible weather, even the training because my form was starting to go downhill.

We arrived in Dunedin for the Third Test and once again the weather had turned the pitch into a mess. It was so bad that the New Zealand Rugby Union even had a helicopter fly over the surface to try to blow-dry it before the game. The All Blacks had dropped Sid Going, and their tactic now was to rush up in midfield as quickly as possible. They had two big-tackling centres in Bruce Robertson and Billy Osborne, both of whom came at me for the whole game. Our forwards again played superbly and won plenty of ball, but the back line, me included, badly let them down. We conceded an early try, managed to get one back ourselves through Willie Duggan, and then Andy Haden scored for the All Blacks to make it 10–4 at half-time.

Our scrum-half, Brynmor Williams, got injured and was replaced by Doug Morgan. But what we really needed as a team, and what I needed as an outside-half was the genius of Gareth Edwards, who could have dictated the kicking game on his own. As it was, our mauling game was delivering up slow ball, which I was making a hash of under pressure. It didn't

137

exactly help the cause that my confidence as a goal-kicker ebbed away with the rain and the mud. Andy Irvine also missed a couple of kicks at goal and we eventually lost the game 19–7.

I was soon back in my room reflecting on our defeat as the rain lashed against the hotel windows. We had lost and I, the captain of the Lions, had been awful. Again I thought about home, but now my homesickness was mixed with guilty feelings. The people I knew back in Llanelli would have gladly given their right arms to be sat where I was on the other side of the world, playing rugby instead of having to work in the steelworks or factories. I was the lucky one and yet I felt demoralised and depressed.

I went downstairs to eat and the menu, which was hardly the best, appeared to be the same as yesterday and the day before that. The New Zealand Rugby Union made a fortune out of the Lions that summer, for we played before packed stadiums wherever we went, but they certainly didn't spend much of it on our food. I looked around the room. Some players were just sitting in silence, others were arguing about the game plan, whilst another group were busy making their complaints about the food. For the first time on the tour I told the hotel manager to forget the set menu; we would all eat à la carte and he could put it down on the Lions' bill. If the management wanted to make an issue of it later on, I thought, then let them try. But it soon turned out that the management were of the very same mind. Plates piled high with our own choice of food, the mood quickly changed and things suddenly didn't seem so bleak. It then dawned on me that I should have been a lot more aggressive and demanding from the moment we had arrived in New Zealand.

We moved on to Auckland for the Fourth Test and a chance to share the series, which I felt would have been a reasonable achievement. The friction between the players and the press had intensified now since as well as all the writers in our hotel some of the pundits who had been firing bullets from back home had also arrived in town. Carwyn James, Barry John and Mervyn Davies were holding court in the bar at night and trying to tell anyone prepared to listen where and why the Lions had got it wrong. As you might expect this went down like a lead balloon with Dawesy, who felt they were trying to undermine the Lions in order to sell a few papers – treacherous behaviour in his eyes since they had been working together in the same place for the same ends, six years earlier.

Things turned really nasty one night when Mervyn bumped into our tour manager, Dodd Burrell. It would have been a frosty encounter anyway but since Mervyn was walking out of the team room – strictly out of bounds to anyone other than squad members – with two crates of the sponsors' beer on his shoulder, there was an almighty slanging match. Insults were flying around and it was not long before an emergency meeting of the management was called. The whole thing would have been best ignored but rather stupidly I was told no longer to talk to Mervyn or Barry. I explained that whatever they were up to now these were former team-mates and friends of mine and no one was going to tell me who I could and couldn't talk to.

Looking back now it all seems incredibly childish, which of course it was. You have to be able to rise above all that, but in 1977 we let ourselves become distracted by such rubbish. This is why I have a lot of respect for Martin Johnson. Any criticism in 1997 and 2001 seemed to bounce off those broad shoulders of his, Jonno simply getting on with trying to win the next game – even when the stick was coming from blokes he once played alongside. In Australia in 2001, with the series poised at 1–1, Johnson had to deal with the whinging Matt Dawson and his infamous diary, followed up by Austin Healey's rant on the day before the deciding Test. Johnson himself, as he has since admitted in print, was not a big admirer of the coach Graham Henry's infamous 'pod system' but he didn't let anything distract him from the job ahead and the Lions came within a whisker of winning the series.

Having gone down the well-trodden road of rugby player turned media pundit myself, I can see both sides of the coin. As a player you don't like to hear ex-players – especially when they are former team-mates – put the boot in. It hurts and can often affect a player's confidence. But once you stop playing you have a less blinkered view. You realise that playing rugby is only part of the whole industry; there are many roles to be played and if newspapers, radio and TV are going to bring the game to a wider audience then it follows that former players will be asked to contribute their opinions. I see little point in those people not telling the truth as they see it. You need to be honest or else you are deceiving your audience or readership.

Back in 1977 we were all amateur players and perhaps more naïve in thinking the media would be supportive. After all, we were doing our best and we weren't getting paid for it. But we should not have worried so much about what was being written and said about us, and we certainly should not have wasted time in management meetings deciding which journalist or which ex-player we were not going to talk to. It was destructive, when we needed to be pulling together.

Having beaten a strong Auckland side I was hopeful, if not

confident, that we could beat the All Blacks for a second time and share the series 2–2. But I was also counting down the days to the flight out of New Zealand. Our approach was far more conservative going into the Fourth Test. Injuries had deprived us of Derek Quinnell, JJ Williams and, most importantly, Terry Cobner. We had decided to bang the ball deep rather then try to play too much rugby, our mistakes having cost us dearly in the previous Test.

At half-time we were leading 9–3 after a try, conversion and penalty goal from Doug Morgan. Our pack was well on top and New Zealand just weren't at the races.

They drew closer with another penalty to make it 9–6 and with a couple of minutes left I struck a clearing kick but if failed to find touch. I wasn't too concerned because although the All Blacks could tackle all day they didn't seem to have the skill to open us up for a try. Bill Osborne kicked it back but Steve Fenwick – normally the most reliable of blokes – half-dropped the ball before feeding it on to our hooker, Peter Wheeler. He was tackled by Graham Mourie and the ball fell for Lawrie Knight to go over for a try in the corner.

I had tried to make amends for my own mistake by tackling Knight as he ran in, but as I got up the crowd's reaction told me he had scored. I just stood there and stared at them as they cheered and I can remember thinking, 'This is it. This is how it's going to end. Four months touring and we're going to lose the series in the last minute by a single point.' It was the lowest I had ever felt on a rugby field. It should have been 2–2 and a creditable draw, but instead it was 3–1 and I had failed in what I had aimed to achieve as Lions captain. All I wanted to do was get home.

That night at the post-match dinner, I shared a few beers

with Willie Duggan of Ireland. We were all off to Fiji for a few days on the way home, where we would combine one Test against the Fijians with a few days of relaxation, but Willie couldn't and because he was a nervous flier he was tanking up so that he could sleep through his flight home in the morning. 'Don't worry, Phil,' he said. 'It's only a game. You'll soon forget about this trip when you win the Grand Slam again next season.' I think he was being genuine, but you could never tell with Willie. He was so battered and bloodied in one tour game that he went off for stitches before half-time. When the rest of us came into the dressing room I saw him sitting there with a fag in one hand and a bottle of beer in the other as they stitched up his face. 'Bad luck, Willie. Well played,' I said. 'What do you mean?' he demanded. 'As soon as this f***er sorts my face out I'll be back on.'

Then there was the strange little kitbag that Willie used to carry with him on his travels. For the first six weeks of our trip I thought it must have held his boots, although I wondered why he was loath to put them with the rest of the squad's gear. It was only after being tipped off by another player that I became aware the bag contained a bottle of whisky, which Willie would occasionally swig from in order to allay his fear of flying. No wonder he sometimes looked a little slow in training on the afternoons we arrived at a new venue. I dread to think what he must have been like by the time he landed back at Heathrow.

The rest of us let out hair down in Fiji and relaxed in the sunshine. It was like getting into a wonderful hot bath after weeks of running through the mud and the rain. Our travelling band of pressmen enjoyed themselves, too, and one night a few of us senior players accepted an invitation to join them for dinner. It was another Lions tradition, seen as a way of burying the hatchet, and although I was ready to bury that hatchet right between the eyes of some of them I agreed to go along. John Dawes refused and I don't think he has ever forgiven me for siding with the enemy.

On the flight home my thoughts drifted back to the 1974 tour to South Africa and the welcome back I had received then in my home village. There had been a huge reception at the airport, and then, having got home and slumped into an armchair, the next thing I knew there was a knock at the door and I was being ushered into a horse-drawn carriage for a ride around Felinfoel. There were people outside their houses along the streets, waving and cheering, a small ceremony in Felinfoel park, and I was also presented with a gift of engraved cut-glass from the people of my village. It had all been very unexpected and proved equally emotional.

This time, I thought, I would be able to sit in the house for a week before anyone wanted to talk to a losing Lions captain. I was right – up to a point. There was no horse-drawn carriage this time. It was a chauffeur-driven car instead. The same faces. The same cheers. It was a lovely gesture and something I will never forget.

Two Lions tours, then, as a player provided me with very different experiences, but both helped me to grow and mature as a person. In rugby, as in life, you have to suffer the bad times to know how to appreciate the good. I learnt a lot about myself in 1977 and I came back home a wiser man.

CHAPTER 9

Australia Rules

Australia has become the hardest place to visit if you are a rugby player – and the best place to go if you're a fan. In South Africa and New Zealand there is always a grim determination to beat you and you can feel it on and off the field. In Australia they certainly want to stuff you, but they would much rather you have a good time while they go about it.

I like Australia and I like Aussies. They are the most passionate and dedicated nation on earth when it comes to producing sporting excellence, but the average guy in the street hasn't forgotten that it's only a game. It's always intense, always high quality, but the social side of sport is not suffocated by the desire to win and at the end of the day – or, more usually, well before – the Aussie fan wants to sit down with you and have a beer or two.

I watched the start of the 2001 Lions tour to Australia at home on television and it made for great viewing. The colour, the spectacle, the great stadia, the superb rugby played by the Lions all left me desperately counting down the days to my departure Down Under, where I was to serve as a pundit for BBC Wales and the *Sunday Mirror* and also as a tour guide for Gullivers. About the only thing that stuck in my craw was the incident in the match between the Lions and New South Wales when the Irishman Ronan O'Gara had his head punched in by Duncan McRae. Eleven times O'Gara was struck as he lay on the ground and not a single Lion came to his rescue. I couldn't fathom that. There was O'Gara taking a real pasting and his team-mates seemed content to let it happen. If the same thing had occurred on the 1974 tour to South Africa all hell would have broken loose. Players would have piled in from everywhere. Maybe that's the benefit of professional self-restraint in the modern era but I felt those other Lions should have tried to protect O'Gara. It suggested to me that too many players were more concerned with looking after themselves rather than with helping the Lions succeed, and eventually I think the Lions suffered because that attitude came to surface more than once.

I first toured Australia in 1969 as a nervous 20-year-old with Wales. It was not what you would call a rugby country and I don't think many Aussies noticed that we were even there. Rugby union was low-key stuff and that was reflected in the very modest facilities and generally lukewarm reception we were given. But by the time I flew out 32 years later it was as if I had landed on a different planet. I was with Gullivers, one of the big rugby travel companies that specialise in carrying thousands of fans all around the world to watch games. As a tour guide you hope that the rugby will meet the expectations of the people you are looking after, but you also hope that the

145

welcome you are given enables them to really enjoy their stay. Australia responded superbly on both counts.

It was only a year after the Sydney Olympics and it seemed to me that the whole of Australia still viewed itself as on trial before the rest of the world and that, in consequence, it was determined to make the right impression. People were always extremely helpful and generous. The hotels, restaurants and facilities were invariably first rate and the sheer friendliness of the place was overwhelming. Whether you asked someone in the street for directions, or a bus driver to identify a landmark, it was always as if they had gone through some government-backed charm school designed to ease the tourists' passage.

This easygoing affability was extended to everyone, even when their own team had just been hammered. The night the Lions won the First Test, 29–13 at The Gabba in Brisbane, was simply unforgettable. Every bar and pub for miles around seemed to be packed with celebrating Lions fans and it was a human sea of red. But where you could spot the odd green-and-gold jersey there was nothing but good humour and warm congratulations. British and Irish fans had invaded their country, swamping their bars and restaurants, and yet there was never any hint of trouble or animosity. They were always the most generous of hosts.

We truly were invaders. I can remember being in one bar and was asked by a guy I recognised from home if I knew the cricket score. I confessed that I hadn't heard the Test score. 'No, not the Test,' he said. 'Sorry,' I said, 'but I haven't heard the Glamorgan score, either.' He looked frustrated and finally explained, 'No, Phil. I was wondering if you knew how Dafen had got on.' There we were 12,000 miles from home and someone was asking me for cricket scores from the next village down the road. Some people might call it homesickness, but for me that typifies the Welshman's regard for his own home town or village.

The match itself in Brisbane was one I will treasure, as the Lions won in style – breathtaking style, in fact. Jason Robinson scored a wonderful try after only a couple of minutes and the effect it had on the Lions supporters, as well as his team-mates, was profound. These Lions were suddenly full of confidence and played with a swagger and a freshness of approach that few people had expected. All we had heard from sections of the Aussie media was how the Lions were a bunch of thugs who were only capable of beating teams by bullying them, by fair means or foul. It all seemed to hark back to the 1989 Lions tour Down Under during which the Aussies were beaten and occasionally beaten up. However, rather than live up to any Aussie-imposed stereotype, the Lions cut loose through their back line and tore the Wallabies to shreds. Robinson's try summed up that adventurous approach and sent the Lions supporters into overdrive. The stadium was a vast sea of red with just the odd splash of green and gold. It could have been Cardiff after a Welsh try, rather than balmy Brisbane. By the time Brian O'Driscoll, Dafydd James and Scott Quinnell had also scored tries it was barmy Brisbane. The Barmy Army, at least 25,000 strong in a capacity crowd of 37,000, went absolutely nuts.

Before the tour O'Driscoll had been compared to Mike Gibson, a Lions legend, which may have been a little premature. Brian still has to go some to match Gibson in terms of his achievements in the game, but that night he justified all the hype with a display of genius. His running terrified the Wallabies midfield and gave rise to the first renditions of

'Waltzing O'Driscoll'; an adopted – as well as an adapted – anthem that we were to hear sung by Lions supporters all around Australia.

It has been said since that the Lions game plan that night bore no resemblance to the one Graham Henry had been striving for on the training field. Henry's plan, according to some, was restrictive and inflexible, while the Lions were adventurous and sometimes off the cuff. I don't know about that. It's a bit mean-spirited to deny a coach his influence on a winning side and if the Lions had gone on to win the series then Henry, I'm sure, would have been given huge credit.

Unfortunately for him, for the Lions, and for all of us watching, he didn't. Australia came back to win both the Melbourne Test and the Sydney decider. Melbourne was a match the Lions should have won because they were well in control. As far as the Third Test was concerned, I always felt that they had suffered too many injuries by then and that key players such as Jonny Wilkinson and Quinnell had taken too much of a physical battering to be quite the influences they needed to be for the Lions to win.

To my mind, Henry was fatally and disgracefully undermined by both Matt Dawson and Austin Healey. I'm not saying he made no mistakes. He made plenty and even if the English boys had kept their mouths shut then the Wallabies might still have won the series. But the message sent out to the Aussies through the three weeks of the Tests was that the Lions were vulnerable because they were divided – and for that Dawson and Healey must take the blame.

They are both fine players but they should have realised that the Lions are even bigger than their egos. By moaning and groaning in print about what a raw deal Henry had given them, they simply handed ammunition to the opposition. I don't mind Lions players keeping diaries, but if they are going to put the knife into the coach they should wait until the series is over, not to spare anyone's feelings, but simply because the overriding consideration during the series should be to win it. As a player, anything that you know is going to threaten that aim should be resisted. In other words, Healey and Dawson should have bitten their tongues until after everyone had walked off Stadium Australia in Sydney after the final game of the tour. It wasn't their complaints that I found galling, simply their decision to voice them when they did. Jonny Wilkinson was carried off on a stretcher in Melbourne, but he did not complain or feel sorry for himself. He concentrated purely on his rugby and training, and he eventually made the Third Test. Admittedly Healey and Dawson had a different set of problems to Wilkinson but their response should have been the same.

As I say, Henry certainly did make mistakes. On reflection he should not have taken charge of the tour. He had enough on his plate in the middle of 2001 with a Wales team that had started to lose its way. Maybe, as Martin Johnson pointed out afterwards, his coaching methods were too rigid and relied too heavily on a pre-programmed approach – that infamous 'pod' system. But for me Henry's biggest mistakes were the ones he made as a man-manager rather than as a coach.

I spoke with most of the Welsh boys in the squad and it was apparent that Henry virtually ignored the midweek team. He treated them like excess baggage.

He took a lot of players on that tour – 37 in all – and both he and they knew that they couldn't all play. But when you are on a Lions tour, you want to make the team, and, more especially, you want to make the Test team. Under Henry and his 13-strong management team – almost as overloaded as the squad itself – talented guys like Healey were not getting a chance in the weekend side and their frustration grew as the tour went on. As a man-manager you have to make those guys still feel very important, but I don't think that happened with Henry. The players were left to fend for themselves. The length of the tour was probably about right, but too many players were taken and those left in the dirt-trackers were not made to feel as if they were part of the show.

Henry's attitude was exposed in an amazing remark he made after the Lions had lost to Australia A in Gosford. It was only the fourth match of the tour, but Henry's response was to say: 'We might just have to concentrate on the Test matches rather than the other games', implying that the midweek team would have to look out for itself. It was an extraordinary and rather stupid thing to say. The message sent out to all the players in the midweek side was that you were out on your own – and, worse still, there was probably no way back into the fold in terms of making the Test side.

No wonder resentment festered. It wasn't helped by the fact that the players hardly saw anything of Australia. They ate, they trained, they met, they ate again and then they went to bed. They were in Australia, one of the most awe-inspiring countries in the world, and yet they could just as well have been in a Holiday Inn at Heathrow Airport.

I felt one of Ian McGeechan's great masterstrokes on the 1997 Lions tour to South Africa was the way he made everyone feel involved and also aware that they were somewhere very different, doing something very special. Geech may have had his Test side mapped out firmly in his mind before he even got on the plane, but he gave the impression to his players that places were always up for grabs. The midweek players always felt they might just get the nod for the Test team if they delivered. It may have been a great con trick on Geech's part, but that's not the point. It kept everyone united because they all felt they were in it together and had a chance of taking a starring role. Even when the Lions went 2–0 up in a three-Test series, the dirt-trackers bust a gut because they felt they had a chance of gaining Test places for the final game against the Springboks. Some did.

Henry, though, was so infatuated with training and preparation that he lost sight of the fact that part of preparation is the importance of keeping players happy. In 1974, our coach Syd Millar also made the midweek dirt-trackers feel important. We, the Saturday side, always supported them and they in turn supported us. I think Henry is an excellent man-manager in dealing with those people he has invited into the inner circle. He motivates and he leads. But if you are not considered worthy of the inner circle then he lacks the skills to still make you feel important and that is why so many 2001 Lions came to feel an antipathy towards him. They got frustrated and angry. I bumped into a number of players walking around Manly who felt demoralised, disillusioned and even quite bitter at their treatment. The midweek players have to feel as important as the Test players. Once you lose their support a tour can split apart, and that's what happened.

Maybe it's simply the New Zealand way of doing things. Perhaps they are just more brutal over there and if you're in you're in and if you're out then you're out. But over here, and certainly in Wales, players respond better when an arm is extended around their shoulders. On reflection it might have

151

served the Lions better to tour with someone other than a New Zealander in charge. But the reality in the summer of 2000, when Henry was chosen, was that there were not too many outstanding candidates around. Clive Woodward? Maybe, but this was a time when Clive was not exactly flavour of the month. I had a few mates within the RFU system who felt back then, that players from the four different nations would not have accepted Clive as the Lions coach.

The Lions lost the Second Test 35–14 inside the awesome bowl of Melbourne's Colonial Stadium and then the Third Test slipped through their fingers, 29–23. In the end it came down to a single score. If the Lions had won that last vital line-out, instead of allowing Justin Harrison to win it, then they might have scored, Jonny Wilkinson might have converted and the Lions might have won the series by a single point. Harrison would not have become an Aussie national hero, the Dawson and Healey diaries would have become about as memorable as a report by the Welsh Assembly and Pat would not have had to put up with my long face over a restaurant table near Sydney Harbour.

Henry's last contribution as Lions coach was to suggest changes for future tours. He claimed that they should be simple almost Test-only affairs: fly in, one or two warm-ups, and then into three international matches. I, for one, would hate it if we ever went down that road. Once the Lions become just another representative team that only plays Test rugby, then it will be the end of a proud tradition. The Lions are special and they need to be kept special. I know all about the crowded fixture lists the demands on the modern player and but it would be a terrible retreat if Lions tours became simply about Test series with virtually no other tour games. A way has to be found to ensure that there is room and time to go to New Zealand on the next tour in 2005 and play against Auckland, Canterbury and the rest. There should be four or five matches at least outside the Test series.

If negotiations with the New Zealand Rugby Football Union are entered into properly, and by the right people, then I feel sure that the whole ethos of the Lions can be preserved. I am convinced that the rugby fans of New Zealand feel exactly the same way. When the game's rulers are sorting out the international calendar then a way has to be found to ensure the 2005 Lions tour is true to the spirit of those of the past.

Anyone who doubts that should ask the supporters who flocked to Australia in 2001. It was a wonderful celebration of one of the great rugby traditions – a travelling jamboree uniting people with a shared passion for the sport across the country.

Australia gave the Barmy Army a fantastic welcome and provided not only me but also thousands of others with some great memories. When I ate with friends at Doyle's restaurant, with the Sydney Opera House lit up on one side and the Harbour Bridge on the other, I thought how lucky I was to be in such a location, thanks to rugby. My mother and father would not have dreamed that playing rugby, watching rugby and talking rugby could take you to a place like that.

While we were in Melbourne, Steven and I went to the MCG, one of the most atmospheric sporting venues I have ever been in. I'm a huge cricket fan and again rugby had provided an opportunity to visit somewhere I had always wanted to see.

We strolled around the place and eventually found the

photograph I had been looking for - one of the visiting England team of 1965 which included Jeff Jones, born two miles down the road from my own home in Felinfoel. Little more than a year on from my visit, Jeff's son Simon, the young Glamorgan fast bowler, would also be on Ashes duty with England until a cruel knee injury wrecked his tour on the opening day of the First Test.

We walked out into the middle and I tried to imagine what it must have been like to open the batting for England on a bright December morning, with Dennis Lillee coming in off a long run and 80,000 Aussies urging him to bash the Pom.

In Sydney I spoke at a dinner alongside Mark Ella, Nick-Farr Jones and Simon Poidevan – three Wallabies who extended such warmth and sportsmanship to the groups of travelling Lions supporters that it really made me marvel at rugby's ability to spark the keenest rivalry but maintain a dignity and camaraderie, even though the physical battle on the pitch can often be brutal.

In Brisbane, Melbourne, Sydney, on the Gold Coast – everywhere we went – the welcome was always extended and always sincere. Australia is a young, vibrant country and it has a youthful charm that unfailingly shines through. It handled the Test series confidently and extravagantly, just as it had handled the Olympics and just as I'm sure it will handle the 2003 Rugby World Cup. I enjoyed the best trip I've had through rugby since I retired in 1982.

When we flew out of Sydney Airport we must have been carrying three times the weight of luggage we had when we arrived. Our cases were bulging and I was prepared to be stung for a hefty bill for excess baggage.

'You guys look as if you enjoyed yourselves,' said the steward. 'I'll ignore the excess. Have a safe trip back and come and visit us again.'

We will, and I can't wait.

CHAPTER 10

Vive L'Europe!

For the first 47 years of my life the European Cup meant only one thing – Manchester United. Whenever United went into Europe I followed their progress by any means available. Every word in the newspapers, each crackling radio broadcast, the briefest TV highlights, or the wall-to-wall coverage offered when it transformed itself into the Champions League, I soaked up the lot.

Like many kids growing up in the fifties and sixties my affections towards United stemmed from the Munich air crash of 1958 when I was nine years old. It was an awful event for all United followers but for those of us who were just starting to form attachments to sporting heroes it had a profound effect. Every game United have played since then, on some faraway foreign field, has always felt partly in honour of the players who lost their lives. Actually winning the European Cup became a cause. More than that, it was a crusade and I often felt that Sir

Matt Busby was a man with a personal mission that was somehow far more important and significant than the ambitions of other managers. Maybe that is why United fans are sometimes accused of arrogance and chauvinism by others who don't carry the same emotional baggage.

For many years the destiny remained unfulfilled and it was left to Celtic to break the mould in 1967 when they became the first British club to conquer Europe. That was a magnificent achievement and I don't think Celtic have ever been given full credit for it outside of Scotland. The following season United also lifted the European Cup and although I couldn't get to Wembley that night I still remember it unfolding on TV as one of the most emotional sporting occasions I can recall. For Bobby Charlton to score in that 4–1 victory, having been a survivor of the air crash ten years earlier, was a perfect ending to a wonderful story. It meant a good deal to me, as a young man of 19. What it must have meant to the United players I can hardly imagine.

Later that year, I was lucky enough to meet those same United players – all heroes of mine – in Argentina, where Wales were on tour. I think the meeting had been arranged by the management of both squads in order to keep us out of the shadier parts of Buenos Aires. United were there playing in the World Club Championship. I would have quite fancied a tour of the city's bars in the company of George Best, and so would a few others in our squad, but those in charge had obviously tried to block any attempts at escape as we all sat in the United team hotel.

It was always going to be a sober affair, but the chance to sit and chat to the likes of George and Paddy Crerand – great guys – was not one any of the Welsh squad were going to miss. They had conquered Europe as a club and now they were taking on the best in South America, Estudiantes, in front of 80,000 passionate Argentinians. But you wouldn't have guessed it by the calm, cool air of confidence that oozed from the likes of Best. If he had been any more relaxed he would have been in a coma.

Regular European competition had taken British club football, and the players, on to a new level and that was why I felt so enthusiastic about the notion of something similar in rugby, when the idea was first mooted. The idea of a Europe-wide club competition had been kicking around for some time, but, just as with the rugby World Cup, those who ran the game always seemed to lag behind those who played and watched. Caution was their watchword, when rugby cried out for boldness and enterprise. It meant that when a European tournament finally did get off the ground, Welsh players of my generation, and many after, had long since hung up their boots.

The first year of the European Cup, which, thanks to the bold backing of the sponsors in those early days, has now become universally known as the Heineken Cup, was 1995. Welsh, French, Irish, Italian and Romanian sides took part and although it might have been 40 years since United and other British soccer clubs first crowded on to small aircraft to make arduous trips to mysterious destinations, there was the same spirit of adventure and exploration about the whole thing. Players, coaches, fans, administrators, media – we were all new to it and it was a journey into the unknown. When you consider how far the tournament has come, how much it has grown in playing standards and commercially, it is remarkable to think that this has been achieved in the space of seven short years. Everything that European soccer encapsulates in terms of prestige, drama, tension and excitement is now there in Heineken Cup rugby.

Take Cardiff, for instance. They are a big club, in many ways the biggest in Wales, but their horizons and ambitions have been broadened by European competition. Their chairman and Peter Thomas, one of the club's financial backers, have publicly stated many times that the ambition of the club is to win the Heineken Cup. They reached the final in the first season in 1995–96 but the tournament was barely into its stride then compared to what it is now. Cardiff know that and they also know that the Cup now carries huge financial rewards. So the competition has become their top priority every season and it is the yardstick by which their teams and coaches have to be judged. So far, they have not measured up to expectations and I'm sure the same goes for leading English clubs who have yet to lift the trophy such as Gloucester, Wasps, Saracens and Harlequins.

For my own club, Llanelli, the desire is even stronger. Having failed to make the final after losing two semi-finals in the dying minutes, I know that there is a restless yearning to become the first Welsh club to win the tournament. Like Manchester United in the footballing equivalent, the European Cup has become Llanelli's holy grail.

In Wales, the Heineken Cup has another important significance. It is the only way at present whereby Wales can match up to and possibly beat England. Wales have fallen so far behind England at international level that Welsh players now have an inferiority complex whenever they come up against the white shirt. The only way I think we can rid ourselves of that is for those same players to take confidence from beating English clubs in Europe. Llanelli went some way towards achieving that when they beat both Leicester and Bath on their way to the 2002 semi-final, where they should really have beaten Leicester again. Perhaps the most encouraging comment made by anyone about the state of Welsh rugby after a dismal 2001–2002 season was Austin Healey's verdict that the hardest matches he had played in all season, for club or country, were Leicester's three matches against Llanelli.

I am convinced that the revival of Ireland at international level was sparked by Ulster's Heineken Cup triumph in 1999 and the growing stature of Munster in Europe. To a lesser extent Leinster have helped, too. In contrast to Irish success, the decline of Scotland at Test level has been merely a reflection of the poor showing of both Edinburgh and Glasgow in Europe.

For France, Europe has enabled their players to grow up, and this fed through to their Grand Slam of 2002. French players now show far more discipline at international level, both individually and as a team. This, too, has come from their experience in Europe, where you need cool heads and calm nerves if you are going to succeed. The French coach, Bernard Laporte, realised this and stressed time and again how important it was for French players to show discipline and self-control in big European matches if they wanted to play for France. In the early years of Europe, the French players could easily be provoked, especially away from home, and they were always able to mask their weaknesses by blaming a foreign referee. But things have changed and it seems to me that the players of Toulouse, Stade Français, Montferrand and Castres are no longer content to seek easy excuses.

As far as England are concerned the effect of Leicester and their back-to-back Heineken Cup Final victories in 2001 and

2002 hardly needs to be stressed. England may have failed to collect the Grand Slam in both of those seasons, but there is no doubt that England's ascendancy in world terms to the elite owes a good deal to the extra competitive edge European club rugby has provided for Clive Woodward's players. Just look at the form Martin Johnson, Neil Back and Austin Healey bring with them to the England set-up.

In fact, I have no hesitation in saying that the major Heineken Cup matches now rival Test matches in terms of standards, intensity and atmosphere, not to mention the demand for tickets. When Wales play Ireland it's normally only during the month preceding the game that a number of my Irish pals, mostly ex-internationals, ring me to ask if I can help them out with tickets, but my phone almost went into meltdown before the 2002 Heineken Cup Final, as even the 30,000 tickets given over to Munster fans for the final with Leicester at the Millennium Stadium seemed inadequate. With the stadium roof closed and Munster and Leicester fans in full voice, it was the equal of any international game.

The final that day is worth reflecting on. It was an afternoon when real fans took over the stadium – not the corporate day-trippers who have infiltrated Six Nations games. Friday night in Cardiff before the game was an incredible sight, with supporters from both teams having taken over the city. The next day, the singing, colour and spectacle all knocked spots off many international matches I have attended in recent seasons. Of course, the Unions all need the income derived from corporate hospitality, but I am inclined to agree with the Manchester United player, Roy Keane, who upset the apple-cart recently by declaring that the prawn-sandwich brigade, as he called them, were reducing Old Trafford to a sterile arena devoid of real

161

passion. If we are not very careful then the same thing will soon happen to the Millennium Stadium or Twickenham, Murrayfield and even Lansdowne Road. That is why the atmosphere at Heineken Cup ties has proved such a breath of fresh air. It's about real fans, with real affinities and real voices.

Paul Ackford wrote a piece in *The Sunday Telegraph* before that Heineken Cup Final in which he suggested that club/ provincial rugby had now become bigger than international rugby. I think he made a very valid point, although my reasons for thinking a shift is taking place are perhaps different to his. I still believe Test rugby sets higher standards and, unlike Paul, I don't feel that the unpredictable nature of the Six Nations championship has been lost forever simply because of the recent success of France and England. These things are cyclical and Wales, Scotland and Ireland will come again even if their strong periods will rarely be sustained for as long as those managed by England and France. My belief that the Heineken Cup is threatening the pre-eminent status of the international game is more to do with the fans. The likes of Leicester and Munster are followed by passionate people with a deep knowledge and respect for the game. The more I go to Six Nations games, the fewer people fitting that description I see around me.

The England–Wales game at Twickenham in 2002 seemed to be watched by people who either had no idea what was going on or else simply didn't really care. There was barely a murmur inside the ground. It was the same when Wales hosted Scotland in the same season. That was a close game, but the two sides were poor and half the stadium seemed indifferent to who won. You can't just blame the suited watchers. The number of people at Wales games who spend half the match wandering backwards and forwards to the bar, or queuing up for soggy pizza, depresses me almost as much as some of the Welsh performances.

In contrast, the Heineken Cup games have become mini-internationals, comparable to the Test matches of old. When Pontypridd play Bath, or Cardiff host Harlequins, there is a bit of bite to the whole thing. Voices are raised. Passions are raised. It matters. The blunt truth is that the 2001–02 season was a pathetic one for Wales, only rescued by our clubs in the Heineken Cup and the Parker Pen Shield.

The change can also be seen in the attitude of players towards club rugby. I went out to France to cover Llanelli's pool game against Perpignan for Radio Wales in January 2002. Perpignan were a strong side and they handed Llanelli a solid beating, even though their own chance of qualification from the group had already gone. In years gone by, a heavy defeat away from home would have been the signal for a serious sorrow-drowning session, maybe until three or four o'clock in the morning. But I saw most of the Llanelli players sipping lemonade in the team hotel at 10 p.m., chatting among themselves – not about the defeat they had just suffered, but about what they had to do to beat Leicester at Stradey Park in order to qualify for the knockout stages.

Three or four years earlier, I happened to have been in Belfast at the same time as Swansea were there after they had been beaten by Ulster. Of course the result bothered them, but afterwards it seemed they couldn't get away from the old mindset that any match outside of their own borders constituted 'a trip' in the old amateur sense of the term. The old rituals and bad habits had to be observed and this applied equally to every club in Wales. A beery weekend in Belfast was fine in the days before professionalism, but is no longer much use if you are aiming to topple the likes of Leicester. I am sure Swansea have since come to recognise that, like every other club chasing the Tigers' tail.

Talking of Swansea, I was reminded of their days of yesteryear on that visit to see Llanelli in Perpignan. Travelling to this part of France, where you are only a couple of hours' drive from Barcelona, seems an unlikely opportunity for tales about old foes back home. But I bumped into Jean-François Imbernon, a massive second row from the French team of the mid-seventies. Having played with distinction for Perpignon, Jean-François now owns a bar in the centre of town where rugby folk tend to meet.

We hadn't seen each other since 1977 when France beat Wales in Paris on their way to a Grand Slam. When I shook his hand, my own disappeared into this huge paw, and, as with all French forwards who had once tried to crush me on the field, he greeted me like a long lost brother. We talked about our clubs and the state of the game in Wales and France, but it was only after the third or fourth bottle that I plucked up the courage to ask him about his nose. I had been staring at it from the moment I met him because it was literally spread over one side of his face.

'What happened to your nose,' I said.

He smiled. 'Ah, it was a Welshman,' he replied, 'the Swansea forward, Geoff Wheel. He caught me with a good one.'

Imbernon had been part of a brutal pack of French forwards along with the likes of the great Robert Paparemborde and Gerard Cholley, who had formerly been a successful amateur boxer. As players they were all lunatics and nutcases, but here

164

I was, sharing some superb wine with this guy, who, 25 years earlier had been trying to tear me limb from limb. It sums up the spirit and tradition of rugby, but in the context of new European horizons. Had Llanelli been purely on the treadmill of the Welsh domestic scene then Jean-François and I would never have renewed our acquaintance.

That is the great thing about Europe as an arena for competition between clubs. It offers something a little different. The players have to cope with new surroundings and the fans get to sample another way of life, another culture, and usually some great food. The welcome from the French clubs has always been lavish. The banquet thrown by Toulouse after they hosted Cardiff a couple of years ago could have kept a small village in food for a week. But it's all done with such style and generosity. The fans and the players, like the great French wing Emile Ntamack and the prop Franck Tournaire, mix together freely and the atmosphere is so relaxed. That connection between players and supporters is something I feel we have lost at all too many clubs in Britain. There appears to be a divide at some places, players preferring to jump into their flash cars and roar off home after a game rather than have a drink with the people who pay their wages.

Perpignan offered fabulous hospitality before and after the game, just as they had done when I first saw Llanelli play out there in 1999. But the Stade Aime Giral is like a bullring. The noise and the vibrant colours of the Catalan flags waved by almost every home supporter make it incredibly intimidating.

Llanelli have come home beaten on both their visits, but they have absorbed so much knowledge from those two games that I am certain they can win there next time. The bank of experience gained from European competition provides the basis for success in this new higher form of club rugby. Leicester lost in the 1997 Heineken Cup Final to Brive and in the following years they also lost away to Pau and to Stade Français. But those defeats taught them so much, the knowledge gained forming the basis of their magnificent victory over Stade in Paris in the final of 2001.

Leicester have undoubtedly set the standards in Europe, having recently become the only team to have successfully defended the trophy. It is a monumental achievement, for which they deserve enormous praise. Leicester have not only been a class above the rest, they have also been involved in some of the epic matches we have seen over the past seven years. Their three matches against Llanelli, played to three packed stadiums in three different towns, couldn't have been more tense. They are virtually unbeatable at Welford Road and they now have the confidence and armoury to go to the French clubs and attack them on their own territory. Dean Richards has assembled a squad with huge strength in depth and they have developed a playing style with far more variety than the Leicester sides of a while ago. It might have been okay for Leicester to dominate in England through the power of their pack, but in Europe they needed something more. Skilful backs, like Geordan Murphy, Steve Booth and Leon Lloyd, have given them that dimension and when a spark of genius is required, they can call on Austin Healey.

Richards can be a bit dour for some tastes. But I like the bloke and he has a wealth of knowledge about the game. John Wells is a fine coach, but the thing that has really impressed me in recent years about Leicester has been their ability to be original and innovative. They have signed players from all over the world, like Rod Kafer and Josh Kronfeld from the southern hemisphere. They have tempted boys from rugby league, like Booth and Freddie Tuilagi. And they have brought youngsters through from their own academy, such as Ollie Smith. They have blended all these influences and made sure every player knows what it means to pull on the club jersey. Maybe most important of all, they breed a winning attitude. Leicester win matches they have no right to win. They just never give up and that is why they have conquered Europe in successive seasons.

Other clubs, such as Saracens and Cardiff, have tried big-name signings, but the thing about Leicester is that all their stars seem to want to die for the cause. You can't say that about Cardiff. They have hugely underachieved in Europe and you have to point the finger at the players.

I know from talking to Leicester players and officials that when they lose or play poorly they don't waste their time with witch-hunts and inquests. They just belt the crap out of each other at training on Monday morning. Cardiff have lacked that spirit in recent seasons and they have suffered for it.

Bath and Northampton are the only other English clubs to have won the Heineken Cup. Northampton edged past Munster in 2000 in a final that never really hit the heights and Bath beat Brive in the 1998 final. Jon Callard scored all Bath's points and one memorable tackle made by Ieuan Evans summed up a very courageous performance. Brive were firm favourites, having beaten Leicester in the previous final, but maybe they had been left jaded by three action-packed matches against Pontypridd earlier in the tournament.

One of those matches packed in a little too much action for most people's liking. Ponty lost 32–31 out in France in the pool stages in a game that regularly boiled over. It was a hard, physical match and Ponty were robbed by a dreadful decision by the Scottish referee Ed Murray. He awarded a late try to Brive, which I was not alone in thinking should never have been given. Unfortunately, the Ponty boys carried their sense of grievance with them to a local drinking spot called Le Bar Toulzac when they should have stayed in at their hotel. All hell broke loose and for a while the mass brawl and its after-shocks seemed to be the only sports news of note in the whole of Britain.

Ponty were wrong to allow themselves to be caught in that predicament, but I genuinely believe the whole episode made them stronger as a team and a club. It bonded them more tightly and the strength of character formed by those three epic games laid the foundation for their wonderful Parker Pen Shield campaign last season, when they reached the final.

Llanelli were involved in an even dirtier match out in Pau in southern France a few years back and for a while it seemed as if every game between French and Welsh sides should carry an EU health warning. But things have calmed down a lot more recently. Players now know that if they go berserk then they will be sent off or sin-binned, and that inevitably costs you points and often victory.

After the Brive and Bath years came the Ulster triumph of 1999. In a ridiculous and petty show of arrogance the English clubs had boycotted the tournament, but that should not detract from Ulster's success. At home that year they were invincible.

Their moment of glory came in Dublin when they beat Colomiers. Thousands of Ulstermen travelled to Lansdowne Road and much was made of the political significance of uniting both north and south through rugby but it was only when I was in Belfast the following week to attend a dinner in the team's honour that I realised what it really meant. David Humphreys, the brilliant Ulster fly-half, sat next to me and told me how moved he had felt as an Ulsterman at the way the whole of the south of the country had got behind his team.

As we chatted together, I felt a little of jealous of David having not only played for his country but also captained Ulster to their European triumph. I was part of a Llanelli side that won four Welsh Cup Finals in succession between 1973 and 1976 and we genuinely felt we were a team capable of giving anyone a game. We had eight Lions in our side and without meaning to sound arrogant we would have fancied our chances against any English or French side we had come across. A European club tournament would have told us exactly where we stood. But in those days, we only played around seven games a season against English clubs and visits to France were very few and far between.

There were no official league tables in Wales or England either and the nearest we came to any kind of cross-border contest was a match against Bedford in 1975. They were the English Cup winners; we were the Welsh holders. Someone had the smart idea to get us together in a challenge over two legs and Carwyn James, our coach, made sure we prepared properly. We thrashed Bedford at Stradey Park, but our plans for the away game on a Monday night were undermined when a few players had to cry off because of work commitments. I was captain and was determined to be there even though it meant driving like a lunatic from a work appointment in Newport. It was my first day with Courage Breweries and half way through an important meeting I suddenly realised

169

I was in danger of missing the kick-off. So I mumbled some excuse and dashed through the door, half fearing I'd probably get the sack. Some other Llanelli players had just got back from Wales A duty in France and the general feeling was one of rushed preparations. It was a freezing night and I came close to skidding the car off the road at least twice before I arrived at the ground with a few minutes to spare. I walked into the dressing room and sensed immediately that not everyone was taking this game as seriously as I was. So I laid it on the line. 'I haven't risked my neck driving across the country on a horrible night for you buggers to lose!' I told them – or words to that effect. The side responded, we gave Bedford another heavy beating and came off the pitch to a standing ovation.

Unfortunately, there were to be no more English–Welsh challenges. Maybe the English thought better of it. Either way, I was disappointed because I think Llanelli could have proved we were the best side around. Thirty years later, and thanks to Leicester, I'm still waiting.

The Heineken Cup is certain to grow from strength to strength. The Parker Pen Shield will always be the little sister and my feeling is that we should do away with it and have one large European tournament with more group games for each team.

The Cup also needs an improved structure. Instead of being played in small chunks, it should be integrated into the season at regular intervals, every few weeks, like they do in soccer with the Champions League. At present the competition goes into hibernation after the pool stages and loses some of its momentum.

Of course, a full-blown European League would be even

better. It would then be more than a match for the Super 12. But at present there are too many vested interests, especially in England and France, and we may have to wait a while for that one.

CHAPTER 11

Scarlet Fever

My father was a steel man. Others worked in the tin-plate industry and some down the mines. There were teachers, preachers, farmers and a few first-timers like me who had never been to Stradey Park before. But even though I was only seven years old and these men looked like giants as I held my father's hand, I could share their sense of excitement at going to see Llanelli. It's a feeling I'm sure Derek Quinnell, Scott Quinnell, Ieuan Evans and others have all felt over the years.

Up until then I had only heard the stories, listening in fascination as the men in my village of Felinfoel discussed the legends and characters of the club. The talk was always passionate and lively even if those telling the stories might have felt tired after a hard-grafting shift. We were only a mile-and-a-half away but it somehow made Stradey seem distant and exotic. Three names were always mentioned. There was Albert Jenkins, who supposedly used to drink five pints on the morning before a game to give him strength. Then there was Ivor Jones, a flanker who toured with the Lions. Finally, there was the great Lewis Jones, the golden boy who became a Lion at the age of 19. These were men who I had never seen play but who I knew plenty about.

Everyone remembers their first time. Mine was against Cardiff. The week had dragged but finally Saturday had arrived and my father let me go with him to see the Scarlets. Cardiff had Cliff Morgan playing for them, while Llanelli's own outside-half was Carwyn James. Little did I know what an influence Carwyn would have on my own rugby career and what a colossal figure he would become in the club's history. I don't remember the score, or even who won. But I can still picture the animated faces in the crowd, the vibrant atmosphere generated by their shouts and urging on of the Scarlets. It was frightening but also wonderfully exciting for a youngster whose only rugby experience had been in the local park. I was hooked.

We went every other week soon after that. When Llanelli were away, then we went to see the soccer team, instead. The Reds might not have had quite the pulling power of the Scarlets, but they could play a bit and they had enough sway to attract a young man down from Scotland called Jock Stein. My hunger for both forms of football was therefore met by what you might call a balanced upbringing: rugby one week, soccer the next.

The only away games my father took me to were the big local derby matches when Llanelli were playing Swansea at St Helen's. There would be a mass exodus from Llanelli station on the train and again my main memories are of intense-looking faces, jokes cracked on the walk to the ground, and blood-stained bandages worn by hard Llanelli men like

Howard 'Ash' Davies and RH Williams who would rather lose pints of the stuff than come off the pitch early against Swansea. We would then relive all the best moments of the game by reading 'The Sporting', except when Swansea City had won. In those circumstances my father would simply refuse to buy a newspaper because he knew it might upset his whole evening.

Llanelli meant something special both to me and to the boys I was growing up with. We were way out west, the farthest tip on the map as far as first-class rugby was concerned, and we were proud of it. We felt it made us special, more Welsh in some way than those lot in Swansea, Cardiff or Newport. They may have had their own arguments when it came to expressing their national identity, but we sang 'Sospan Fach' when the Scarlets won and you couldn't get any more Welsh than that.

By the time I was 14 I had my own heroes that I had seen regularly with my own eyes and whose talent I had been able to discern for myself. There was the wonderful DK Jones and the exceptional Terry Price, who was better at 18 than anyone I can think of before or since. Terry made the game look ridiculously easy because he was a natural athlete who appeared as though he didn't even need to try. He was lost too soon to rugby league and then tragically killed in a road accident when he was still a young man.

It was around this time that I was given the chance to come under the guidance of Carwyn James – and promptly turned it down. After seeing me play in a schools tournament, Carwyn asked my parents if they would like their son to leave the local school and go, instead, to Llandovery College, a private school with a long rugby heritage. I would have received a scholarship and the chance to gain a wonderful education, but I was far less interested in the idea than my parents. I wanted to start working, not stay in school. My father had suffered an accident at work that had restricted his earning capacity and my mother was now working in a factory. I felt I should be pulling my weight and so I rejected the idea of Llandovery College and ignored Carwyn's advice. Besides, I'd seen the photos of the College and thought the teachers looked a bit strange with those square-shaped black hats on their heads. I've never regretted my decision because I don't think I could have stuck studying for long. In those days, unless there was a picture of a sportsman on the cover, I would rarely open a book. In fact, the only regret I have from that time is that I didn't work harder at trying to become a professional soccer player.

Swansea Town, as they were in those days, had me playing for their Colts teams when I was 14 and West Ham United also invited me for trials. I didn't go because the idea of spending a fortnight on my own in London frightened me to death. If it had been my beloved Manchester United then I would have held my nerve. Soccer continued to go well, though, and at one stage I was playing rugby every Saturday morning and soccer in the afternoon. Trevor Morris was the Swansea Town manager and we got on well. But rugby finally won the day through a strange combination of factors. I played one match for Swansea Colts on a gravel surface and tore the skin off my backside making a sliding tackle. It made the train journey back from Swansea to Llanelli even more lonely than usual, while at the same time the rugby boys of Felinfoel Youth seemed to be both winning and having fun. As I was limping back to the house after a painful trip home, I could hear my pals celebrating a Felinfoel victory in the clubhouse. My father also edged me towards rugby, not, I think, because he didn't enjoy football but because he didn't like the idea of any son of his wearing the white of Swansea. In a way, I regret giving up playing soccer at that age because I've often wondered how far I could have progressed.

Professionalism was always there in football and although I turned down being paid to play rugby league, I would have loved to have given it a crack as a professional soccer player. In the pecking order of my dreams, playing football for Manchester United came a very close second to playing rugby for Wales. It still does!

Having plumped for rugby, I spent my late teenage years with Felinfoel Youth. I owe the club and everyone associated with it a huge debt of gratitude for the guidance and opportunities they provided. Being club president these days has given me the chance to help pay something back. We had a very strong side in those days, with a sprinkling of future Welsh internationals, and one of the clubs we used to thump regularly was Llanelli Youth. But when it came to senior rugby only one club in the area really mattered, and I duly made my way to Stradey Park with nothing but encouragement and good wishes from my own village side.

It was 1967 and Barry John had just left Llanelli to go to Cardiff. It provided me with half an opening for the outside-half position and I was determined to take it. But the truth is that Llanelli were not a strong side in those days. Even mild-mannered, ever-so-polite sides like Harlequins came to Stradey and gave us the occasional beating. I spent most of my early games in awe of the players around me, but the organisation of the club then was not the best and sometimes before away games we would be scrambling around needing to borrow players from local village sides in order to make up a team.

Change was in the air, however. Peter Rees breezed in as chairman and brought with him some much-needed fresh ideas. One was to enlist a fitness expert called Tom Hudson. Before Tom's arrival the nearest anyone came to measuring fitness was to decide whether a player looked more or less tired than he had done the previous week after five laps around the field. Tom had charts and clipboards as well as a strength of character that demanded we submit to the new regime. Before long, we were the fittest side in Wales and other teams were being blown away in the last quarter of games as we kept going and they faded.

Of the many inspiring figures I looked up to in those days, perhaps the biggest was Delme Thomas. He was a magnificent forward with an aura few players could hope to match – tough, uncompromising, but with a quiet dignity that meant he didn't need to act aggressively for the sake of it. Some players act hard. Delme just was. His presence could lift any side and when he came back from the 1966 Lions tour I was in complete awe of this dark, tanned, athletic man who destroyed opponents but never boasted about it. He was quiet, modest and didn't drink, yet you knew that playing for Llanelli meant everything to him. Delme went on three Lions tours and in my book that qualifies him to be called a true great of Llanelli RFC – a legend, in fact. I sometimes have to laugh when I hear more recent Llanelli players described as 'greats'. Even blokes like Rupert Moon, Phil May and Lawrence Delaney, who gave Llanelli fabulous service but never had a sniff of a Lions cap, have been labelled alongside Delme, which shows an alarming lack of perspective by some people.

With the odd man-marvel like Delme, some other experienced campaigners, and a smattering of youngsters, Llanelli began to emerge again as a real force in Welsh rugby. But at the start of the seventies it needed something extra to turn a good side into a great one. It also required someone very special to fuse the traditional flair of the Scarlets with a competitive, more ruthless modern approach. That someone was Carwyn James.

When Carwyn arrived as coach everything at Llanelli fell into place. He laid the blueprint not just for Llanelli's success in those years but for the whole playing ethos and style of the club in the years since. He was our Bill Shankly – an inspiring man, a motivator, an eccentric, but also a meticulous planner with a ruthless streak. It's a sporting cliché to say someone is ahead of his time, but Carwyn really was. If he was still alive today, and had simply spent the last 30 years in cold storage, then he could coach any modern team without a problem. I know what an influence he has been, for instance, on the club's current coach Gareth Jenkins, and although they coached the club in different eras and had very different personalities, I can see strong parallels between the two of them.

It was Carwyn, of course, who masterminded one of Llanelli's greatest-ever moments, the victory over the All Blacks in 1972. He had planned for that match from the previous summer. At the very start of the season he had told the players, 'You're going to beat the All Blacks in a few months' time.' I think most of us thought he was daft, but Carwyn believed it because he had already planned it all in his head. He knew we needed to become more ruthless so he encouraged us to show no mercy to any team we came across, whatever the circumstances. It was an exciting new approach and the players took to it.

When London Welsh came down to play us very early in the

season, they had only just returned from their tour of the Far East. They were under the false impression it would be gentle exhibition stuff but we smashed them out of sight. JPR Williams and John Dawes, heroes of the triumphant 1971 Lions tour the year before, were in their side and they were both battered. I had wound up Ray Gravell before the kick-off with all the usual red-rag stuff about stuck-up poncey Londoners who weren't really Welsh. When Grav hit Dawesy hard with his first tackle, which was maybe a little late, John complained to me. I knew John well but I gave him a mouth-ful of abuse and told him to shut up and stop moaning. We murdered them, showing just the kind of attitude Carwyn knew we needed to have instilled in us if we were going to beat New Zealand.

Carwyn was shrewd enough to strengthen the team, too. He wanted to sign Tommy David from Pontypridd so he asked me to be the go-between. I suggested a meeting but Carwyn said, 'No. Give him an invite to the Barbarians game and we'll talk afterwards.' The Baa Baas match was a 15,000 sell-out and created a fantastic atmosphere to celebrate our centenary season. Tommy was given the best seat in the house and the full VIP treatment, with a succession of people instructed to shake his hand before kick-off and tell him what a good player he was. We won by 30-odd points. Within a few minutes of the end of the game, Carwyn shook Tommy's hand and told him, 'We're going to beat the All Blacks. Would you like to be part of it?' Needless to say, Tom was sold.

Chico Hopkins, who had toured under Carwyn on the 1971 Lions tour, was brought in and a couple of others. It was hard on some of the existing players, but this was all part of the mili-tary strategy and, as in any battle, there were going to be some casualties. Those who remained were given a reminder of great Scarlets heroes of the past when those very heroes were invited along by Carwyn to attend our training sessions. I can remember Ash Davies talking to the forwards about scrummaging. The players were inspired and appreciated more than ever what the jersey meant to the whole town. So many coaches have used this kind of psychology since. Graham Henry had Willie John McBride giving a pep talk to the 2001 Lions in Australia, but Carwyn was doing it over a quarter of a century ago.

Carwyn was also full of surprises. There was one occasion, just before a Cup final, when we had trained one Sunday morning at Llandovery College but he ended the session early. 'Right,' he said, 'I've booked lunch for all of you down the road and the girls are invited too.' After we had picked up our wives and girlfriends, we arrived at a country hotel, where Carwyn rolled out some barrels of beer and announced it was time for everyone to have a well-earned drink. We talked about the forthcoming game and as the beer flowed so our self-belief and confidence in each other increased. A few hours later and we were the greatest team in the history of the game, ready to slaughter everyone we met. In fact, Carwyn's only oversight was that he had forgotten to book a bus to take us home. Foolishly, I attempted to drive home, despite having drunk my fair share of beers, the result being that I ploughed into a hedge while manoeuvring out of the car park into the dark country lane beyond. Eventually, my wife Pat drove us home, despite not yet having passed her driving test, the journey taking somewhat longer than usual due to her failure to get out of second gear! First light revealed innumerable scratches to the paintwork, testimony to the previous evening's escapade, but it was worth it, for it was at our get-together that night that we first began to believe we were something special – a team that was not going to be denied.

Nowadays, coaches call these 'bonding sessions' and give you a load of psychobabble, but Carwyn understood then the simple power of pals getting together to enjoy a few jars.

When the big day itself arrived, a Tuesday, we went down to the Ashburnham Hotel in the morning to escape the tension in the town, which had already become a sea of red and white at 9.30 a.m. Carwyn had filled every hour, every minute, every second. There had been a strange atmosphere around Llanelli. No one spoke to me for fear of saying the wrong thing. It was all nervous smiles and glances. But as soon as Carwyn took charge at the hotel, the hours remaining to kick-off stopped looming like years ahead of us and we settled into small talk, followed by a short walk and more reassuring words from Carwyn. He believed we could win, and in those wonderful lyrical tones of his he convinced us that we would win. He reminded us that we had been preparing for months, and that we had a plan – a winning plan – to take them on again and again up front. We were about to put that plan into operation and win the game.

We got to the ground, Delme gave an emotional speech in the dressing room, and we were ready. We were determined not to be intimidated, and we weren't. In fact, it was the All Blacks who flinched. Our forwards were ferocious that day, the crowd carrying us through the last 20 minutes, and we won 9–3. Roy Bergiers scored the try, I put over the conversion, and Andy Hill kicked a penalty. And yes, it's true; the pubs did run dry. Hardly surprising, since everyone came out to celebrate. Work was abandoned for the rest of the day – and most of the next day, too.

I felt more emotional after that match than after any game I ever played for Wales. This was my town, my club, my work-mates who had desperately wanted us to win, and we had done it for them. Only once did a match move me as much. That was in 1974 when I was part of a Lions team that won the Third Test in South Africa to clinch the series. That victory, though, was more for myself and for the squad. The Llanelli victory was for everyone who had an emotional stake in the club. Carwyn understood this more than anyone. He cultivated it. It was a driving force for the team. That was why he didn't mind grown men coming into the dressing room afterwards to ask for the mud from our boots, or the boys who just wanted to come in and stare. I can clearly remember two policemen playing rugby in the street outside a pub later that evening, using a helmet as a ball. Another man, who had sent his wife off to give birth on the morning of the game, told her in the evening that he wanted to name their son after the entire Llanelli fifteen. It was that kind of day. It felt like VE Day. And Carwyn had proved himself. Not only could he coach a Lions side to conquer New Zealand, as he had shown a year before, but now he had also done it with his own club side.

We were away to Richmond on the following Saturday, and we lost. I was still trying to sober up from our celebrations and one of my kicks at goal almost struck the corner flag. Carwyn ordered another crate of beers for the train journey home and told us, 'Boys, this is the end of our partying. There is just one final thing to celebrate. I've just heard on the radio that Cardiff lost today against the All Blacks.' There was a huge cheer and we honoured our own victory one more time.

Carwyn was always one step ahead. Sometimes, for example, he would ring the Met Office before a game (or so he claimed) to learn the expected wind direction for later that evening, and he would then instruct me which direction to play towards if I won the toss? He never once, though, told me or anyone else how to play the game. He would advise, suggest, offer insights and so forth, but he always left his players to make their own decisions on the field. He loved flair and adventure. It was how he had played the game, and the only way he wanted Llanelli to play.

Major victories were rewarded with meals out for the players and their wives, often with an overnight stay thrown in for those like JJ Williams who lived out of town. If a committee man raised an eyebrow at the cost then Carwyn would turn on him and deliver a sharp rebuke, reminding him and everyone else just how much money the team was bringing in at the gate. He'd then order more wine for the ladies and another gin and tonic for himself. He held such sway in the club that soon after Pat and I lost our first child, he booked a week away in Spain for the two of us. He knew we needed it and he also knew it was something we could not afford to pay for ourselves. A coach could only get away with that kind of thing if he held huge power in the club. Carwyn's power was immense.

He was also, though, a complex man and there was a dark side to Carwyn that I always suspected was full of loneliness and frustration. He had his rugby, he had his life as an academic at Llandovery College and then as a broadcaster, but he lived with an elderly sister and sometimes he appeared to be the loneliest man in the world. Pat and I would often hear a knock at the door in the evenings and Carwyn would be there seeking conversation and company. Here was the greatest rugby coach in the world, who would have been welcome anywhere the game was played, sitting on my couch late at night because he had no one to talk to and nowhere to go. It was tragic. He drank more than he probably should have, yet even that sometimes failed to disguise his unhappiness.

When Carwyn eventually left the Llanelli area he went to live in Cardiff, alone. One night after we had played away at Bedford, I drove back with Carwyn and our flanker Gareth Jenkins, who would one day go on to take up the coaching reins at the club and achieve wonderful success himself. We dropped Carwyn at his door and he asked us to join him for a drink. It was 3 a.m. We both had to work in the morning but there was a sense of desperation in Carwyn's voice. The idea of being alone in his small flat was obviously something he dreaded. We went in, and it was all-too obvious that this was the home of a solitary man for whom companionship was sadly missing in his life.

There had been rumours about Carwyn for years. I don't know about his sexuality, but I do know he was deeply lonely in his personal life. He had people who worshipped him for his talent in so many spheres – rugby, politics, literature, all aspects of Welsh life and culture – but few he could really talk to. He was hugely popular and yet so often alone. Carwyn was a riddle – and one I was never able to solve.

When the news came through in 1983 that he had died of a heart attack in a cheap hotel in Amsterdam, I cried. Carwyn should have died at home in his beloved Gwendraeth valley, not in some lonely room in Amsterdam. I didn't want to know the details and circumstances. I hated the rumours that followed. All I knew was that the greatest rugby man I had ever known had died a sad and lonely death, and it broke my heart.

They came to Carwyn's funeral from all over the world. Ex-players and administrators, academics and the rest stood alongside the miners' families of his own community to pay their finals respects. The words spoken and hymn sung were beautiful, but overall it was a sombre occasion, quite different from the joyful celebration of life that marked the more recent funeral of another legend: Gordon Brown, the great Scottish forward.

Carwyn's life was unfulfilled and perplexing in so many ways and his death was simply another unsolved mystery, yet his influence on Llanelli is there in the record books. We made the first five Welsh Cup finals after the competition began in 1972 and we won four of them. We beat the best teams in England, won Sevens tournaments and the old un-official Welsh leagues, won against French clubs in one-off games, and beat the All Blacks with a team that included seven Lions. Between 1972 and 1975, I think Llanelli were the best club side in Europe and had there been a tournament like the Heineken Cup then I've no doubt we'd have proved it.

Carwyn's influence on the club runs much deeper than mere statistics. Without knowing it at the time, he created guiding principles for other coaches, both in playing styles and man-management. Carwyn's sides always strived to play attractive running rugby and that has become the blueprint for Llanelli since. Before games against sides like Pontypool or Cardiff he would say to us, 'This lot are strong, but you'll beat them. You can match their strength but they can't match your style.'

Gareth Jenkins has frequently paid tribute to Carwyn's influence on him, and when building his own teams he has striven to remain true to his ideals. On several occasions when we have been talking rugby, he has commented concerning some problem or other, 'Phil, how do you think Jamesy would have solved this one?' His stint as Llanelli coach has been long and

185

successful, and, aided by a superb team around him – people like Allan Lewis in the past and, more recently, Nigel Davies – he has achieved wonderful things. In the main, he has got the team to play with great style, which is just as important, both to me and to every other Llanelli supporter. The year Llanelli won the League and Cup Double in 1993 I felt they played some of the best rugby any Scarlets side has ever played. Phil Davies, Lyn Jones and Emyr Lewis linked wonderfully with their backs, and were complemented by great finishers out wide in Ieaun Evans and Wayne Proctor. They won games and they entertained. They were magnificent.

I have to confess that I have been amazed at the length of time Gareth has spent in charge as coach. He was there in the eighties after he retired as a player, there throughout the nineties, and he is still there now. Most coaches lose their enthusiasm or worse still their players become stale listening to the same voice. Gareth, however, always seems to find enthusiasm and inspiration from somewhere at the start of every season and Llanelli are right up there as one of the best clubs sides in Europe, just as they have been for a number of years.

Gareth has always had a wild streak to match his wild dark hair. As a player we knew him as 'Gypo' because he looked as though he had gypsy blood in him somewhere along the line. He was raw around the edges, on and off the field. As players, he and Carwyn could not have been more different. Carwyn was a craftsman, an outside-half with neat hands and jinking feet. Gareth was a rough, tough flanker, lean but with bucket-loads of determination and guts. I loved playing alongside Gareth because he would fight anyone all day if it meant Llanelli would win, and he would invariably be first in when things boiled over.

186

Both of them were emotional men, so the way Gareth has become far more thoughtful and shrewd has surprised me. I thought perhaps he would be too impulsive to be a successful coach, too headstrong. I knew he would be all heart, but I doubted he would use his head. I have to say he has proved me completely wrong. Not only is he a great tactical thinker and man-manager, but he is also always at the forefront of new coaching ideas and techniques. He uses the latest technology, with computers and video analysis now the norm at Stradey in the team's build-up to a game. Although he has developed this side to his coaching, however, he has lost none of the passion and soul that he has always felt for the game and the club. He has learnt from his mistakes and mastered his trade. He has been the best coach of his generation in Wales and I am sure he will one day fulfil the role that many people would love him to take and become national coach.

Just as success brought Carwyn power in the club as well as respect, so it has been with Gareth. He has delivered trophies and there is a feeling that he could yet deliver the Heineken Cup. He may have a board to answer to, but generally what Gareth says goes – just as it did for Carwyn. There have been those within the club, petty committee men with short memories, who have tried to undermine Gareth when the times have been less successful. Thankfully, they have not yet had their way. Gareth deserves his success. He has steered the club through some stormy waters, especially some of the financial crises that arose after the game went professional.

Llanelli have always enjoyed a healthy support base but the management of the club has sometimes not matched the fervour or expertise of the fans. When I played we always seemed to have healthy crowds, often full houses, but so much of that income must have been squandered. Certainly, the players never saw it. We made do with a few quid from expenses and the only real spending I ever saw evidence of was a new stand and floodlights. When I was captain in the late seventies and early eighties I continually urged the club to pay for undersoil heating for the pitch. I pointed out that it would pay for itself once it saved a couple of games from being postponed. But it was viewed as extravagance and I was given the impression that I should keep my nose out.

Committee men made similar mistakes throughout my playing career, but nobody really noticed and it wasn't too much of an issue because amateurs were running what was still an amateur game. But things changed after 1995 when the game went professional. Suddenly, Llanelli were obliged to have expertise in financial management, sponsorship and all kinds of commercial activity that would help to pay for getting a successful team on to the park. I'm afraid to say that such expertise, for the most part, just hasn't been there.

One day in 1996 I had a phone call from a wealthy man called Mel Davies. He told me he wanted to invest money in the club. The figure mentioned was £1m. I told Llanelli's chief executive, Stuart Gallacher, an old team-mate of mine who had gone to play rugby league in the seventies before coming back to run a small business in the town. 'Phil, this could be the answer to all our dreams,' said Stuart. I urged the club to be cautious and to take their time in checking all aspects of any deal. I was purely the messenger. But it was not long before Llanelli were signing players on astonishing salaries. One deal, for a young second row called Steve Ford, from Bridgend, was so excessive that the player's own father admitted to me he thought it was crazy money. 'He's not even a cap, Phil, but they've offered him half of Port Talbot.' Other ordinary players arrived on big wages as a kind of panic buying seemed to grip the club. The feeling seemed to be that if you didn't buy now you'd regret it later, since others would snap up all the talent. While all this was going one, another potential white knight suddenly appeared on the horizon. A business-man, Ian Walters, said he also wanted to put £1m into the club. Now people's heads really did start to spin. There was talk in the club of a combined £2m investment from both men. Walters sent his accountant, a blunt Yorkshire-man called Brian Laws, to check out the club's facilities and for a time it was like Father Christmas had turned up; we were promised new training pitches, indoor arenas, the club's fitness coach, Peter Herbert, was going to be sent away on courses in America. Both Walters and Davies attended club meetings and Mel told me he wanted me to take a place on a new board of directors. The atmosphere was feverish. Mel and I even visited Northampton where the coach, my old Lions team-mate Ian McGeechan, explained how their benefactor, Keith Barnwell, was transforming the club.

Then came the deal to end all deals – and it almost ended the club for good. Frano Botica was a former All Blacks outside-half, a gifted player and a peerless goal-kicker. But he had cut short his rugby union career long before the game went open in order be a pro in rugby league. He'd made a good living and a great reputation with Wigan. But now he was winding down his career in the north of England with Orrell. Llanelli paid a transfer fee of around £70,000, but failed to find out that Castleford had also got a binding agreement with the same player. This rather important oversight meant that they had to pay out almost the same amount to Castleford before taking into account Botica's own wages, which were enormous, big enough for Frano to tell me later that Llanelli were paying him more than Wigan had done, and Wigan, at the time, were the richest and most successful club in rugby league. Frano played on and off for a couple of seasons and someone worked out when he left that his appearances for Llanelli had cost around £13,000 a game. It was the economics of the madhouse.

As suddenly as he had appeared, Walters drifted away, while the Mel Davies deal never materialised. An agreement was made and there were people at Llanelli rubbing their hands together in anticipation but, due to unsubstantiated rumours suggesting he didn't have the required money, Mel pulled out of the deal on principle, leaving Llanelli with half a squad of players that they couldn't afford. I must admit I feel guilty at having made the initial contact. But I also feel angry that mud was flung in my direction when it should have been the job of others to check the small print. This was a job for the accountants and the trustees to sort out, but to this day I still don't know who sanctioned the Botica deal when the money clearly wasn't there. I had made my reputation with Llanelli as a rugby player, not as a lawyer or a financier. The problem, unfortunately, was that people like Stuart Gallacher had done the same. Stuart was a fine player and I'm sure he cares about the club's fortunes, but he has never made fortunes himself and is not really the kind of person you want making crucial decisions involving the running of a rugby club. Llanelli need greater financial expertise. They are a big business nowadays and if they want to compete with the best clubs in Europe then they need the best financial management available. The club has already had to sell the land it sits on and now leases it back. In the amateur days, bad decisions simply lost you matches, but these days there are people's jobs at stake. I'm not convinced that Llanelli's financial management is as sound as it should be and for that reason I ended up buying only £100 worth of shares in the club when there was a flotation, instead of the £5,000 or so I had originally considered.

The team has been successful over the last few seasons, but I generally feel the commercial arm of the club is lagging badly behind. The place should be packed out every week. With players like Scott Quinnell and Stephen Jones in the side, gaining major sponsors across the board shouldn't be a problem. But only last season fans were being let in for nothing for a vital Heineken Cup match in order to boost the gate. It may have been portrayed as a nice gesture to supporters, but the hard facts are that crowds are dwindling. Compared to the rapid strides clubs like Newport have made in recent times, with packed crowds back at Rodney Parade, Llanelli look as if they are still waiting for the starter's gun.

I've been asked a few times to take a seat on the Llanelli board, but I've always declined. First, and most importantly, there is the obvious conflict with my work in the media. I enjoy contributing to newspapers, radio and TV, and I like to feel the opinions I offer are sincere and well balanced. I try not to make criticism too personal and I attempt to keep praise in perspective. If I didn't feel I was being honest with people then I wouldn't see any point in opening my mouth. But I know that if I was on the board of Llanelli it would place limits on my judgement when it comes to the club and its players, and I don't want to feel restricted in that way.

Secondly, the dealings I have had with some board members have left me unimpressed. Those with business brains seem to want to involve themselves in rugby matters. On the other hand, the rugby folk seem to think they can also do the sums. I think the best-run clubs are those where both sides stick to their own area of expertise, each given plenty of rope to either climb or hang themselves with.

It still gives me the most enormous pleasure to see Llanelli succeed on the field. I feel huge pride when they do well and I love nothing better than to hear people from outside Wales talking in respectful terms about the Scarlets. Thanks to Gareth Jenkins and others we've had plenty to enjoy in recent years. I love the supporters and what the club means to the town. But I've been disappointed and hurt by the way Llanelli have conducted much of their business off the field when it could have been done so much better.

CHAPTER 12

Scarlet Thread

At the risk of viewing the world through Scarlet-tinted spectacles, I think the future beckoning my old club in playing terms could be just as spectacular as the past. In any era, rugby clubs are really all about two things; you need players and you need fans. Exciting players bring in excited fans. The more good players you have, the more fans you can attract – and I include backers, benefactors and sponsors in my definition of fans – meaning, in turn, you can bring in more good players. Some will come through the ranks if a club invests in a sound youth and schools policy. Others will have to be attracted to join from outside.

Llanelli have always produced talented players. The catchment area is huge and so is the interest in the game among youngsters. The club have also always had an ability to garner some additional recruits from outside. At present, the current squad is strong – good enough, I reckon, to have another two or three bids at conquering Europe before it will need to be broken up. The players have ability and pride in their inheritance, and they normally strive to remain loyal to the style demanded by the great Carwyn James.

If you are going to emulate the past, and hopefully build on it, then you need links with those years gone by. In the current Llanelli side there is no more obvious link with the team of the seventies than in Scott Quinnell and his father Derek.

I was in the same class as Derek at Coleshill Secondary Modern. We played together for Wales Schools and Wales Youth and then joined Llanelli at about the same time. I then spent ten seasons playing alongside him for the club, as well as for Wales and the Lions, so I feel well qualified to make a judgement on Derek. In my view, he was an outstanding natural talent – good and versatile enough to play in any position in the second or back row. He was as effective at the front of the line-out as he was at No. 8 and if anything, his adaptability probably obscured just how great a player he was.

Derek had great skills for a big man and was extremely mobile around the field. He also had great heart and courage. Three Lions tours between 1971 and 1980 says it all, especially when you consider he didn't go with the 1974 Lions. Durability and versatility were his stock-in-trade. Training sessions, however, were not. His nickname was 'Sloppy' and that perfectly covered his attitude to turning up on time for training as well as his dress code. Derek had a variety of skives, those most commonly used being work commitments and niggling injuries. But even if you hadn't seen him train for a week you could guarantee that when the big games came calling Derek would pull out a big performance.

When he first arrived at Llanelli Derek was quite slight and had to be put on a diet of milk and steaks to build him up. Once he put on that extra muscle there was no stopping him – in matches, at least. One week he hardly showed up for training at all, even though we had a major Cup game coming up against Cardiff. I was captain and had grown accustomed to his methods, but two days before the match, in a selection meeting, the other selectors wanted to drop him. I dug my heels in and refused to allow it but I made sure that the issue reached Derek's ears. On cue he had a magnificent match and from that time on most people in Llanelli allowed him to work his own little system when it came to training.

There was something of Barry John's character in Derek. He was passionate about the game, but not obsessed by it and there were aspects he had little time for. Both he and Barry would yawn their way through team meetings. When Derek did train, he trained hard, but I always felt he had one eye on the clock and the chance of a gin and tonic and cigarette in the clubhouse.

In my opinion, Derek's son Scott was the one true world class player Wales had throughout 2001 and into 2002 before his decision to step down from international rugby – the only contender who could seriously expect to make any kind of World 15. Yet I feel Scott shares so many of his father's characteristics and they were all apparent from an early age. For a few years after I had retired in 1982, I continued to train with the Scarlets, just to keep fit. Scott was a young boy of tremendous potential and made a massive impact in youth rugby, but when he began training with the senior squad it was case of Derek revisited. I can remember one session where fitness coach Peter Herbert told everyone to do a sequence of ten sprints, with very short rests in between. 'Ten!' yelled Scott.

195

'Why can't we do six?' Talk about a chip off the old block. But just like his father, I could see he had enormous raw talent. I had admired Scott's progress through the ranks. More than anything I was impressed with the way he had handled all the kids who had seen the name 'Quinnell' on the opposition team sheet and tried to knock Scott's head off. It was the kind of thing my own boys, Steven and James, had to cope with throughout their school days.

Scott broke into the Wales team and his reputation, not to mention his value, soared after he scored that magnificent individual try against France in 1994. He looked the image of his father as he brushed past French tackles to plant the ball down in the corner. The image, though, was reflected in other ways. Scott was not as fit as he could have been but shared his father's view that it was not what you did on a Tuesday or Thursday night that mattered, but how you performed on a Saturday. That try of his changed his life because soon afterwards he was made an offer he couldn't refuse by Wigan and he went to play rugby league. I was told they didn't think Scott was anywhere near as fit as he could be, but they planned to work on their investment. They were true to their word. His body shape changed as he lost his puppy fat and became toned and muscular. His stamina also shot up and he rapidly became an excellent rugby athlete. In rugby league there is no room for shirkers.

I'm a big armchair fan of rugby league and the progress Scott made week by week was impressive. But financial problems led to Scott being sold back to rugby union when the game went professional and he found himself in England with Richmond. His recall to the Wales team was inevitable, although there were some contractual rows to sort out before

196

he pulled on the jersey. Since then, his influence for Wales and, in recent years, for Llanelli has been difficult to overstate.

The truth is that both Wales and Llanelli became far too reliant on Scott Quinnell. He was the only ball-carrier, the only player battering a way forward – minute after minute, match after match. He's paid an obvious price for that. His body is now wrecked. His knees are so bad that some mornings he struggles to get out of bed. Llanelli have become fully aware of this and it's rather ironic that the way they cope is hardly to train him during the week. In the early days they tried everything they could to get Derek to train; now they are just as determined to make sure he doesn't. Like his old man, he has become the ultimate big-game player – coaxed and cajoled from week to week and then taken out of cotton wool for the matches that really matter. Sometimes when Scott goes down injured I have to laugh because I know he's looking for a breather, or for time to let an ache or pain subside. I've seen it all before with Derek. But like Derek, there is a bravery and a courage that shines through Scott's performances. They have both been willing to take the bootings, shoeings, rakings and punches, each refusing to hide away from the heat of the battle.

What worries me is that Scott will be forced to retire in a couple of seasons, not much beyond his thirtieth birthday. He will probably have a painful old age to look forward to and the game is doing very little to ensure that the next generation of players do not go the same way.

Scott has matured a lot through captaining both Llanelli and Wales. He is more open and honest, and less defensive than he used to be. His wife and children have given perspective to his life, and it's remarkable to think that after going off to earn

197

his living in Lancashire, and then London, the best years of his professional career have been spent in the town where he grew up. I can best sum up Derek and Scott as players by saying that when it really mattered they both delivered – for Llanelli, for Wales and for the Lions. Derek was probably the more naturally skilled rugby player, but Scott has shown he has more application and determination to make himself an even more formidable player than his father.

You know you are getting on in years when you recall not only the current players' fathers but their grandfathers too. I was thrilled to be in South Africa in the summer of 2002 to see Dwayne Peel play scrum-half for Wales. Dwayne is a lovely kid who has looked very impressive since breaking into the Llanelli side. His grandfather, Bert Peel, would have been very proud of him. Bert was a legend at Stradey Park when I played. He was our trainer, the original rub-a-dub man. A miner from near Tumble, he was a strong man with firm opinions but a wonderful warmth. I'll always owe him a debt of gratitude, for he delivered me from the new training method that was taking off in the seventies – weight training. I worked in the steel works and thankfully that was good enough for Bert. Whenever someone suggested I get down to the gym, Bert would look up from pummelling my body on the massage table and say, 'Weights are for poofs. Real men get strong through a proper day's work.' Miners, steelworkers, farmers and labourers were okay by Bert. Anyone else was viewed with suspicion and as for gaining strength through a gym, well, that was very odd behaviour. Maybe the scientific approach to rugby we see nowadays would have left Bert behind, but there was a skill and an expertise to his work that you struggle to find nowadays.

Bert would give massages to the players at the baths of the colliery in Cwmgwili near Tumble. There were no machines or equipment – just Bert and his hands. A session would consist of a huge miners' cooked breakfast with a mug of tea, a rub from Bert, and a hot shower. Whatever injury I might have suffered on the previous weekend Bert could get rid of it. When I left there, I would feel like a new man. Bert was also used by Glamorgan cricketers, and later became Viv Richards' regular fishing partner.

Dwayne must have inherited Bert's magical hands because he has just about the fastest pass in the game right now. To see Dwayne form an all-Llanelli half-back partnership for Wales with Stephen Jones has been very satisfying. Stephen is fast becoming one of the better-known faces in European rugby. His performances – and especially his goal-kicking – for Llanelli against Leicester and Bath during the 2001–02 season were exceptional. I think Steve could become the natural successor to Neil Jenkins for Wales, although I also have a suspicion that inside centre could still prove to be an occasional option.

Stephen is not the typical Welsh outside-half, but then neither was Neil. They share many attributes – accuracy with the boot, tactical awareness, a great temperament under pressure and a willingness to work hard in order to succeed. I talk occasionally to Steve and he is a good listener who is keen to take advice on board. Not so long ago we discussed his kicking out of hand. I'd noticed he was kicking the ball too high and sacrificing his distance. Now he's put that right. We've also been working on his speed off the mark. Stephen doesn't have great natural speed, but if he can improve his footwork then he can make that up.

Whenever former players are asked to give help and advice

to current ones there can sometimes be a sense of awkwardness, a feeling that normally stems from suspicion and misunderstanding. But I must say that working with Stephen has been an absolute delight. The only thing that I see holding him back at the moment is the way both Llanelli and Wales tend to use him. He is playing far too flat, too close to the opposition. It means he is taking the option of carrying the ball himself into the tackles instead of passing or running for space. Both Gareth Jenkins and the Wales coach Steve Hansen need to use Stephen standing deeper if they are going to get the best out of him. Those two coaches will probably tell you that the game has changed, that No. 10s now need to carry the ball themselves into the contact areas. I don't agree. Space has become so restricted that it makes more sense for the outside-half to stand deeper and avoid early physical confrontation. Jonny Wilkinson does not stand that flat for England. If Stephen can improve his speed off the mark, just as Wilkinson has done, then the sky is the limit. There's no doubt that he could become one of the very best. He's got huge strength of character and I'm delighted with his obvious determination to do his utmost for the Llanelli cause. But his coaches must encourage him to take charge on the field, and you do that by being alert and on your toes, not by being trampled on at the bottom of a ruck.

If Stephen makes those adjustments to his game then I think he will not only take over from Jenkins as the Wales No. 10 for years to come but will also take over the captaincy. In fact, I can see a Wales–England fixture in a couple of years' time when both Stephen and Wilkinson are not only calling the shots but are both captaining their country; a situation that could continue for a long time to come.

To see Dwayne Peel and Stephen Jones dictating the game for Wales against the Springboks in South Africa reminded me of just how many quality international players Llanelli has provided over the past decade or so. Phil Davies, Nigel Davies, Wayne Proctor, Gwyn Jones, Neil Boobyer, Emyr Lewis, Robin McBryde . . . they have all served the club with distinction. But the player who stood out throughout the nineties was Ieuan Evans, who was a constant source of pride to everyone at Stradey.

Ieuan's image was always that of the ultimate professional who looked after himself and prepared well. But when he first came to the club it was a very different story. He was quick, but he had a little beer belly on him and after two or three surges down the wing he would be knackered for the next 20 minutes. You could see the potential, but it was all going to waste. Gradually, he improved his attitude and commitment, and he became one of the world's great players. For a long time during the mid-nineties he was the only true world-class player Wales had. As a finisher, he was in the same class as JJ Williams, and I can pay him no higher compliment because I know from playing alongside him just how good JJ was.

Ieuan never lost sight of his roots with the club and gave Llanelli his best years before going on to Bath. His career just caught the era of professionalism and I was glad that someone who stayed loyal to club and country managed to make a few quid from the game before he retired.

At the same time that Ieuan became a fixture at Llanelli, so too did Rupert Moon. In truth, Rupert was an average player but I've never seen anyone make as much from the cards he was dealt. Determination and enthusiasm carried Moony a long, long way. He captained the team with pride and distinction and was a major component of the side that won the Double in 1993 and also beat the then world champions Australia. He may have been an outsider from the Midlands, but I have nothing but admiration for the way Rupert threw himself into the community and became such a firm advocate of the club's history and traditions. In a small place like Llanelli there will always be those who turn their backs against outsiders, but Rupert won over so many people he became something of a folk hero. His influence on the side was huge. He took innumerable physical batterings, but he was so resilient he always bounced back, playing on with injuries that would have had lesser players carried off. I would never describe Rupert as one of the most gifted players to play for Llanelli, but I would say he was an outstanding servant. Along with team-mates like Phil May, Lawrence Delaney and Nigel Davies, he gave great service to the club for many years.

All those players were characters – some extrovert like Moony, others more introverted like Nigel. But they all shared a loyalty to Llanelli that saw them play hundreds of matches and develop a wonderful rapport with the supporters. That's the thing about Llanelli. The supporters cherish both the club and the players who wear the jersey. They expect high standards and success, but so long as there is passion, desire and some panache they will always back you.

One player perhaps sums up that special relationship between the players, supporters and town. He was a team-mate of mine for both Llanelli and Wales in the seventies and he is now club president. He's Ray Gravell or just 'Grav' to everyone who knows him. If ever you wanted someone to express what the passion of playing for and supporting both

Wales and Llanelli is all about, then you would turn to Grav. If there was some way of wiring him up to a generator then the electrical charge that seems to run through him whenever he talks about Llanelli could keep the whole town alight for days.

I had been with Llanelli for two or three years when I first bumped into Ray. Or rather, he bumped into me. It was a training session, and as I tried to make a break this lump of a boy battered into me and I fell in a heap. 'Sorry, Mr Bennett,' he said and he looked genuinely concerned as he picked me up. I asked someone who this nutcase was that was trying to injure me and I was told his name was Ray Gravell, my biggest fan. Mind you, he was the biggest fan of every other Llanelli player in the side, too!

He soon made the team and I don't think I was the only one who was a bit unnerved by this young man who used to enter the dressing room with a wild look in his eye. The passion and nervous energy he brought to the room would leave me feeling tired out even before we had taken the field. There was a certain Welsh humour to his routines. He would rubbish the opposition one moment and then, in the next sentence, be seeking reassurance that he was up to the job. I think underneath all his bubbling enthusiasm and bravado there was a nervous player trying to find a way of dealing with his own anxieties. He fascinated and wore me out in equal measure.

His father, a miner, had died when Ray was a boy. The circumstances were peculiar and it was only years later that Ray admitted his father had, in fact, committed suicide. A proud miner, his father suffered ill health and had been given a job above ground. His inability to continue to work alongside his mates down the mine led to problems with depression and one awful, bleak night he went missing. A search party went out into the night and there among the mountains near his home it was Ray, aged 14 at the time, who discovered that his father had taken his own life. The emotional impact was something that Grav had to carry with him, and I think he found a release for all that emotion within rugby, and, in particular, through playing for his father's beloved Scarlets.

Grav would be laughing, screaming, shouting and crying, all within the build-up to a game. One minute he would have the rest of us in stitches, the next he would be driving us all nuts. He would breeze in late and then occupy the toilet for the 20 minutes before kick-off, reading the match programme with the door wide open, singing the songs of Dafydd Iwan – a Welsh folk-singing hero of Grav's – at the top of his voice.

Delme Thomas, the most respected Llanelli player of the era, became Grav's father-figure and if Grav wasn't allowed to get changed alongside his hero he would go into a strop. Delme found it all a bit baffling and could sometimes be embarrassed. Once, in a tight Cup match, Delme was taking a pounding as a fight broke out among the forwards. Delme was 6ft 3inches of solid muscle and had the streetwise know-how that comes from three Lions tours. We all waited as he was about to put one of these upstarts in their place. But before Delme had time to size up who had hit him, Grav was pushing past me and had run 30 yards to the aid of his hero. Fists were flying everywhere with Grav in the middle of it. Delme looked astounded. The referee eventually calmed things down and the incident ended with Delme glaring at Grav – a look that simply suggested neither he nor any other Llanelli forward needed a little centre to fight their battles. Grav looked heart-broken.

Not that Grav was small in any way. He and Roy Bergiers were two rocks that I came to rely on alongside me. Roy was lovely player, full of intelligence and subtlety and a privilege to play with. Grav was a big, powerful centre who caused no end of problems to the opposition. He was the original crash-ball man. No one has run as hard, as straight and as forcefully, taking the ball directly up the middle of the field, as Grav. Yet he could also be a bit of a softie. He was forever complaining about injuries, worrying that a twinge in his shoulder or his back was about to end his career. JJ Williams vowed never to share a room with him again after one night spent with Grav at the Angel Hotel before a Cardiff international. Grav had woken up sniffing at 6 a.m. on the morning of the game, and shaken JJ awake to ask him if he thought he had bronchitis. 'Don't ever put me in a room with that lunatic, again,' JJ demanded the management.

When he got on the field for Llanelli or Wales though, Grav could be immense. Big forwards were knocked to the ground and he would smash through the opposition line time and again. He actually became a better player as he got older, adding more subtlety to his game. Yet before a match he would continually be asking, 'Hey, Phil. These are no good are they? Because I've heard they're strong, and quick, too. What do you think? Can I handle them?' He had this constant need to be reassured even though he was normally one of the players the other team would fear. Once, when we were playing Bridgend, Grav was up against Steve Fenwick, also a Welsh international centre. I put Grav into space with a pass and he rounded Steve and left him for dead before putting JJ over for a try in the corner. It was obviously a moment of great pride for Grav who didn't seem to notice that JJ had badly injured himself in the act of scoring. As JJ writhed in agony and told Grav he thought he'd broken his foot, Grav said, 'Never mind that. Did you see that break I just made? Did you see that pass? Fenwick, was nowhere. I left him behind, didn't I? Who's still the best centre in Wales?' Even on one leg, JJ had to be forcefully restrained from whacking Grav before he was helped towards the dressing room.

He may have wanted reassurance but Grav knew his own mind. When John MacLean became Llanelli coach in the 1978–79 season, Grav was rebuked for arriving late for a team meeting before a game. John was not the greatest coach in the world, but he was a good organiser and thorough in his preparation. One of his innovations was a tactics board with magnetic discs to represent players on the field. John was quietly explaining some or other ploy and illustrating it by moving the discs on the board when Grav burst into the dress-ing room with a loud greeting of 'Shw Mae' (Welsh for 'How's things?') to all the boys. 'You're late, Grav,' said John. 'Sit down and listen!' Instead, an angry Grav kicked the board into the air, scattering small coloured discs across the dressing room. 'It's men we're playing against out there, not f***ing discs on a board,' said Grav. John's team talk had come to an abrupt end.

I travelled the world with Grav and there was never a dull moment. He was the proudest Welshman I've ever met and Llanelli summed up everything he felt was close to his heart. Others went north but he wouldn't have lasted a week in rugby league. He'd have got homesick after two days. But he served Llanelli with distinction as a player, just as he does now as club president. A great player, a real character, it was a privilege to have played with him. If the club can attract the same loyalty, passion and commitment from the next generation of players, then the future of Llanelli is in safe hands.

CHAPTER 13

The Top Ten

There is just something about the No. 10 jersey. It looks good from the sidelines. It feels even better on your back. In most rugby-playing countries the debate over who should wear No. 10 for their national team generates plenty of heat. In Wales, it is not a debate; it's an obsession. Walk into a bar in Sydney and you might find a group of blokes arguing over who should open the bowling for Australia. In Rome, it could be a row over who should be the Italian centre-forward. In Cardiff, it's always about who should wear No. 10.

Outside-halves, fly-halves, stand-offs – it doesn't matter what you call them – the position has always held a certain mystique. The guy there is the fulcrum of the team, the decision-maker. More important to me as a kid on the playing field at Felinfoel, it was where the glory boys played. Felinfoel kids in those days were divided into two camps: those who wanted to be Carwyn James and those who wished they were Cliff Morgan.

Asking a Welshman to select his best outside-halves is a bit like asking Joan Collins to name her favourite husband. So many look great, until you clap eyes on the next one! But since it's a pastime that rugby folk in every clubhouse in the land love to indulge in I may as well join in the fun.

In no particular order, those in this chapter are my favourites, and I use the word 'favourite' rather than best. They are the players I have enjoyed watching, who have made me gasp, smile, shout, rave and generally get excited. It's not always about pure skill. It can equally be about character and dedication. Not all of them are the most capped or celebrated, but I would rather go and see this bunch than any other.

Had I been born a little earlier, and seen him play, I would have included the great Irish hero Jackie Kyle. Even when I was a small boy, Jackie was held in awe throughout Wales. His name would invariably crop up when adult conversation turned to great players of that era. I have had the privilege of meeting him on half a dozen occasions and can testify that he's a real gent. I've also seen flickering black and white images of him jinking through defences, but since I never actually saw him in the flesh I'll have to leave him on my subs bench. The same goes for others before my time, men whose deeds I read about as a youngster, like Cliff Jones and Willie Davies.

My first No. 10 was a contemporary of Kyle's but a player I was lucky enough to see as a young kid in Wales in the late 1950s: Cliff Morgan. In 1955, when he was still only 25 years old, Cliff scored a try for the Lions against the Springboks in South Africa and went on to captain the Lions in a Test on that same tour. So, by the time I was taken to Llanelli by my father to see Cardiff play, he was already one of the great players of his era.

Cardiff were the elite, the establishment club. While some were ordinary working men, others had careers in the professions, public school educations, and the right connections. It was said in West Wales that if you played for Cardiff you were already halfway towards a Welsh cap. They were the city slickers and the Llanelli boys always wanted to stuff them. We had Carwyn James at outside-half. They had Cliff Morgan.

I was seven years old and a little unnerved by the passionate atmosphere – especially when Llanelli supporters shouted loudly at their team to get stuck into Cliff Morgan. Llanelli had a flanker called Peter Evans who was big and strong, and who chased Cliff all over Stradey Park. I was a little worried what might happen to the Welsh outside-half if Peter caught up with him, but it never happened. Cliff was always two steps ahead of him, and three moves ahead, too.

He was brilliant. His running with the ball in-hand was quite breathtaking. In those days there was no ten-metre rule at the line-out and defenders could be on top of you before you knew it. But Cliff was so elusive that nobody got near him. He jinked and danced his way out of trouble time and time again. The crowd were mainly working men who had come from Saturday morning shifts at the steel or tin-plate works. Dressed in their working clothes they were there to let off steam and it made for a raucous atmosphere. But despite all the desperate shouts and screams for this Fancy-Dan Cardiff outside-half to be dumped on his backside, Cliff was rarely tackled, and long before the end of the match a respectful quiet had descended on the ground. It was almost as if his sheer talent had smothered the hostile energy of the crowd.

I must have seen Cliff play in the flesh on only another three or four occasions, but what always struck me about him was his pace. He was lightning quick off the mark. Though small, he caused panic on the field. Carwyn had been my hero. He was a more crafty player than Cliff, with beautiful hands. But once I saw Cliff Morgan I became aware of how a No. 10 could cut and slice a team to ribbons. I wanted to do the same.

I wasn't the only one who reckoned Cliff was a half-decent player. Nearly 20 years later when I was in South Africa with the 1974 Lions, I had countless people come up to me and tell me that if I was half as good as that bloke Cliff Morgan who had toured there in 1955, I would do okay.

All of us who have worn the Welsh No. 10 jersey since Cliff owe the man an enormous debt. He created the mould. He flirted with danger, skirting that edge between the opposition and where the space was, between glory and disaster. Perhaps more than anyone he helped invent the Welsh outside-half.

If Cliff Morgan created the model, then Barry John turned the model into mythology. Barry was unquestionably rugby union's first superstar. Football had provided George Best. Rugby's reply was Barry John.

I knew early on how good Barry was going to become because I was in on the secret from the beginning. Barry came from a mining village, Cefneithin, just down the road from my village of Felinfoel. He had talent at an early age but he also had lots of ambition. He spent a brief time playing for Llanelli, but the club was not a glamorous one in those days. Cardiff had the glamour. That was where Barry wanted to be; he dreamed of being on the biggest stage under the brightest lights.

I was about 17 or 18 at the time and had just joined Llanelli from Felinfoel Youth. So, to be frank, I was pretty pleased to see the back of Barry John. Had Barry stayed I would have been forced to make a decision. Either stay and wait my turn or join another club. Thankfully, Barry was the one who left and Llanelli asked me to go straight into their side.

At Cardiff, Barry was in his element. He thrived alongside Gareth Edwards but I still feel the making of him as a player was not the Lions tour to New Zealand of 1971, but the Wales trip to the same country two years earlier. Wales had won the Triple Crown, with Barry and Gareth as the young princes at half-back. We were a confident squad and young Barry, aged just 24, was the most confident of the lot. I was four years younger and there to make up the numbers but we were stuffed by the All Blacks in both Tests and it was an eye-opener for all of us.

Barry realised that if he wanted to beat the likes of the All Blacks he had to become a stronger character, both mentally and physically. Like the rest of us, he worked harder on his game and set higher standards for himself. Within two years he was back in New Zealand with the Lions, proving himself the most influential player on a winning tour and the best outside-half in the world.

Barry had improved dramatically. He had found his feet in Test rugby and that simply gave him the confidence he needed when he went out on to the field. There was an arrogance about Barry, both on and off the park. After 1971 he knew he had become the best there was and it was almost as if the challenge had now gone. He seemed to become bored with rugby, even though he and Edwards were probably the two best rugby players in the world.

It was all too easy for him. Around that time Llanelli had beaten Cardiff at Stradey and in our team that day were Barry's brothers, Alan and Clive John, two of our back-row forwards. Alan dumped Barry on the ground a couple of times and words were exchanged which seemed to hark back to similar contests in the family back garden. Barry seemed to take it all in his stride, but it obviously stuck in his craw. The following season Cardiff beat us and Barry dropped four goals in the game. As the fourth kick sailed between the posts, he was trying hard not to laugh as he taunted us about how we shouldn't have upset him 12 months before. It was typical Barry; he could be brilliant, cocky, and genuinely very funny all in the same game.

There had been no rugby player before him with a profile as big as Barry's. He was 'The King'. After the 1971 Lions tour his picture was forever in the newspapers. One minute he would be trying on clothes in Carnaby Street, the next he would be on the panel judging a beauty contest. Barry was showbiz. He got to know and became friends with George Best, and they had much in common, maybe too much. Perhaps Barry unwittingly sowed the seeds of George's problems, which were to lead to his early retirement from football. Unquestionably, Barry got fed up with the grind. He couldn't be bothered with weekend training sessions and if anyone asked him to think about the opposition he would look at them as if they had asked him to mop the floor. Intense-looking coaches would be talking earnestly to a group of backs about running angles and alignment and Barry would be yawning or gazing off into the distance wondering how to spend the afternoon.

By 1972, it was all over. Barry had packed in playing for Wales at the age of 27. I must admit I wasn't that surprised when I heard about his decision. I could sense that he was finding it all rather a strain. Everyone wanted a piece of him and he found it difficult to say no. On the field, for whatever reason, he was not getting the same thrill out of playing as he had felt before. Maybe he found it frustrating to discover that not all players were on the same wavelength.

I was given a big hint of what might follow when we played Ireland at Lansdowne Road in 1970. I was on the bench – still the apprentice while Barry was the master – and we were gunning for a Triple Crown. But it was a poor Welsh performance and everything Barry tried seemed to go wrong. Ken Goodall scored a memorable try for the Irish and we eventually lost 14–0 in the days when 14–0 was a thrashing. At the post-match dinner some of the selectors were openly critical of Barry's performance and he got to hear about it. These were the so-called 'Big Five', the selectors you were expected to bow and scrape to and certainly not take issue with. But Barry was having none of it and he went beserk, screaming at them that they knew nothing about rugby and even less about playing outside-half. He tore them to pieces while other players looked on in amazement and silent admiration.

A fortnight later we were playing France and Barry dropped out with flu on the Thursday before the game. I was chuffed because it meant I came in to partner Gareth Edwards at half-back for the first time and win my fourth cap. Perhaps his decision to do so was made easier by the fact that he had clearly little motivation left to play, given his loss of respect and disillusionment with the selectors at the time. Within two years he had packed it in for good.

But what a player he was. I had never seen an outside-half like him and there hasn't been one since. He had such confidence in possession of the ball, seeming to have all the time in the world. People have said Barry John wasn't quick, but their eyes deceived them. He *was* quick but he would glide over the ground, and that gave the impression he wasn't as fast as some.

So often I would see Barry running towards a defence and wonder where he was going. Then, suddenly he would be floating through a gap that no one else had even noticed was there. He held the ball out in front of him and it seemed to mesmerise the opposition. He could also defend, and he made his share of try-saving tackles because he could read the game so well. He was from mining stock and so had a natural hardness.

Few players have had such natural ability. Even his goal-kicking seemed to be something he was born with. He certainly didn't spend much time practising. Before he went to New Zealand in 1971 he was rarely asked to kick goals, but he came back from that Lions tour hardly having missed a shot and with 188 points in the bag.

I used to love playing against Barry. You knew he would torment you, but he was never an overly aggressive player. There was always time for a smile and a wink and once the game was over that was it. No recriminations, no regrets, and certainly no discussing the game until late into the night. That wasn't Barry's scene at all. You had fun while it lasted and then you did something else, which I suppose sums up his career.

David Watkins was different – from another era and in complete contrast to Barry. He was more in the mould of Cliff Morgan. If Barry was a glider and a drifter, then Dai was a jinker and a darter. If Morgan had been the prototype typical Welsh outside-half then Dai was the upgraded model. He was short, dark, extremely quick and had that fabulous awareness of what was going on in the confusion that seemed to reign around him.

Barry could look so relaxed that there was an almost casual air about him, but Dai was the exact opposite. He was intense, full of explosive energy and had a visible single-mindedness about the way he played the game. Where Barry would run with the ball held out in front of him, like a wand, Dai would have the ball clutched to his chest. He didn't ghost through gaps; he burst through them. He was a bundle of energy, had a great sidestep, and must have been a real handful to play against.

I first saw Dai play in a sevens tournament in Swansea and I was absolutely dazzled by him. He was part of an outstanding Newport team that thrashed every side they played and David was simply unstoppable. He had such pace and acceleration that once he gained a yard on an opponent the race was over. He rarely did the outrageous thing, but he seemed so often to do the right thing.

I watched Dai play many times for Wales in the mid-sixties, an impressionable time for me as I was making my way in schools and youth rugby. He was inspiring because I could relate to his lack of size and bulk. He was small but so determined, and he knew his natural tenaciousness could make up for any deficiencies.

As well as watching him play for Wales, I saw Dai give some wonderful exhibitions of fly-half play with Newport whenever they came to Llanelli. The pity was that Dai had not yet reached his peak for Wales when he opted for the financial security of rugby league at the age of 25. Many people thought he would fail miserably, expecting the hard-nosed rugby league forwards to eat this little Welsh boy for breakfast. How wrong they were. He took some fearful physical hammerings, because rugby league back then was a much dirtier game than it is now, but his fierce competitiveness meant that he always bounced back. His skill with a rugby ball shone through. Not only did

216

Code-breaker: Jonathan Davies made history when he became the first player to return to rugby union in Wales after a career in rugby league. As always, he made the break and others followed in his wake.

Black magic: The wonderful All Blacks No.8 Zinzan Brooke playing against Wales at Wembley in 1997. He is tracked by Gwyn Jones in his last match for Wales before a neck injury sadly ended his career.

Joost on the loose: South African scrum-half Joost Van Der Westhuizen was one of the key players who helped turn the Springboks from international outcasts to world champions in 1995.

Lions unleashed: Danny Grewcock leads a Lions charge against Australia during the 2001 series which was strife-torn and eventually won by the Wallabies.

Jason and the arguments: The doubters questioned the ability of Jason Robinson to convert from rugby league to rugby union, but he has proved his worth for both England and the Lions.

Gypo: With his shock of black hair, boundless energy and real passion for the game and the town, Gareth Jenkins the Llanelli coach, is no different from Gareth my old clubmate.

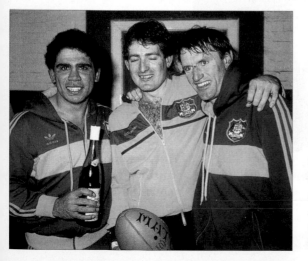

Pure genius: David Campese (centre) excited fans all over the world, but made a real impact on me during the 1984 Wallabies tour. He is pictured with another Aussie great, Mark Ella (left) and Andrew Slack after their victory over Scotland had given them a Grand Slam triumph.

No going back: Vernon Pugh (right) and Bernard Lapasset declare an end to the amateur regulations in Paris in 1995 and a thousand journeymen players join the gravy train.

Feeling the strain: The frustration, anger and anguish of being the Wales coach proved too much for Kevin Bowring. It has become an impossible job.

Firm foundations? Welsh Rugby Union chairman Glanmor Griffiths shows off the partly constructed Millennium Stadium which was built in time, just, for the 1999 World Cup. The national team on the other hand, are forever rebuilding.

The Rainbow Nation: President Mandela hands over the World Cup to South Africa's skipper François Pienaar at Ellis Park, Johannesburg in 1995. This was perhaps the greatest moment in rugby's history.

Ecstasy: Colin Charvis feels the joy and relief at scoring Wales' first try of the 1999 World Cup at the Millennium Stadium, Cardiff, against Argentina. Charvis missed the next game through suspension.

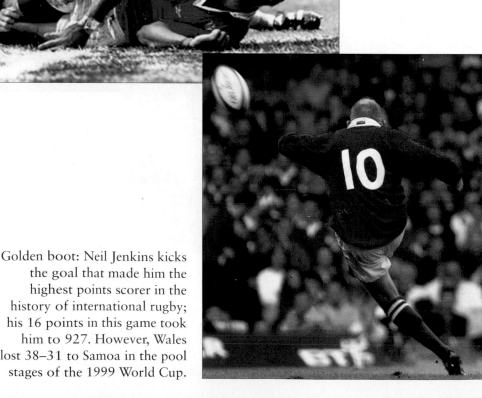

Golden boot: Neil Jenkins kicks the goal that made him the highest points scorer in the history of international rugby; his 16 points in this game took him to 927. However, Wales lost 38–31 to Samoa in the pool stages of the 1999 World Cup.

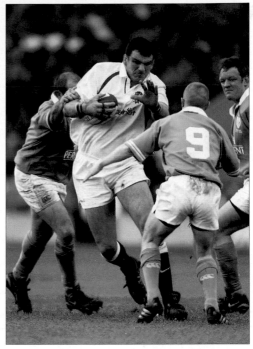

England expects: Every England fan expects Jonny Wilkinson to score hatfuls of points and win matches whenever he steps on the field. He is a phenomenal player, but I fear for his long-term ability to avoid injury.

Get out of my way: And who wouldn't? Martin Johnson shows the power and determination that has made him one of the greatest players and captains in England's history and very bad news for Wales.

The real deal: Some players can play in more than one position. John Eales, the brilliant Australian forward and World Cup-winning skipper, could have played in them all.

Say yes to the Euro! Martin Johnson shows the Heineken Cup to Leicester's jubilant fans at the Millennium Stadium in Cardiff in 2002. The tournament has transformed European rugby at club and provincial level.

Great Scott: Scott Quinnell has been one of Wales' very few genuine world class performers over recent years and his decision to retire from international rugby is a grievous blow to his country.

Don't believe what you read. The advertising slogan at Lansdowne Road urged Graham Henry to keep the faith, but the Wales coach decided to quit after this match in 2002 and return to New Zealand.

The writing on the wall. The scoreline in Dublin in 2002 which persuaded Graham Henry it was time to go. It was probably the worst Wales performance I can ever remember.

Leap of faith: Scott Gibbs scores one of the most memorable of all Welsh tries in the final minute against England at Wembley. It denied England the 1999 Grand Slam and Scott's exploits were written into Welsh folklore.

Pointing the way ahead. Steve Hansen, another New Zealander, took over as Wales coach in 2002 and has attempted to rebuild the national team around a group of promising youngsters.

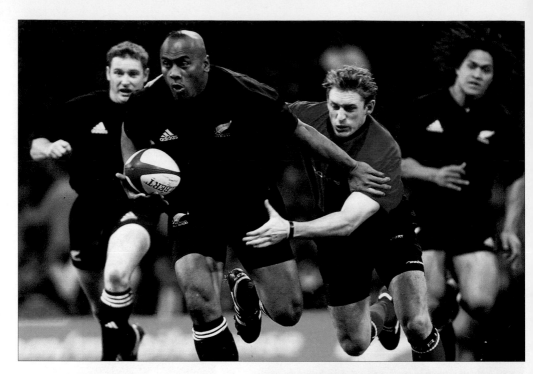

Jonah and Wales: The great man Jonah Lomu in full flight as Jamie Robinson of Wales tries his best to stop him. Lomu re-wrote the book on wing play and his celebrity status around the world took rugby into new territory.

New breed: Born in New Zealand, but definitely Welsh-qualified after living in his adopted country for more than three years, Sonny Parker of Pontypridd is one of the band of youngsters Welsh fans are pinning their hopes on.

he prove himself with Salford, but he went on to captain Great Britain. Few players have represented both the Lions in rugby union and Great Britain in rugby league, but Dai was one of the first; a fitting tribute to his ability and courage.

I have no doubt that David played his best rugby in the north of England rather than in Wales, but he still comfortably finds a place in my personal top ten. Newport supporters still rave about his ability and whenever I find myself at places like Wigan or Warrington they always want to tell me what a great player he was. They're right.

That's enough Welshmen for the moment. Let's change tack and also move the clock on a few years. One of my favourite overseas outside-halves was Michael Lynagh, a player I would put into the Barry John-type category. I'm not suggesting he was as good as Barry, but he did have the same unflappable air of calm about him. No matter what the match, or the situation, Lynagh always looked the coolest cookie on the field. Australia might be losing, the minutes could be ticking away, but Michael never seemed to break out in a sweat. I'll never forget that try he scored against Ireland in the dying minutes of the 1991 World Cup quarter-final in Dublin. The Aussie fans may have been chewing their fingernails, but Lynagh was the calmest man in Lansdowne Road.

He was by no means the quickest outside-half in the world. But he read a game perhaps better than any No. 10 who has ever played. Lynagh was a real general and his marshalling of the Wallabies World-Cup-winning side of 1991 cannot be underestimated. He was so shrewd. Every time he took possession he had worked out what was the best option and then delivered it. When he was waiting for the ball you could sense his brain was rapidly making all the right calculations. David

217

Campese was the instinctive genius in that Aussie side, the showman and entertainer, but Lynagh was the professor.

I felt Lynagh never perhaps gained the credit he deserved, but those who belittled his ability were normally not watching closely enough or didn't know what they were looking for. He was not flashy, but he did the right thing over and over again and kept the wheels of the team turning. He just went about his job quietly but the effects would be devastating, his lightning and canny decisions so often the key factor in what went on to become try-scoring moments. His passing was very sound off either hand, his tactical kicking was first rate and he was an excellent goal-kicker. All these attributes came together to form a complete picture of composure. Everything about Michael Lynagh told you that he was in control. His forwards might be keen to keep it tight, and Campo screaming to spin it wide, but Lynagh would keep his cool and play it the way he believed it should be played.

The statistics do not lie. Lynagh played in 72 Tests between 1984 and 1995 and scored 911 points; a world record that stood the test of time until Neil Jenkins came along. There have been many great Australian players over the past 10 or 12 years, but Lynagh compares with any of them.

Another Aussie who makes my list is Mark Ella. I saw him play in Wales as a schoolboy and I wrote his name down in order to try to keep track of his career when he went home. I needn't have bothered. Mark made sure his name stayed on everyone's lips, and by the time he came back to Wales to tour with the 1984 Wallabies he was one of the finest players in the world.

The essence of Ella was that he was quite simply the most naturally talented player I have ever seen. I am not saying he was the best outside-half – I think others worked harder to create an ability that possibly overtook him – but Ella had more raw talent than any player I can think of and it was all there when I saw him on that outstanding schoolboy tour. He was the equivalent of a Brazilian soccer star who had developed his range of skills on the beaches of Rio de Janeiro. Whatever sport Mark had chosen he would have succeeded without much effort, and done so with style. He had all the tricks at a young age. He could dummy, feint or pass the ball from behind his back, all with a seemingly effortless ease. There was a lovely flow about his game. The ball would move across the field, hardly appearing to stay in his hands for more than a fleeting instant. He played the game with flair and a complete freedom of expression.

Mark rarely kicked the ball. He would always try to pass his way out of trouble and had an almost naïve belief that if he kept playing the way he felt the game should be played, then something would come of it. He never had the blistering pace of someone like Jonathan Davies. He was more of a Michael Lynagh type, but with far more flair and extravagance.

Away from the field, Mark was a real gentleman and I had the pleasure of spending an hour in his company when I was in Australia for the 2001 Lions tour. We chatted about players past and present, and although he was a big admirer of that Lions squad he was as baffled as I was by the untimely publication of tour diaries by Austin Healy and Matt Dawson. Mark was an individualist, but he knew that the team had to come first. The 1984 Wallabies team that toured the UK was an exceptional side, laying much of the groundwork then for their triumph in the World Cup seven years later. Mark was crucial to it.

Let me bring things right up to date and say that one of my favourite No. 10s is England's Jonny Wilkinson. A year or so ago I would not have included him in my list because he seemed more functional than inspirational. But Jonny's all-round game has come on in leaps and bounds recently and now he deserves to be seen as one of the greats which is extraordinary for a young man who is still only 23.

Jonny is already tearing up the record books as a goal-kicker and if he stays fit I am sure he will go on to score more points in Test rugby than anyone else in history. He could set a new landmark that will stand for years after he has retired.

There is now so much more to his game. The defining characteristic is his pure guts. He is the bravest outside-half I have ever seen. When he was carried off on a stretcher in the second Test against Australia during the 2001 Lions tour, he looked as though he had no chance whatsoever of making the final game. There were even fears he had broken his leg. But his courage and determination ensured he was there again, wearing the Lions No. 10 jersey just a week later.

Wilkinson's tackling is another aspect of his game that I feel sets him apart from other No. 10s. By rights he shouldn't really be allowed into the fly-halves' union because he tackles too hard. Over the years, most fly-halves have tackled because they had to. Jonny does it because he loves it. His tackling and his defence in general is on a par with any international inside-centre, which gives both England and Newcastle a formidable level of defensive security in midfield. I shall never forget the power and aggressive force of Jonny's tackling when England beat France in Paris a couple of seasons ago. It was almost like watching Scott Gibbs against the Springboks for the Lions in 1997. Jonny not only stopped the big French runners, but he lifted them off their feet and dumped them on their backsides.

The thing that has really impressed me about Wilkinson, though, has been his attitude towwards improving his own game. When he first came on to the scene he did not seem to have a great deal of pace. He was okay, but not top-notch. But I know that training alongside the likes of Jason Robinson opened Jonny's eyes to what can be achieved. He has worked on his basic speed and added an explosive edge to his running game that wasn't there before. If he continues to develop these parts of his game then he could be a fixture in the England side for another seven years, at least.

The way England currently play suits Wilkinson. He has the ability to vary his distribution, so England have threats all over the park. He can throw out very accurate long passes to split the defence out wide. He can also pop up passes to his forwards, enabling them to attack closer in. And now that he has worked on his speed, Jonny can also surge through gaps himself. His vision and control of games is also improving. In short, he is on his way to becoming the complete, modern-day outside-half.

I like the mature way Jonny handles himself off the field, too, even though the level of attention focused on him is huge. He is modest and very self-critical. Others may heap lavish praise on him, but he always suggests he has a long way to go. How far he progresses is entirely up to him. There are no limits to what this young guy can achieve. My only concern is whether he can stay clear of injury. He is such a gutsy character that he can put his body on the line too often. For example, just before the Lions left for Australia in 2001, Jonny played in a club game for Newcastle against Harlequins. It was a tough, hard-fought semi-final of the Parker Pen Shield and Jonny had gone into the match with a neck injury. After almost every big tackle he went down and looked half-concussed. Yet he kept jumping up to slam into the next big tackle. Eventually, Jonny had to go off and it left me fearful. Unless he becomes a little less reckless he could pay a heavy price. If I was Rob Andrew at Newcastle I would be trying to adapt Jonny's game slightly so that the physical demands are not quite so risky. If Jonny doesn't do that then I fear he could simply take too much of a pounding and be lost to the game through injuries long before he has reached his peak. That would be a tragedy.

I'm sure Clive Woodward is also aware of this and that is why Clive has been campaigning so vigorously for strict limits on the number of games England players are allowed to play in one season. But sometimes it's not just how many games you play, it is the way you play. Jonny might find that a little bit more faith and cooperation with his back row and inside-centre would enable him to keep his body intact.

Scotland have produced some wonderful outside-halves over the years right up to Gregor Townsend, but the one that I was always a big admirer of was John Rutherford, who is now part of the Scottish coaching set-up under Ian McGeechan. What I liked about Rutherford was his consistency in a Scotland side that could be very inconsistent. John was a silky runner who was also very adept at putting others into space. Unsurprisingly, he was a fixture in the Scottish side throughout most of the eighties. Like Barry John, he had that wonderful ability to look as though he was going nowhere, before suddenly ghosting through a gap that only he had noticed. His hand-ling and kicking skills were excellent. He could beat a man over a couple of yards through going at right angles rather than relying on pure pace, and he had a great knack of turning defence into attack. Sometimes, he was not only physically but also mentally a yard or two ahead of his team-mates.

John was an all-rounder. He wasn't fantastically quick and his goal-kicking was not always deadly, but he was composed and could do most things very well. He was also a very effective general, organising his team-mates and choosing the right options in the same way as Lynagh did for the Aussies. He toured New Zealand with the 1983 Lions, and I felt he was un-lucky not to have made the Test side ahead of Ollie Campbell, who was a better goal-kicker but a less effective runner.

From another part of the world entirely, my next choice is the great Argentinian outside-half Hugo Porta. He was a few years younger than me but our paths crossed when he was part of the Pumas team that toured Europe in 1976. I also played against him for Wales in Cardiff.

As with most of the Argentina team, I had never heard of him. This was long before the days of Argentinians earning a living by playing their rugby in Europe, so it's fair to say they shocked us with their ability and commitment. They gave us a real going over and we were rather fortunate to escape with a narrow 20–19 victory. They were a strong all-round side but the man that stood head and shoulders above the rest was Hugo Porta. They played some great football that day and this tall fly-half was at the heart of it.

He was deceptively quick. Sometimes tall players take a while to get into their stride, but Porta was very fast off the mark and proved a difficult man to contain. He linked well with his three-quarters and was a key figure in a Pumas side that genuinely rattled us that day.

It was his kicking, though, that really left us all open-mouthed. Wales would be near the Argentinean 25-yard-line but when we lost possession Porta would belt the ball 60 or 70 metres down field and into touch. He was outstanding that afternoon and unsurprisingly stayed in their side for years, eventually earning 42 caps and scoring 408 points. He became Mr Argentinean rugby and was their most admired and respected player. At his peak, he had a complete game. He could run, kick for position, and create openings for others. But he stayed in the side even after he lost his pace, and that was mainly down to his wonderful reading of the game. He proved that a shrewd No. 10 can still control matches even when he no longer has the speed to make breaks himself.

Porta was also a deadly exponent of the art of kicking drop-goals and would regularly put them over from long distance. Rather like Diego Dominguez has done in recent seasons for Italy, Porta was able to carry an ordinary side at times through his own skill and experience. He set the standards for players that followed and the fact that Argentina have developed so much in recent years is a tribute to his influence.

I return to Wales for one of my very favourite players, perhaps the best to have pulled on a Welsh shirt over the past twenty years: Jonathan Davies. Jonathan grew up in Trimsaran, a village not too far from Llanelli, but a tough old mining community where you had to fight your own corner if you were going to survive. His father died when Jonathan was very young and this circumstance, I feel, moulded a character for whom self-belief, self-reliance and determination were second nature. Add to that all his wonderful natural abilities as a rugby player, especially his devastating pace, and you have all the attributes you require to reach the top.

I saw Jonathan play many times when he was a kid. Even when he was around nine years old, the word in the area was that this boy was a bit special so I went to have a look.

He was small, scrawny even, but he was incredibly competitive and very, very quick. His school team used to just give the ball to Jonathan and wait for him to score.

But things didn't always run as smoothly off the field. There has, I think, been a bit of a rebellious streak in Jonathan all his life. He doesn't always conform. In fact, he could be something of a hell-raiser as a youngster. I can remember one occasion when, Jonathan having been prevented by Gwendraeth Grammar School from attending a Welsh Schools trial, a tearful Mrs Davies rang to ask me to have a conversation with the school about the situation.

It turned out that his PE teacher Allan Lewis – who went on to coach Llanelli and Newport and is now at Bridgend – had banned Jonathan because he had played a game for Trimsaran Youth instead of representing the school. It had been the latest in a series of misdemeanours. I told Allan he had overreacted but he was determined to dig his heels in, and I got the distinct impression that this was not the first time Jonathan had defied authority. 'He never listens to me, Phil. Who the hell does he think he is?' said the exasperated voice on the other end of the line. It wasn't to be the last time Jonathan insisted on doing things his own way.

But that kind of attitude obviously helped Jonathan to become a great player. Without his father he had to learn to stand on his own two feet, an ability that stood him in good stead when he joined Neath. They were a pretty wild bunch in those days and I know from chatting with other Neath boys of that era that Jonathan wasn't the only one to find the bus journeys to and from games far more dangerous and gruelling than the matches themselves.

Here, then, was this young man who was quick, skilful, fiercely determined and playing in a pivotal position for a very strong club side. It was quite a combination. I saw that Neath side of the early eighties play Bath at the Gnoll. Bath were the best side in England and fancied their chances but Neath tore them to shreds that day and Johnny gave Stuart Barnes the biggest runaround of his life. There was a ruthless arrogance about Jonathan that day. He knew how good he was. He scored one try when no Bath player laid a finger on him but he couldn't resist smiling broadly at every player who had tried to tackle him as he walked back to take his kick.

Johnny went on to play for Wales and was the inspiration behind the team that won the Triple Crown in 1988 by beating England at Twickenham. We all thought it a team that would bring Wales back to the fore but it broke up soon afterwards as Jonathan and so many others went north to play rugby league.

That is the great pity of Jonathan's career in Wales. He played at a time when Wales were a volatile team run by a volatile bunch at the WRU whose regular knee-jerk reaction to setbacks was to sack the coach. So he got out in the autumn of 1988 and spent his best years playing rugby league. Others followed and Welsh rugby lost a gold mine of talent. If Jonathan had stayed one more season in rugby union then I reckon he would have become the complete player and captained the 1989 Lions to Australia. He really was that good. He could have helped the Lions win the series, laughed in the face of David Campese, and come back with his market value even higher than it finally was when he turned professional.

When Jonathan went north there was a lot of two-faced criticism and sneering at his decision – as was typical at the time in Wales – but that was nothing compared to the reaction in rugby league circles. They thought this kid was just too cocky by half and they predicted he would be eaten alive. Old lags were wheeled out regularly in the newspapers to predict his stay in rugby league would be a short and painful one. But like Dai Watkins before him, Jonathan overcame the doubters and the prejudice to be a massive success, going on to become a star of the Great Britain side. I never thought he would be anything less.

Jonathan scored some brilliant tries in rugby union and between 1985 and 1988 he was the outstanding player in British rugby. But his very best days were spent with Widnes and Warrington or playing rugby league in Australia. It was soul-destroying to see Wales go rapidly downhill while this Welshman was taking rugby league by storm.

At his best, Johnny had the lot: blistering pace – as he showed with that famous try for Great Britain against the Aussies at Wembley – vision, flair, outrageous cheek, courage and determination. And on top of that, he became a brilliant tactical kicker and deadly goal-kicker, too. His Wembley try in 1993 summed up Jonathan perfectly. There had been talk before the match about the speed of the Aussies and how unwise it would be for Jonathan or anyone else to try to take them on for pace. Within a few minutes Jonathan had shredded their defence and beaten their entire back line in a race to the corner. It was as if he needed to prove people wrong.

A couple of years later and Jonathan became the first big-name rugby league player to return to rugby union, when he left Warrington to join Cardiff. It should have given the entire Welsh game a massive shot in the arm but his return was appallingly handled. Cardiff allowed their players to openly snub Jonathan, and it was embarrassing to watch. Players who were not in the same class were denying him the ball because of some petty little agreement they had devised to satisfy their own jealousies. Some of those games, when Jonathan wouldn't get a single pass, made me squirm. It was shameful to watch a great player being treated so badly.

I was also saddened, though, by Jonathan's relative decline. He was 33 and the years and the injuries had taken their toll. Gaps would appear on the field and I would wait for Jonathan to blast through them, only for some bloke who wouldn't have got within five yards of him at one time, to pull Jonathan down.

Jonathan was mainly used as a replacement by the then Wales coach Kevin Bowring, generally kept out of the team by players who would not have held a light to him during his prime. It was all summed up by Jonathan's last appearance for Wales, when he was given the No. 10 shirt for the 1997 match against England, the last at the old Cardiff Arms Park. Jonathan tap-tackled Jeremy Guscott to deny England a try and earned plaudits for the effort. But I winced when I heard the applause because I knew that Guscott had been getting away from Jonathan at a rapid rate of knots – a race that Jonathan would have won hands down without breaking sweat when he was in his prime.

Those last few matches were not the glittering end to his rugby union career that Jonathan deserved, but in the years when he sparkled few have shone as brightly as he did. He reached the top in rugby union and rugby league, and did it also in Australian rugby league, which is as tough as it gets, making a good living out of rugby along the way.

My final favourite No. 10 is the man who has taken more criticism and abuse over the years than any other. In his more recent years he has won over most watchers, but there was a time when Neil Jenkins was vilified almost whenever he took the field.

And yet this is a player who has scored more points than any other player in the history of international rugby. There is no pleasing some folks, not in Wales, anyway, and certainly not when it comes to outside-halves.

Neil has been the most consistent and dangerous goal-kicker I have ever seen, but his general play has always been a source of much debate, especially in his own country. His style has never been that of the classical Welsh outside-half and I'll admit I have been critical of him after some matches for Wales. When he was nervous in his younger days, the mistakes used to flow, and when he had those poor games he was probably more exposed than most because his style was never orthodox in Welsh terms. He is far nearer the Grant Fox than Barry John mould of outside-half. That meant he perhaps never gained the sympathy he might have enjoyed had he been more acceptable to the purists.

What really marks Neil out for me, however, is his durability. He has withstood all the flak and kept going. He may have been dropped at many stages during his Wales career, but he has kept playing, kept coming back, and kept winning matches for his country.

Neil has made a massive contribution to the Welsh game, not just at Test level, but also for both Pontypridd and Cardiff. That he has achieved so much in the face of criticism is a huge testament to his inner strength and determination. He could easily have packed in years ago, but he has not let himself be deflected from his personal goals and ambitions, and his achievements now stand comparison with any player in the game.

Neil was first capped when he was 19 but the Welsh public never took to him as they did to most No. 10s. He was pale and red-haired, he did not have a dramatic change of pace, and he rarely made breaks that relied upon stealth and cunning. In short, he was not the jinking, weaving inheritor of the Welsh tradition that could be traced all the way back to Cliff Morgan. He was more like a New Zealand outside-half – reliable, functional and very disciplined. Perhaps that was why he was such a favourite of Graham Henry.

But I can remember another side of Neil. While his passing and distribution skills have never been in doubt, there were many matches for Pontypridd when he showed he could run and make breaks. Perhaps we saw the free-running player so rarely for Wales because he was generally playing in poor Welsh teams who were on the back foot. In those circumstances, he opted for safety and security, which maybe reflects his nature.

On the few occasions when Wales boasted a strong side around him, Neil has flourished. When Henry enjoyed his ten-match winning streak in 1999, Neil was just about the best No. 10 in the world at the time. He controlled matches through knowing exactly what options to take, what players to bring into the game and where to put the ball, either with his hands or with his boot. His tackling and covering were superb. He even made breaks, as those who saw the first Welsh win in France for 25 years can testify.

Two years later Neil went back to Paris and had an even better game, as Wales won again. He just sat back and destroyed the French with one of the best tactical displays I have ever witnessed.

When Neil went on the 1997 Lions tour of South Africa he became a national hero for his goal-kicking in the Tests, even though he was playing out of position at full-back. He hardly missed a kick. To see the looks of fear and apprehension on the Springboks supporters faces every time Martin Johnson handed the ball to Neil to kick for goal was an absolute pleasure for me.

It was a far cry from four years before when Neil was taking terrible stick in the Welsh media. My old pal JJ Williams got stuck into Neil after one particularly bad display against Scotland up at Murrayfield. JJ, I think, was trying to make the point that Neil didn't have a mindset that allowed him to see openings like a traditional Welsh fly-half. But the newspaper headline simply said, 'Brainless!' and went on to brand Neil as having nothing between his ears. It was fairly typical of the stuff said about Neil at the time. Much of it was hurtful and abusive and I really don't know how Neil coped. Had it been me I think I would have emigrated. Neil, however, has proved himself extremely thick-skinned. In his younger days he would snap back at his critics, but he has long since adopted a shrug of the shoulders as his best form of defence. He has been a role model and a fantastic ambassador for Wales. He is also just about the most modest, unassuming guy you could ever wish to meet.

That, then, is my list of top No. 10s. What about you? Who would you choose, given the chance?

CHAPTER 14

Legends

There are times when, listening to some members of the media, I feel like hitting them over the head with a dictionary. It's when I hear them use the word 'great' to describe some current player who we all know is only marginally above average. For instance, Mike Catt has been a very good player for England over the years. So have Matt Dawson and Will Greenwood, and before them, Rob Andrew. Similarly, Dai Young and, more recently, Colin Charvis have given sterling service for Wales. All six have toured with the Lions, but they are not among the greats of the game. Those are few and far between. For me, the greats are players whose achievements live in the memory as well as in the record books. The contemporary greats of English rugby are the likes of Martin Johnson. In Wales, it has been Neil Jenkins. A handful of the greats can be called legends of the game – men who contributed brilliance and box-office appeal, and who helped shape and define the way the game has been and will be played. There haven't been many true legends but I was lucky enough to play with a few.

I count it as one of my privileges in life, rather than simply in rugby, to have known Willie John McBride. I had played against Willie in Wales–Ireland games for a couple of years before I went on tour with him to South Africa in 1974. He was captain of the Lions and I was a young man completely in awe of the bloke, even though I had been on the winning side against him. Maybe it was because he was on his fifth Lions tour while I was on my first. He had so much knowledge and wisdom about the game that you could learn more in five minutes in his company than in an hour spent talking to most coaches.

It was his strength of personality that made Willie such a magnificent captain; a player you would follow to the ends of the earth. He knew visiting South Africa in the mid-seventies would be fraught with problems, being well aware that our trip would be a focus for concerted protest, but he had a way of gaining personal respect that made you willing to take all the criticism because you wanted to be part of this great adventure led by a man who seemed capable of doing anything. There was a personal charisma about him. It didn't matter whether you were a Test regular or someone struggling to get a match with the dirt-trackers, everyone respected Willie John and was willing to bust a gut for him. I don't think any Lions captain since has commanded that kind of loyalty. Personal gripes and grudges were never allowed to surface because players thought too much of McBride to bother him with anything like that. Even if players were unhappy with their personal situation, they wouldn't rock the boat lest the skipper should think they were undermining the Lions' cause. Matt Dawson and even Austin Healey would have buttoned their lips if they had found themselves left out of the Test team in 1974. In fact, there *was* no Test or midweek side, just 30 British and Irish Lions all in it together.

Willie John knew his capabilities as a player. In order to save energy when we were doing our warm-ups, he would jog around at the back of the group. Sometimes, he would have a nap in the afternoons because he felt tired. In the evening, though, he would talk consummate sense about the game, in between puffs on his pipe. Calm words, but spoken with quiet authority. He knew how to get the best out of players. When the tension was it its highest, he would be at his quietest, for he always knew that the right words at the right time counted for far more than any ranting and raving.

He had a presence that inspired you before the game and made better players of those around him. He still has it now when he meets up with old team-mates and I'm told from players who were in the dressing room on the 2001 Lions tour that it was one of the real highlights when he came in before the First Test against Australia. They said he was an inspiration and the decision to involve him like that was one of the shrewdest made by Graham Henry.

Willie John could make you believe in yourself as a player. He would soothe the most frayed nerves, whatever the circumstances. I can remember once playing for an international 15 in a charity match on Willie John's home patch in Ballymena in County Antrim. It was at the height of the troubles and there were soldiers with rifles hiding behind sandbags on the street corners around our hotel. Willie John must have sensed my anxieties and those of a few other players, too. So he gave us a short history on conflict in Northern Ireland, which ended with a balanced account of what life was like in the city and why the soldiers were on the streets. I felt a little less tense. 'Oh, and besides,' he said as an afterthought. 'If one of their flankers comes in at you from offside, then I've arranged for the snipers to take him out.'

One night in South Africa in 1968, Willie John wanted to celebrate a hard-fought victory with his room-mate, Delme Thomas. But Delme was not much of a drinker, or a party man, and he'd turned in at around 10 p.m. Willie John was unimpressed. He asked Delme to join in the celebrations in the bar downstairs but Delme insisted he'd rather just go to sleep. Willie John appeared to have lost the argument but later in the evening Delme did indeed join the rest of the squad for a pint. 'We thought you were staying in bed,' we said. 'I was,' he replied. 'Until the captain set fire to my sheets.' Years later when Delme was feeling unwell, Willie John rang me from Northern Ireland. 'How's the great man from Carmarthen?' he asked. 'Tell him, he had better recover soon, otherwise I'll be over with my matches'.

The only player I can think of who had the same influence on those around him was Colin Meads when he played for the All Blacks. Like Willie John, Meads was a big man with a stature to match. Meads was also a magnificent player, a real athlete, and a forward who was in a class of his own during most of his playing days. Willie John may not have had the same aura as a player, but he always rose to the big occasion and was a very good forward. But Willie John's status as a legend comes from his longevity and the success he achieved with the teams he led. Five Lions tours – it sounds even more remarkable now than it did back in 1974. And no matter what anyone says, you don't get picked for five Lions tours unless you can play a bit.

Willie John wasn't the most skilful or the fittest, but he was a hard grafter, won his short ball in the line-out, and was a very strong scrummager. He also knew the basics and insisted that the forwards establish territorial dominance and control before the backs cut loose. For him, scrummaging was a weapon and the Lions used it to undermine the physical and mental strength of the South African forwards. He destroyed them at what they thought was their strongest point.

Willie John's last match for Ireland happened to be against Wales at the Arms Park in 1975. We beat them 32–4 and scored five tries to their one. It was one of our most ruthless displays of that period and I felt rather sorry for Willie as he trudged off at the final whistle. He deserved a better send-off than that. Like many great players he paid the price of going on for one season too many. The right time for him to have got out was after coming back from South Africa a hero in 1974. He admitted as much to me some time afterwards when he told me about his encounter with two Irish fans as he came out of the dressing rooms alone, the last to leave after slowly packing away his kit. They had both drowned their sorrows during an increasingly painful second-half. 'Ah, never mind, Willie John,' said one. 'It's the Irish centenary season so we've all a lot to be grateful for.' 'Thanks, boys,' said Willie. Then he heard the other say, thinking that Willie had walked out of earshot ''Tis still a shame he had to play like a f***ing founder member.'

If Willie John had reached the end of his best years in 1974, then Gareth Edwards was just approaching his own peak. I spent a good deal of time standing alongside Gareth during that tour of South Africa, and for much of it I was simply open-mouthed. He reached standards that were higher than anything I'd ever seen on a rugby field. A couple of years ago, Gareth was voted by one leading rugby magazine as the greatest rugby player of all time. Had there been any other result then I don't think I'd have been alone in demanding a recount. Other players have been more skilful players than Gareth – quicker, stronger or more determined – but in terms of overall attributes and the application of those in big matches year after year, I think he stands alone. He was never a one-man team, but he was the one man every team would have killed for.

Gareth toured with the Lions in New Zealand in 1971. It was his second Lions tour and he was only 23 years old. He had hamstring problems on that trip but still managed to emerge as one of the key men in helping the Lions make history. By 1974 Gareth had a swagger and self-confidence about him. He knew just how good he was and was well aware that he had got himself into the best physical shape of his life. So much has been said and written about his contribution in the Tests against the Springboks, but he did more than anyone to set the tone for that tour early on. I can remember him destroying South West Africa in the second match of the tour. In unbearable heat, as part of a group of players who hardly knew each other, Gareth ran the show. He ran, passed, kicked and tackled the life out of the opposition. They didn't know how to cope with him. He was unstoppable. Our forwards were out on their feet after 15 minutes because of the heat, but Gareth carried them for the rest of the game and made sure we won. He was so majestic that day that the word went around South Africa that Gareth had to be stopped – by any means. The sparks flew in a few games subsequently but Edwards was never intimidated and never less than a huge thorn in the Springboks' side.

Gareth had been outstanding for Wales for a good while before 1974, but sometimes the team had failed to bring out the best in him. After the Grand Slam of 1971, Wales went through something of a rebuilding period and Gareth was perhaps unable fully to utilise the whole range of his skills. By 1974 his kicking game had improved immeasurably and I felt from then on he became the complete scrum-half.

His service in South Africa was just a dream. When we played at altitude I felt we could have stood on either sides of the field and the ball would still have reached me. It gave me all the time in the world. I dropped two goals in the Third Test, largely because Gareth was giving me the time to do as I pleased. The supply was so perfect that I could have signed my name on the ball before lining up the kick. He gave me one reverse pass in that game, while he was off-balance, which wrong-footed the entire defence. I still feel only he could have thrown it.

That 1974 tour brought us together as friends and as players. We lived in each other's pockets and developed a rapport, just as Gareth had enjoyed a special rapport with Barry John. Ours was a different sort of understanding, though. Barry was more laid back than me and famously told Gareth on their first meeting, 'You pass it. I'll catch it.' We worked on our partnership day after day in South Africa until it became second nature. We reached a stage where he always knew where I was, without having to look. I could move anywhere, without having to worry. We maintained that understanding for the next four years.

As Gareth grew older he adapted his game. The pace was

still there, but he couldn't sustain it for 60 or 70 yards. So he improved the accuracy of his kicking and made sure his team were in the right areas from which he could attack from within the opposition 22. He was shrewd enough to know that over the shorter distance his power, especially his upper-body strength, still made it an uneven contest for anyone trying to stop him.

In those later years, Gareth's presence alone would unsettle the other side. When I was Welsh captain and Gareth had been struggling with an injury during the week, I would always urge him to strap the injury and get on the field. Even a half-fit Gareth Edwards was enough to put doubt in the minds of the English, the Scots, the Irish or the French. On the other hand I knew the opposition would get a massive psychological lift if they heard Gareth had pulled out.

We became good friends. We were young men, playing for our country, seeing the world and having the time of our lives. About the nearest we ever came to a cross word was when a coach urged me to stand closer to Gareth to avoid crowding our outside-backs. Gareth hated that. He wanted to show he had the longest, straightest, fastest pass in the game. If I moved closer to him in a training session he would mutter his displeasure under his breath and the ball would come fizzing towards me like a guided missile. After five minutes, simply in order to catch it, I would be standing as far away from Gareth as before. He never liked losing – even arguments.

Sometimes that could produce an explosive atmosphere, especially when there were others who also liked to dictate and who were not used to giving way. If JPR Williams felt Gareth was trying to do too much on his own, then a voice would come booming from behind the back line, 'Tell Edwards there

239

are 14 other players on this field and we might find it easier if he used them.' Gareth would scowl and mutter something back towards JPR before Gerald Davies would come in from the wing and use his calming influence to smooth things over. Gareth and JPR were two enormous talents with big egos to match, and clashes between them were not uncommon.

But those kinds of disputes never lasted too long. Gareth would soon shrug his shoulders, crack a joke and normal service would be resumed. In his case that meant making the most of his extraordinary talent. He was always a lively, bubbly character on the field, but he wasn't one of those scrum-halves who would spend time trying to wind up his opposite number. He didn't need to. He'd be destroying them with his talent, so why waste words? Gareth would talk a lot to his own forwards, but referees and other No. 9s were generally not worth bothering with.

Everyone recalls Gareth's famous try for the Barbarians against the All Blacks in 1973. It was a classic; a match that all rugby fans never seem to tire of watching or talking about. However, the memory that sticks in my mind of Gareth and the Barbarians took place at Lansdowne Road. We were playing the Lansdowne club as part of their centenary celebrations. That afternoon I saw the sheer power of Gareth Edwards at its most raw and brutally destructive. He took a pass at pace and ran at their outside-half. This guy tried to tackle Gareth who simply ran over him on his way to the line. Twenty years later I saw Jonah Lomu do the same thing to Mike Catt in the World Cup semi-final at Cape Town. Gareth jogged back after scoring while this poor Irishman tried to get off the floor. Blood was pouring from a huge gash across his nose. Gareth and I went over to make sure he was okay and he slowly struggled to his feet. He looked as though he'd been run over. 'How did you manage that?' I asked. 'I don't know,' said Gareth. 'I think he must have got his nose in the way of my legs.' I looked down at Gareth's legs. His thighs were all rippling muscles, like an Olympic sprinter's. His knees looked as though they'd been chiselled from marble. It must have been like trying to stop a racehorse. I just felt glad I didn't have to tackle him.

One of my most satisfying victories as a player was when Llanelli beat Cardiff 30–7 in the 1973 Welsh Cup Final. It wasn't the fact that I had played well and didn't miss a kick all day that pleased me; it was pride in convincingly beating a team containing Gareth Edwards. After all, he was a seasoned match player who loved the big occasion. He went on three Lions tours and was a genius in two of them. He would have made it four had he wanted to go in 1977. He thrived on pressure situations.

Once he had come off the field, however, either for Wales or for Cardiff, then that was it. He rarely wanted to talk about rugby. He'd rather tell you about where he had planned his next fishing trip, or something about his family. Looking back, I suppose drawing a line under the matches when they had finished was his way of coping with the level of expectation. He could keep rugby in perspective, rest his body for the next big test, and switch off. It was perhaps ironic that during the years when rugby was a national obsession, the most important player of that whole decade was someone who never treated it as more than a game. But what a game he could play. What a player!

While Gareth could relate quite easily to Barry John's detached, almost casual view of everything that surrounded top-level sport, JPR Williams had an intensity that was always

241

intimidating and quite often frightening. I played alongside John for Wales schoolboys when we were both 15, and I played against him at the same age. It didn't really matter whether he was on my side or not, he still scared the living daylights out of me.

John was a natural sportsman, a gift most clearly displayed when he won Junior Wimbledon. He was not all that big when he was young, but he still had a presence about him that must have worried those poor tennis kids on the other side of the net as much as it worried his opponents on the rugby field. A lot of people considered John arrogant and aloof, but they were those who didn't understand that it was his competitive streak that drove him. He had to win everything, but once the game was over he was gracious and magnanimous. He always had a deep respect for everyone who gave their all on a rugby field.

I once saw JPR and Gareth Edwards play a doubles match in Japan against two very talented members of a well-to-do tennis club in Tokyo in 1975. Gareth was playing because he thought it might be fun. The rest of us went to watch for the same reason. But JPR went to win. He had to win. He put as much effort, energy and determination into winning as when playing for Wales against England – a fixture he never lost in 11 encounters. There were forwards sipping beer on the club balcony overlooking the court who thought JPR was insane. But John thought they were the mad ones for choosing to drink and socialise when they could have been beating some poor sod into the ground with a tennis racquet.

JPR radiated confidence to those he played with. He was certainly the bravest player I ever saw as well as the most deeply determined. The clenched fists after a particularly good tackle, the flowing hair as he knocked players aside when he counter-attacked, the pure relish with which he lunged into clattering contact – he was a one-off. An inner strength and self-belief emanated from somewhere deep within him.

I saw the courage John had at an early age. When we were both very young we toured New Zealand with Wales in 1969. The All Blacks had a mighty side, with Colin Meads in his pomp. It was the first Test in Christchurch, the weather was atrocious and Wales were being destroyed up front by the New Zealand pack. They thought this 19-year-old kid at full-back must be a weak link, but JPR was as hard as nails and he proved it. We lost the match 19–0 in the days when 19–0 was a horrible thrashing, but I saw the All Blacks pay JPR a strange kind of respect I've never seen since. After taking high balls all day without flinching, after bumping off tacklers with his shoulders every time he took the catch, JPR stationed himself under another up-and-under with about five minutes to go. Meads could have flattened John had he wanted to. He had the perfect chance to smash into the Welsh full-back and take man and ball. But JPR took the catch, bravely as ever, and Meads simply ran to the side of him. Perhaps Meads simply pulled out because he had heard JPR call the mark and didn't want to commit a late tackle. But something about the way Meads avoided an easy target said something more to me. JPR had won the respect of the All Blacks for 75 minutes as he stood, covered in mud and bruises, taking catch after catch. Perhaps he'd done enough as far as Meads was concerned and didn't deserve to be flattened in the final few minutes.

Perhaps Meads should have taken the chance to give John a good battering, though, because when JPR went back to New Zealand in 1971 he wore the Lions No. 15 shirt in all four

Tests and was a 21-year-old colossus. He dropped a goal to help win the series in the final Test and New Zealanders everywhere still talk of the man's raw courage and his fearsome will to win.

JPR was big and strong, but he also had a mental toughness that stood him apart from most players. He almost willed forwards to come and run at him because he wanted to impose himself on them, take them on physically. I can hardly remember him ever missing a tackle. In every game we played together for Wales he anchored the team through being the rock at the back, the player you knew would never flinch and never let you down. More than that, his tackling and his fearsome running would demoralise opponents. They knew that to score they had to get past this lunatic in a red shirt.

He played hard on the field and he played hard off it. John liked the social side of rugby and could match anyone drink for drink when the occasion required. But while most players would need to spend the next morning trying to recover, John would be up at 7 a.m. and off for a run before training. He was unbeatable in every respect. What's more, that warrior spirit is still there. Just try going for a jog with him or see him play in a golden oldies game. It wasn't that long ago that JPR could still be seen playing every Saturday afternoon for his local club, Tondu – a 50-year-old surgeon smashing and crashing around a rugby field every week against players who were half his age but twice as nervous about the physical confrontation.

I played in one memorable golden oldies game with JPR a few years back against Llandovery. It was a couple of years after I had retired and it was billed as an exhibition game featuring some past Welsh players from the seventies. We all rolled up, looking forward to a gentle afternoon of more or less touch rugby. But far from playing against a Llandovery side of veterans like ourselves, we were rather shocked to discover we would be playing their first team. Some of our side were a bit unsure, but JPR started pumping himself up in the dressing room. There was a decision to be made. Play the game or tell JPR we were crying off. It felt safer to play the game. We drew 28-all and it was one of the most physically demanding matches I've ever played in. JPR was in our back row and his commitment was both extraordinary and quite frightening. He threw himself into every tackle and every ruck. When he came off at the end he looked as though he had gone 12 rounds with Mike Tyson, but there was no way he was leaving the field before the final whistle. I looked at him, standing there smiling with blood running down his face. The same hands he was using to stem the flow would be performing an orthopaedic operation on someone on Monday morning. I thought, 'John. You haven't mellowed with age. You're more insane then ever.'

Like Gareth Edwards, JPR comfortably measures up to the status of a rugby legend. He played on for Wales for too long, I felt, because there came a time when his pace no longer matched up to his spirit and commitment. But I count myself as fortunate to have had a playing career that ran in tandem with his. I was a steelworker's son, while he was the son of a doctor who learnt his rugby at public school. But we hit it off and shared some great times together, as we still do when we meet up now.

JPR, Gareth, Willie John – they all confirmed their greatness on Lions tours, and so did another man I would class as a real hero and a legend of British and Irish rugby: Fran Cotton. Before I went away with the 1974 Lions I spoke to some former Welsh internationals who claimed that the English were self-centred and aloof on Lions tours, even snobbish in their attitude towards the rest. On both my Lions tours, however, I have to say I never found anything to back up that accusation in the slightest. Bill Beaumont, Peter Wheeler, Tony Neary, Roger Uttley, Mike Burton and others were all fine by me. They had the Lions at heart and they would graft and scrap and fight their corner. You can't ask for more than that. But for me, one man stands out among those Englishmen as a true legend and that was Cotton. He went on three Lions tours and he held the England pack together at times in the days when there was not always much else keeping it intact.

It's often said of props that they become the cornerstone of the team. It's usually just a cliché, but Franny really was our cornerstone in 1974. He was a huge, indomitable northerner, as solid as the red-brick Victorian buildings of Lancashire, both in body and in spirit. Fran was a massive man, with enormous power to match. Lions parties had been going across to South Africa for years before 1974 and finding themselves up against giant Springbok forwards who we were unable to match. But Fran was someone they had to look up to – tall, strong, broad across the shoulders and very competitive. Suddenly, the boot was on the other foot.

Fran was steeped in a Lancastrian rugby tradition and held a high regard for rugby league and their players, as well as rugby union. Wigan was his club and he knew the 13-man game well enough for much of their professional approach to rub off on him. He trained hard, worked on his skills, and became simply an outstanding forward. The Test front row on that 1974 tour was one of the best there has ever been – Fran, Bobby Windsor, the best hooker I ever played with, and Ian 'Mighty Mouse' McLauchlan. They had strength, great technique, fitness and the resolve not only to get the better of the Springboks' front row but also to keep that grip tightly held for three months. It gave everyone else a massive psychological lift.

Those Lions forwards would practise their scrummaging for hours on end. Eight versus eight. No machines, just blood, sweat and tears until they got it absolutely right. I would go along and watch these sessions after the backs had finished our routines. It was raw and brutal stuff. By the end the skin was peeling off their foreheads from the constant scrummaging and the friction didn't end there. Often, there would be a punch-up between the Test pack and the midweek eight. They were all fighting for Test selection and no prisoners were taken. The star of the show, though, was usually Fran. He was awesome in training but the perfect gentleman off the field with a smile on his face and real enthusiasm for the whole business of touring. The local South Africans loved him.

Fran was hard, but he was never a dirty player. He could punch his weight, which was considerable, but he wasn't the kind of forward who would be stamping and kicking players on the ground. There was always a dignity and respect about his game. He was forceful without being overbearing – on or off the field.

As Lions skipper in 1977 I lent heavily on Fran's knowledge and experience. He knew what needed doing among our own forwards, what needed saying, who was pulling their weight and who wasn't. Like JPR, he had an intensely competitive streak. On that New Zealand tour in 1977, we lost 21–9 to New Zealand Universities and Fran was devastated. But we then went on a ten-match winning streak that took us into the Tests, our final pre-Test victory being against Auckland. They were a very good side but we beat them 34–15 after destroying them up front. Our front row was taking theirs to the cleaners so they opted for a three-man scrum to try to get the ball out as quickly as possible. It was the first time I'd ever seen that tactic used and it blew up in their faces. The Lions front row simply held on to their three forwards and proceeded to walk right over them – nothing nasty, just a good honest shoeing. Fran then noticed that Auckland were warming up another prop on the sidelines to take over from one of his battered and bruised colleagues. It just happened to be the same prop who had played against Fran for the Universities team some five weeks before. When Fran recognised him his eyes lit up. He gestured over and shouted, 'Oi, you! Get on here, now. I owe you one.' The prop had to be almost dragged onto the field and obviously wished he could stay on the bench. Years later I met that prop and he confessed that Fran had scared him to death that afternoon.

Fran was equally revered as an England forward, a player who gave an edge to the English pack at a time in the seventies when they sometimes struggled for athletic and committed forwards who could last the pace of a tough international. Every England player respected him because they knew he could scrummage, hit rucks and mauls, and be very destructive all over the field.

Fran was streetwise and knew how to conduct himself in any company. He could be very persuasive and it hasn't surprised me in the slightest that he's become an extremely successful businessman in his own right as well as a leading administrator within the RFU. If only Welsh rugby had more men of his calibre in positions of influence. He also did a superb job as Lions team manager in South Africa in 1997, being a key element in a successful tour. Yet despite all those entries on his CV, Fran has not changed one jot. He's still an amiable and knowledgeable rugby fan who loves to discuss the game with anyone.

So far I have selected two Welshmen, an Irishman and an Englishman. So it's only fair I end with a Scotsman. I could have picked three from my own playing days – Andy Irvine, Ian McLauchlan, or Gordon Brown. Scottish sport lost a real hero when Gordon died recently and his funeral was one of the most moving but inspiring days of my life. It was a wonderful celebration of a marvellous man. So many famous faces from Scottish sport were there including soccer stars such as Kenny Dalglish and Ally McCoist, everyone had their favourite story about the big man, and when the lone piper played as he walked away into the distance it was profoundly emotional. I had seen Gordon only two or three weeks before he died at a fund-raising dinner for him in London. It was packed out and the evening raised over £200,000. We all knew it was a farewell occasion, and so did Gordon, but I shall never forget how stunned I felt at seeing this giant of a man so terribly struck down by cancer. As I shook his hand and we embraced I could feel how frail and icy-cold he had become and I knew that rugby was saying goodbye to one of its great men. Mighty Mouse was also a truly great performer. How many other players can boast they played in eight Tests for the Lions and only lost once? But I've gone for Andy Irvine because my thoughts haven't changed since I first played alongside him for the Lions in 1974; he's one of the most talented and exciting rugby players I've ever seen.

Some said Andy was weak under the high ball. Maybe he was. Perhaps he dropped the odd catch now and again, but it was never a significant weakness in his game and he had

249

so many attributes that more than compensated. I always regarded Andy as one of the great entertainers, a fantastically balanced runner from full-back who had enough pace and finishing power to be equally at home on the wing. So many of his tries for Scotland combined that precious gift of real flair with tremendous pace. I rated him as one of the quickest men I played against. In South Africa in 1974, he was the only player who could run JJ Williams close and JJ was a former Commonwealth sprinter. Over 50 yards it would be John by maybe half a yard. But whereas JJ was a pure speed man, Irvine had more vision and variation to his running.

It was a tribute to Andy's ability that he made the Test side on that tour. No one was going to remove JPR from the No. 15 shirt, but Andy was such a good footballer that a place simply had to be found for him and so he gained a spot on the wing. He was also an excellent goal-kicker, capable of scoring from long distance, and his pace made him invaluable as a last line of defence when it came to cutting off the angles. But the one gift he shared with Gareth, with JPR, and with other great players who loved the ball in their hands, was an unshakeable belief in his own ability. He loved the ball kicked to him because he wanted to prove to his opponents that he was more dangerous with the ball in his hands than they were. JPR would tackle anything that moved, but Andy had more gas and more confidence in his own pure speed than JPR could dream about.

I loved playing alongside Andy because his first impulse was always to launch a counter-attack. In 1977 on the Lions tour to New Zealand he scored five tries in one game against King Country and was unstoppable. I always knew that if I could get back to support Andy when he ran from deep then he would chance it. Kicking was used only as a last resort and although that might have frustrated some of his Scottish teammates at times, it was an attitude I deeply admired. He was the David Campese of his generation – a genius. I don't use that word lightly, but in Andy's case it was appropriate because it was a self-made talent. Scottish club rugby didn't compare to Welsh club rugby in the seventies and yet here was a player that Wales would have loved to have had in their ranks.

I always got on well with Andy. He was a genuine sportsman on and off the field. He played the game the way it should be played and did so with great skill, and then, when it was over, he was always the most courteous and engaging company. Whenever I am at Scottish clubs in the nights before a Scotland–Wales international, then any excuse to share talk about Andy Irvine is worth taking up.

CHAPTER 15

My Favourite Fifteen

The most common criticism thrown at former players offering opinions on modern rugby is that we are forever harking back to the past. Perhaps we do. Maybe we are all a little guilty of eulogising about our own era at the expense of the present day. I know I enjoyed playing rugby when I did and the truth is I'm not so sure I would have liked it as much if I were playing today.

When it comes to comparing standards from one generation to another, I accept that the pundit is always on difficult ground. It's like comparing the performance of a new VW Golf with what of an old Morris Minor. Times have changed, the game has moved on. Pitches, balls, training methods, diet, and general preparation for the game have altered dramatically from when I stopped playing in 1981. It makes it almost impossible to make judgements on how most players would have performed had they played in a different time.

I'll admit I do make the odd exception to that rule. There are, I believe, certain legends of the game, like those I have talked about, who would have survived in any era. People sometimes say to me, 'Barry John would never have found space among modern defences,' or 'Gareth Edwards would not been such a threat against the big, fast men of today.' But my reply is that they would have found a way. That's what set them apart in their own years. They had the vision, determination and imagination to rise above the players around them, and they would do just the same if they were playing today. If Gareth Edwards was 18 years old now and able to use the back-up that professional rugby can offer then I shudder to think how good he could have become.

But players like Edwards only come along very, very rarely and in general it's almost impossible to imagine how players from 30 years ago would have succeeded now or how modern-day players would have fitted in years ago. As someone once said, the past is a fine place to visit occasionally but only a fool chooses to live there.

With that in my mind I've decided to pick my favourite fantasy 15 from within clearly defined boundaries. And since it's easy to favour your old mates, and claim that they were all the bees knees compared with today's bunch, I've decided to restrict my own choices to players from the modern era. So, taking the past 20 years – since my own retirement, in fact – as my selection era, this is my favourite team. Another explanation is due at this point. I'm using the word favourite rather than best. These players are my personal choices because I enjoyed witnessing their talent. They may not be the best in terms of winning matches. In fact, if it was a case of picking a team to win the World Cup during a wet and rainy winter in

New Zealand then I might have gone for an entirely different bunch altogether. But I feel grateful to players who have given me pleasure watching them and so I've decided to indulge myself. Here then, with my own entertainment firmly in mind, is my favourite 15 from the past 20 years.

At full-back I would have no hesitation in naming Serge Blanco. When I first saw him play as a kid for France B he blew me away. He was raw, untutored, but massively talented and he scored a couple of fantastic tries that day. Blanco rewrote the rulebook. He counter-attacked from outrageous positions, but he had such pace and skill he would terrify the opposition even when he was 80 yards from their try-line. Off the field, he smoked like a trooper and wasn't the most dedicated trainer in the world. But when it mattered for France he could be relied upon to regularly deliver brilliant performances. Gavin Hastings was another full-back I greatly admired for his solidity and the security he spread through a team, but Blanco took my breath away. He also left me frowning because it seemed he used to save his most devastating performances for his encounters with Wales. The number of times I thought Wales had plugged all the gaps only for this silky runner to suddenly make off across the field to exploit some space that no one else had noticed. Serge played 93 times for France between 1980 and 1991 and although he perhaps wasn't the most destructive tackler, he rarely missed his man. He had great hands, could kick well when he needed to, and was blessed with that extra flair and vision that could decide matches.

My right wing is David Campese, probably the most exciting player rugby has seen over the past 20 years. Campo could be guilty of the most extraordinary lapses, such as when he dropped the ball for Ieuan Evans to win a series for the Lions, but these were very much outweighed by his incredible individual talent. Campese had more natural control of the ball than any player I've ever seen. It was his wand. He could do anything with it and he could have played any position behind the scrum. He chose to play on the wing and although he was never the fastest at finishing off tries, he was quick enough.

What made him special, though, was not pace but disguise. Opponents could never tell which direction he was heading, when the change of pace would come, or where the ball was going. He was impossible to read, which is a very rare attribute indeed. Supporters loved him because no one could read him from the sidelines either. Because of that, and bearing in mind the ten-year span of his Test career, I would suggest he's been the greatest entertainer the game has ever known.

Ieuan Evans, John Kirwan and a few other wings all had their attributes over the past 20 years but Campese was the master. He baffled people. He could sidestep, jink, and change angle and direction, but he also had other tricks, like his trademark goosestep, that were all his own. Some individualists are unable to fit into a team pattern, but Campese always did the basics well for Australia and realised he had to mould his talent for the good of the team. The Wallabies were the best team in the world in the early 1990s and much of that was down to David's influence and ability. He may have lost a yard of pace in his later years, but he made up for it in the pure genius he had for the game.

Away from the field, I must admit I've always enjoyed Campo's outbursts and wind-ups. It was all part of the act of a great showman and was good for the game. For example, he branded English rugby as boring and mercilessly taunted Will

Carling, but in doing so he made headline news on the back pages and helped to put rugby on the map.

If there is one player whose profile in global terms eclipsed even that of David Campese, then it is Jonah Lomu, my choice on the left wing. Quite simply Lomu became, and perhaps still is, the biggest box-office draw in the game. He didn't ask for it. It just happened at the 1995 World Cup and since then, wherever the big man has gone, there is always a crowd of kids following him around as though he's the pied piper.

I can't believe any rugby player will have an impact at a World Cup that compares with the one Lomu made at that tournament in South Africa. It was extraordinary. He destroyed Ireland, Wales, Scotland and finally England in that epic semi-final. Will Carling called Lomu a 'freak' but the reality is that he was a novice blessed with incredible natural attributes for the game; no expectations and no nerves.

Things had altered by the final against South Africa. The Springboks had worked Lomu out and suddenly there was enormous pressure on his shoulders from an expectant New Zealand public. Lomu was contained that day and it was the first sign of vulnerabilities within his game, especially when the ball was kicked into space behind him. But the havoc he caused with the ball in his hand still far outweighed his deficiencies. It was South Africa's brilliant defensive display against him that won them the Cup, not Lomu's shortcomings.

When he has been fit – and he has suffered terribly with kidney-related illnesses at times – Lomu has been the most devastating player the game has ever seen. There has never been such a blend of power, strength and speed. In a 15-man game few players have ever been capable of destroying teams almost single-handedly, but Lomu had the ability to do just that.

Trying to tackle him head-on is virtually impossible, so you have to narrow his space and take him side-on, but then you run the risk of simply being outpaced. A weapon like Lomu would be a massive asset to any team you care to assemble because it can sometimes take three or four men finally to deal with his threat, by which time there is plenty of space elsewhere. Jonah also has good handling skills for a big guy. People sometimes dismiss him as a battering ram, but he is astonishingly light on his feet. It's been a major sadness for me that his health problems have interrupted his playing career such that we have maybe never really seen the kind of player he could have gone on to become. But I have loved watching him, repeatedly having been thrilled at the menace and mayhem he has brought to games, and he would be one of the first names down on my team sheet.

I hope we see more of Jonah in the years to come. He did not have a good Super 12 tournament in 2002 but if he can stay fit and healthy then I can nonetheless see him being one of the stars of the 2003 World Cup in Australia. It might be his swansong as an All Black before he cashes in by playing in England, but it would be wonderful to see him at his peak again in a major tournament.

Inside Lomu and Campese I have gone for two centres who lack the spectacular impact of that pair, but who, to my mind, were both magnificent players – Tim Horan and Philippe Sella. Horan was a youngster in the Australian side that won the World Cup in 1991. Eight years later and he was voted man-of-the-tournament at the 1999 event, which the Aussies won again, and that neatly sums up the man's stature – he has sustained the highest quality over many years.

Horan was impressive enough for the Wallabies in 1991,

when there was a lot more space to be found in the international game than there is now. But to have an even greater impact eight years later, when midfield space has shrunk as the game has changed, says so much about his ability. He never had electrifying pace, but he picked such beautiful lines when running that the gaps somehow opened up to him. Allied to that has been Horan's sound reading of the game and his superb temperament. In attack he always seemed to know the right option, while defensively he was a rock. If you were a captain then you would love to have 15 players like Tim Horan. He never had the exquisite skills of Jeremy Guscott and he certainly lacked the blinding pace of Brian O'Driscoll, but his all-round game and the way he could read defences in order to break them down, make him my natural selection at No. 12.

Everything Horan did on the field had the stamp of quality and in some ways he reminded me of Steve Fenwick who played in the centre for Wales during my time. The likes of Gerald Davies, Gareth Edwards and JJ Williams would catch the eye but Steve would be the one to supply the telling pass, finding the right angle at the right moment. Horan has been like that for Australia, although I'm sure Steve would admit that Horan has taken those kinds of skills and attributes on to a different level.

Outside of Horan, I have gone for Sella. A big, tall, powerful Frenchman, Sella also had pace and flair in abundance. Despite the fiercely committed, whole-hearted approach he brought to the French team, Sella was rarely injured. He often seemed indestructible, testament to which is his world record of 111 international caps earned between 1982 and 1995. Former French coach Jacques Fouroux summed up Sella neatly when he said he had 'the strength of a bull but the touch of a piano player'. He was a bustling, physical centre who would run through brick walls every time he pulled on the blue jersey, but he had that touch of finesse we have come to expect from the greatest French three-quarters. He had incredible leg and shoulder strength that allowed him to burst out of tackles, but then the presence of mind and necessary skill to make the decisive pass.

Sella packed in Test rugby when he knew he was in decline, but there was still more than enough left in the tank for him to have a successful time playing in England for Saracens. In the past 20 years I would say there have been few French backs with real longevity, but Sella was outstanding for over a decade and I cannot think of anyone better to put alongside Horan. I've combined the alert, pragmatic mind of an Aussie with the instinctive and athletic presence of one of France's greatest-ever players.

The centres that come close to this pair as favourites of mine over the past 20 years would be Guscott, Scott Gibbs, Walter Little, and Frank Bunce. O'Driscoll has the potential to be even better than any of them, including Sella and Horan, but he needs perhaps to confirm his world-class stature at a World Cup finals or on another Lions tour.

Obviously, I had to think long and hard about my outside-half. I narrowed it down to about a dozen and then came down to three – Michael Lynagh, Mark Ella and Jonathan Davies. Had Jonathan stayed in rugby union then I am convinced he could have become better than either of the two Aussies, but the fact is that he spent his best years playing rugby league. Instead of captaining the 1989 Lions to glory in Australia, Johnny was getting bashed around while he found his feet at Widnes. That leaves Ella and Lynagh. If my team were playing for high stakes, then Lynagh might shade it, but since they are only playing for my own pleasure I have gone for Mark Ella. He was such a natural player that the ball seemed to obey his every command. He might not have had the tactical control of Lynagh but my side is hopefully going to be so good that the only tactic will be to attack. When you have the likes of Campese and Lomu on the flanks, and Sella and Horan in midfield, it would be a criminal waste not to have a fly-half with the vision and creative flair to make the most of the talent around him. Ella had that in abundance.

As I said earlier, I realised Mark was something special the first time I saw him, when he toured the UK as a young kid with the Australian schoolboys. He played with such a natural feel for the game that his vision and his basic skills, such as his passing, were sublime, effortless. He was a joy to watch. He may not have had the devastating pace of Jonathan Davies, or the hard-nosed approach of Lynagh, but I wanted to go for a creator and distributor in order to get the utmost out of the great players I have chosen along the back line. Ella was just that.

The scrum-half position presented a tough choice. Wales have had more than their share of top quality scrum-halves, even since Gareth Edwards retired. Terry Holmes was a fabulous player and Robert Jones was a class act along with Rob Howley. Then there have been Nick Farr-Jones and George Gregan in Australia. But the No. 9 I've gone for is South Africa's Joost van der Westhuizen, who was at his peak between 1994 and 1999. He was the most competitive, most determined player I've ever seen – rugby's answer to Roy Keane. He scored tries out of nothing, often at crucial times when the Springboks were being completely outplayed. He was dynamic, fast and as slippery as a bar of soap. But like Keane, there was always an abrasive edge to his game. He could be a nasty little so-and-so and the more riled he became, the more determined he seemed to be to finish on the winning side.

At his best, Joost reminded me of Gareth Edwards. He was capable of the same surging runs, with fantastic acceleration that took him right into the opposition danger areas and often all the way to the try-line. Like Gareth, when he was five yards from the line he was virtually unstoppable. He perhaps did not have the precise passing ability of Edwards or Robert Jones, but the way he was virtually like a ninth forward, and this, combined with his other abilities, made him a devastating opponent. Like Blanco, Joost seemed to save his most destructive performances for when he was playing Wales, and he buried us so many times under his tries and sheer will to win. The Springboks were on the wane by the time of the 1999 World Cup, but Joost gave a vintage display to knock England out at the quarter-final stage and over the years he also turned it on against the All Blacks and the Aussies. So maybe Wales were not the only ones on the receiving end. He poses such an individual threat that to name him as my scrum-half should open up a bit more space outside him for the rest of my back line.

Now we are on to the forwards and when it comes to my front row I have a confession to make. As a player I remained blissfully unaware of the technical differences between a loose-head prop and a tight-head. To me they were all just prop forwards and whether or not they were holding up their own scrum, attacking the opposition prop, driving in towards the hooker, or trying to bring their opposite man lower to the ground, remained a complete mystery. As long as the ball came back on our side I didn't care what they got up to. Even now I'll admit that my knowledge of front row forward play is gleaned from conversations with the men who played there – blokes who worked at rugby's coalface game after game, like Graham Price, Bobby Windsor, Charlie Faulkner and Fran Cotton. It's a dark art in many ways, often shielded from prying eyes, and I honestly think that the only players who know what it's really all about are those who have played in that position.

I was aware as a player that Pricey was ahead of his time as a prop because he could run and handle like a back-row player, as well as kick and put in saving tackles. I saw those same attributes in my loosehead choice, Steve McDowell, the New Zealand All Black of the eighties. McDowell could scrummage well but he was also wonderfully mobile and had genuine pace. Typically of a Kiwi forward, he was always fit and strong enough to be up with the action, but that never seemed to drain his energy as a scrummager. I watched McDowell a good deal on the 1989 All Blacks tour of the UK and he was rock-solid and tremendously useful all around the field.

On the other side of my front trio I have gone for Christian Califano of France. Like McDowell, he had all the attributes any coach would ever require from a prop forward. Califano was immensely strong in the scrum, but remarkably light on his feet for such a big man and he handled quite beautifully. Like a number of truly exceptional props, Califano could play loose or tight-head; it made no real difference to him because he was such a natural. He was part of formidable front row at Toulouse and having made his reputation there he went on to become one of the most feared forwards around during the mid-nineties. Like McDowell, Califano could be found all over the field. I can remember one explosive run he made in a Test against Wales in Paris when he must have made 40 yards, a number of Welsh back-line players seemingly unable to keep up with him. It was that kind of ability that sets him apart from good solid performers at international level like Jason Leonard and David Young, and the South African Os du Randt.

My choice at hooker would also be my captain – the wonderful All Black Sean Fitzpatrick. Although I rate Keith Wood as one of the best hookers the game has ever seen, I cannot bring myself to pick anyone ahead of Fitzpatrick. In many ways, when Fitzpatrick first came on the scene, he was a typical New Zealand hooker. Hard, abrasive, a good scrummager, but not someone you would necessarily expect to see popping up all over the field. But as the game changed, Fitzpatrick changed with it. He became far more like a loose forward in broken play, offering support all over the field, running alongside his wings and taking passes to score tries in the corners. He never stopped and some of his displays for New Zealand in the Tri Nations were simply inspirational.

After the All Blacks had lost the 1995 World Cup Final to South Africa, Fitzpatrick led New Zealand back to that country on tour. He didn't talk about revenge. He just talked, in the quietly determined way of his that became his trademark, about wanting to win. He was superb in matches in Cape Town, Durban and Pretoria, the All Blacks winning all three of them. Despite their World Cup Final defeat, that New Zealand team was one of the very best, with Fitzpatrick proving a charismatic leader as well as superbly talented hooker.

If Fitzpatrick was an easy choice at hooker, then John Eales breezes into my favourite 15 in the second row. Eales was superb at the 1991 World Cup as part of the winning

263

Australian side, but eight years on, as captain of the 1999 World-Cup-winning side, he was still there and just as influential. That's the measure of a truly great player – consistency at the very highest level over a long period.

Eales was unquestionably the most naturally athletic forward I have ever seen pick up a rugby ball. He was very quick, had magnificent skills – especially his ability to leap and catch a ball dropping from any height at any angle – and he could even kick goals. He was a laid-back character off the field, a real gent, but that masked a fierce competitiveness when he strode on to the pitch. He did all the basics exceptionally well and I'll never forget the match-saving tackle he pulled off on Rob Andrew as the Wallabies hung on to win the 1991 World Cup. John could have played Test rugby in almost any position on the field, which is a remarkable thing to say about a tall, lanky lock-forward. The only question over his selection is who to pair him alongside in the second row: Ian Jones or Mark Andrews?

In many coaches' eyes, Jones would be too similar to Eales – another tall, stylish forward with a similar range of skills – and I can understand that view. The more traditional selection would be to complement Eales with a hard, dogged performer who would be a real nuisance at the front of the line-out. Andrews fits the bill perfectly, having fulfilled that role for the Springboks over many years, and for me he is very slightly ahead of England's Martin Johnson. But as this team is all about class and entertainment I've decided to go with Jones. My side is going to be so pacey around the field that once we have won the ball I want players who can keep up. Jones consistently did exactly that for the All Blacks, his influence on the side in many ways underrated. He hardly ever looked as though he was breaking sweat because he knew how to anticipate play; a marvellous talent to have on a rugby field. So Jones it is.

When it came to the back row I thought long and hard about several players before eventually deciding to leave them out – men like England's Peter Winterbottom and Neil Back, the Australian Simon Poidevan and another Aussie, David Wilson. I eventually went for three All Blacks; Wayne 'Buck' Shelford, Michael Jones and Zinzan Brooke. Together, these would give any coach pretty much everything he could ever want from a back row. The only possible problem would be if the game were scheduled for a Sunday, as Jones's religious convictions would not allow him to play. Since I'm the coach, however, I've decided we are a Saturday-only outfit.

Shelford was primarily a No. 8, but in order to accommodate both him and Brooke I've moved him across to blindside flanker, a position he occasionally occupied. Captain of the all-conquering 1989 All Blacks that stormed through the UK winning every game they played, Shelford was the heartbeat of the side. He was a hard man, who didn't tend to go in for the fancy skills of Zinzan, but every back row needs a real dog of war. Shelford was just that. On that 1989 tour, New Zealand played Swansea, a team that, full of youthful enthusiasm, rose magnificently to the occasion that day. The club side would have won had it not been for the sheer physical bravery and resilience of Buck Shelford. A few of the All Blacks forwards went missing in action, but Shelford was always in the heat of the battle, often putting his body on the ground to win ball despite some of the fiercest rucking from both sides I've ever seen. He took it all and didn't bat an eyelid. Shelford was ruthless in his own rucking but he always led from the front, always doing the very things himself that he demanded from his players. With Shelford in my side, I can afford the luxury of some of the ball-playing forwards like Brooke, Jones and Eales. Shelford and Fitzpatrick will be the men who hold everything together when the going gets tough.

Brooke is my No. 8 and I can safely say he was the most skilful back-row forward I have ever seen, with the widest range of skills. He could throw 40-yard passes, dummy and jink his way through defences, and even score the most amazing drop goals like the one against England in the semi-finals of the 1995 World Cup. Like Campese, he was a great crowd-pleaser. In some ways he went against the New Zealand tradition of hard, raw, no-nonsense men who simply served up the ball for others to play with. Zinzan wanted the ball in his own hands because he knew how well he could use it. In that sense, he had more the style of a Fijian or a Frenchman. But he could also do all the basics, as he showed in that extraordinary match against England. If he hadn't been able to do the bread-and-butter jobs like ruck, maul and carry the ball, then he would never have got anywhere near the All Blacks side, whatever other talents he was blessed with.

At open-side flanker I have plumped for Michael Jones, a flier with the basic speed of a three-quarter. Jones suffered a lot with injuries and illness, but at his peak he was a devastating forward. He would be down on the loose ball before anyone else, constantly setting up the next phase. And like all great open-side flankers, Jones had that sense of anticipation that gave him half a yard over his opposite number. He just edges out Josh Kronfeld, Winterbottom and the likes of Finlay Calder who was so effective for both Scotland and the Lions. There are so many other great back-row forwards I could have included; men like Neil Back, Lawrence Dallaglio, and, before their time in an England shirt, Mike Teague. But I've gone for the three New Zealanders, not because of any leaning towards that nation but simply because these three have set standards that left a lasting impression.

In fact, now that I have pencilled in the names from 1 to 15, I notice that there is something rather striking about my selection. I have not included a single player from any of the home countries. Not an Englishman, Welshman, Scotsman or Irishman to be seen. Perhaps if England win the 2003 World Cup I will change my mind. Players like Dallaglio, Martin Johnson, Jonny Wilkinson, even the rugby league convert Jason Robinson, would be hard to ignore. They are all close, but on both an individual and a team basis I'm pretty happy with the guys I've gone for. Take a look at the teamsheet.

1   Steve McDowell (New Zealand)
2   Sean Fitzpatrick (New Zealand)
3   Christian Califano (France)
4   Ian Jones (New Zealand)
5   John Eales (Australia)
6   Wayne Shelford (New Zealand)
7   Michael Jones (New Zealand)
8   Zinzan Brooke (New Zealand)

15   Serge Blanco (France)
14   David Campese (Australia)
13   Philippe Sella (France)
12   Tim Horan (Australia)
11   Jonah Lomu (New Zealand)
10   Mark Ella (Australia)
 9   Joost van der Westhuizen (South Africa)

I've included seven New Zealanders, four Australians, three Frenchmen and one South African. I might be labelled unpatriotic in some quarters, but even though so many British and Irish players have impressed me over the past two decades I simply cannot find a slot for them ahead of the men I've chosen.

Numerous players from the UK came close, and if I was choosing a Best of the Rest from inside the four home countries – a sort of Lions-qualified best 15 from the past 20 years – it would look something like this:

1 David Sole (Scotland)
2 Keith Wood (Ireland)
3   Jason Leonard (England)
4 Martin Johnson (England)
5 Wade Dooley (England)
6 Lawrence Dallaglio (England)
7 Peter Winterbottom (England)
8 Scott Quinnell (Wales)

15 Gavin Hastings (Scotland)
14 Ieuan Evans (Wales)
13 Jeremy Guscott (England)
12 Scott Gibbs (Wales)
11 Rory Underwood (England)
10 Jonathan Davies (Wales)
 9 Terry Holmes (Wales)

CHAPTER 16

Day Jobs and Night Terrors

I expect to receive a sackful of letters from outraged fans everywhere who cannot understand why their favourite player has not made either of my favourite 15s. I'll look forward to them. Rugby is about opinions, and the moment a writer, broadcaster or pundit stops provoking a reaction then it probably means people have stopped caring what he or she thinks. I've been commenting on the game since I retired in 1981 and I must admit I enjoy the arguments and debates it can spark. Sunday wouldn't be Sunday without someone or other ringing the house to tell me what a load of rubbish I've come out with in the paper.

Very occasionally, the business can get nasty. JJ Williams once made critical remarks about Neil Jenkins following a particularly awful Welsh defeat to Scotland at Murrayfield. The newspaper concerned took a few liberties in its headlines and the result was a rather uncomfortable reception for JJ when he arrived back at Cardiff Airport and bumped into some Pontypridd supporters, who were obviously very loyal to Neil. For some time after, Ponty fans kept gunning for JJ, and the abuse he received the next time he went to Sardis Road overstepped the mark.

I've taken some stick myself at various places. Pontypool fans never let me forget that I suggested John Perkins should be dropped by Wales and I had another rather frosty reception at Pooler, one day, for what they perceived as a slight against their folk hero, David Bishop. Neath fans in Paris once told me to stay out of the way of their prop, Brian Williams, and Swansea supporters are rarely shy in telling me what they think of my remarks about their club. But it has all been pretty good-natured stuff, banter rather than anything more sinister. Despite all the harsh words and blunt truths I've never once been threatened with physical violence – either by a fan or a player – which is about as much as you can ask for as a professional critic.

During my days as a player, I never contemplated working in the media. It just happened. After I retired I was invited to offer my thoughts for a column in the *South Wales Evening Post*, ghost-written by their rugby correspondent, the late Ron Griffiths. Ron was great fun and the fact that he was a Swansea Jack and I a Turk from Llanelli made for some memorable arguments whenever the two clubs met. I then had a lucky break when Onllwyn Brace, the former Wales international who had become Head of Sport for BBC Wales, offered me some work as part of their TV commentary team. Initially, I found live TV terrifying as well as stimulating. The nerves before a programme were as bad as anything I suffered as a player. But like everything else, the more you do it, the more confident you become and in the end it helped provide me with some of the buzz on match-day that I was missing as an ex-player. I was also extremely fortunate to be able to work with some consummate old pros of the business like David Parry Jones, our commentator, and the producer Dewi Griffiths.

Working for BBC Wales, either on radio or TV, has continued to help plug the gap left in my Saturday afternoons since I retired from playing. There is never a real substitute for being out there on the field, but working with a dedicated bunch of people who are all trying to bring the sport to life for a wider audience has its own excitement and disciplines, just like playing. Sometimes broadcasting can be hard work, but on other occasions it flows like the best action on the pitch. Getting around the grounds also keeps me in touch with teams, coaches and players, and provides another angle for my newspaper columns. It's easy for a former player to sit sniping on the sidelines in the press, but if you are still around the sport then you obviously have a clearer understanding of the modern game. I've written for the *South Wales Evening Post*, the *Daily Star*, and the *Sunday Mirror* and I've enjoyed working for them all. The popular tabloids are not normally seen as rugby papers, but I've got nothing but praise for the *Sunday Mirror* because they have given the game extensive coverage in Wales where it means a great deal to the working man. They have also never tried to influence anything I say, allowing me a free rein to cover what I've considered the important issues of the day. I know of other columnists who have sometimes been led by the nose, but my experience has always been that the column was my space in which I could say whatever I wanted.

Perhaps I would have found even greater fulfilment – and certainly stayed closer to the action – if I had gone into coaching.

But apart from the fact that the regulations concerning amateurs prevented me from doing so for many years, I'm not sure I would have felt entirely comfortable. I have coached many players on a one-to-one basis when I've been asked, but that's always been as far as I've wanted to go. I have huge respect for the likes of Gareth Jenkins, Dean Richards, Rob Andrew, Dai Young and all of the other coaches operating in high-pressure jobs at some of the most demanding clubs in Europe. But I'm not sure I'd want to swap places with them and take that level of stress home with me every evening, especially when the livelihoods of many are dependent on the whims and wishes of board members who sometimes know nothing about the game. I might make the odd howler on air or in print, but neither keeps me awake at night. I spent 16 seasons worrying about Llanelli when I was a player, which is probably long enough for anyone in one lifetime.

In a sense, I was lucky when I first picked up a microphone. By the time I began working in TV and radio most of my contemporaries as players had also retired. It meant I didn't have to criticise my own mates. I was able to keep a distance between me and the players I was discussing and felt, as a result, that anything I said should not be taken too personally. Over the years I know that I have offended players, making some feel uncomfortable and occasionally angry, but I have always felt I needed to be truthful. If I wasn't giving an honest opinion, then there was no point in me offering an opinion at all. Professionalism changed a lot of things in 1995, one being the status of players in the eyes of others. They are now hired tradesmen and if the quality of their work is not up to scratch they should expect to be criticised. It doesn't mean those dishing out the criticism think any less of them as people.

I find it particularly hard not to be critical when I watch Wales lose to opponents I feel we should beat. Every international match I attend, I want Wales to win and to do so in style. When we don't win, I feel there is nothing wrong with a discussion and an examination of why it didn't happen. In recent times, certain players and coaches have tried to dismiss all criticism by labelling those who dare to question them as 'negative'. It was a favourite tactic of Graham Henry. But I care so deeply about Wales that I think the truly negative thing would be to pretend everything is okay when it obviously isn't. All successful teams will vouch for the fact that self-criticism leads to improvement and I see nothing wrong with similar criticism being expressed by people outside of the team environment. So long as it's genuine and not malicious then it can be a positive influence. Sometimes truth hurts, but it's still the truth.

As I've said, professionalism has altered the picture. No current international player has to go out on to the field on the back of a night shift with the police or the fire brigade. None has just finished a shift down the mine or on a factory floor. If players make mistakes it's because of poor preparation or possibly because the physical demands on them from the game itself have not been carefully thought out. But it's no longer because they've still got coal dust in their eyes or an aching back.

When I was growing up in Felinfoel, everyone who played rugby at club and country level did it as a pastime. It was not a career. Often it would conflict with work and sometimes players would turn up late for Llanelli matches because they had been down the pit or driving a truck. I can remember playing games over at Newport or Pontypool where team-mates

273

would arrive late and come into the dressing rooms looking absolutely knackered because they had just done a hard day's physical work. They would also have driven like a madman across the country in order to make the kick-off. Today's players arrive at games by luxury coach having spent the week preparing for the game, so sloppy standards on the pitch are down to no one but themselves.

I always had to combine playing for Llanelli and Wales with a variety of jobs throughout my career and that could often be difficult. My father had worked in the local steelworks and at 15 I followed in his footsteps. I was a kind of odd-job boy, fetching and carrying for the men working the furnaces. I had never been the keenest academic at school and the job seemed like the natural thing to do because steel was the biggest employer in the area. It was either that or work down the mines strung out along the Gwendraeth valley.

I have to say I loved it. The works were full of men who either played for or supported Llanelli RFC and rugby dominated our conversation. I would listen to the older workmates chat about the game and the great characters within it, just as I had listened as a small kid when my father sneaked me into the local pub. It was inspiring stuff for an impressionable youngster. But the steelworks was never a secure form of employment and redundancies were a regular event. I left after a while and worked in a car plant, but that, too, hit hard times and I soon found myself back at the steelworks. As my standard of rugby improved, then so did my network of contacts and potential employers. In my mid-twenties I had a variety of jobs as a sales rep, for Courage Breweries and other firms. One job as a rep with an oil company lasted precisely five days, that being the time it took for me to realise my role there was less about gaining new business and more about picking up arrears from existing customers. I had no wish to be a debt-collector, so I left.

A job as a rep was the fashionable choice for a Welsh international rugby player in the seventies. There were loads of us. The money was generally good, the work was not too strenuous, and your employers were usually fairly flexible in accommodating your rugby demands, because your profile as a player was important. Oh, and you had a nice new car. It certainly beat working down a mine, but being a sales rep was never really me. I didn't have the patter, the bluff, the ability to move from breezy chit-chat to clinching a deal. I didn't use the jargon. I would rather chat rugby and then just leave. I suppose I just wasn't pushy enough to be a salesman. Many's the time I squirmed as I listened to other blokes pleading to customers how they needed a deal in order to feed their kids.

I was grateful for those various jobs, though. They enabled me to put food on the table and allowed me to combine working with playing rugby. Pat and I raised two boys, Steven and James, who were both sports mad like their father, and it was a happy home with good friends and family close by. Towards the end of my playing career, I went into business with a friend and we opened a sports shop in Llanelli. It was reasonably successful but not as much as we had hoped. I had started to do the occasional bit of after-dinner speaking on the rugby circuit, which was great fun and brought in a few extra quid, and then I went back to work as a rep for a chemical company, but it was not until 1990 that I finally found a job that gave and continues to give me real satisfaction. Working for the local authority in Llanelli as a sports development officer allows me to combine my primary passion, sport, with doing something

275

I feel is worthwhile and important – trying to ensure that all young people in our area have the widest possible opportunities to take part in, and enjoy, sport. It's a link-up between Carmarthenshire County Council and the Sports Council and as officers we liaise with all the schools and colleges in the area.

That suits me perfectly because I feel very at home in a teaching and coaching environment, around kids who often need the stimulus and opportunities sport can provide. Rugby in Wales merely reflects what is happening in our schools throughout the country. Kids are desperate to get involved in sport at the age of nine or ten, but the challenge is to keep them interested by the time they get to mid-teens when other interests kick in and peer pressure can drive them away. The real buzz for me is when a young boy or girl comes through our local schools and goes on to play sport at an elite level. I was thrilled when Simon Jones, the young Glamorgan fast bowler, made his debut for England, but I get as much satisfaction from seeing a young girl from my area represent her county or country at hockey. Sport can give children a wonderful sense of self-worth and achievement, and it dismays me to see so many educationalists nowadays who don't put a high enough priority on kids getting out into the fresh air and doing some physical activity.

I've enjoyed every minute spent working as a sports development officer and the truth is I wished I'd moved into the field years before I did. I'm also very glad that the job involves all sports rather than just rugby. Not only would a constant diet of rugby drive me round the bend, but I also love so many other sports – especially cricket, boxing and soccer. If I hadn't been a rugby player then I might have done more to try to follow my dreams of playing in midfield for Manchester United or opening the batting for Glamorgan. When I played for Llanelli, and even for Wales, the first thing I wanted to find out after showering and getting changed was how United had got on. I still follow their results and watch them whenever I get the chance, but I'll admit the love affair has cooled a bit since my younger days. I think it's the number of foreigners in the side. I just don't feel as attached to them as I used to. I shudder to think what it must be like being a Chelsea fan.

You can admire sports stars from any part of the world, but real emotion, I believe, is saved for those from your own community. That's certainly the way I feel. I was in awe of Muhammad Ali, but I loved Howard Winstone because he was fighting for Wales. All my family loved boxing, including my father and my father-in-law, and we all crowded around a black-and-white TV set to see Howard become world feather-weight champion in 1968. Before that, I had listened on a crackling radio set to those three brilliant and unforgettable fights against the Mexican Vicente Saldivar, and like so many other people in Wales I was captivated by this proud man from Merthyr who was putting our nation on the map. Howard was a genius of a fighter, someone who literally had to box clever and work out how to beat an opponent through sheer skill, because he lacked the big punching power to knock people out. Away from the ring, he was a lovely, modest man with a sharp dry wit, a character who would always enliven any sporting gathering. When Howard died a couple of years ago, Wales lost one of its greatest-ever sportsmen.

There's something about boxing that fascinates me. It's the combination of hard, sometimes brutal combat with the mutual respect that exists among the fighters. There is obvi-ously a nasty side to the sport, but the pride and dignity of boxers at every level is remarkable. Between fights, I once climbed into a ring on a bill in Merthyr to receive a miner's lamp presented to me by the great trainer and manager Eddie Thomas, in recognition of a Welsh Triple Crown. The heat, the lights, the noise, the smells – the whole atmosphere inside that ring – was incredible. My legs almost buckled under-neath me. It was far more intimidating than anything I had ever witnessed on a rugby field. They say boxing is the hardest game, and I reckon they're not kidding. Winstone, Joe Erskine, Brian Curvis, Johnny Owen the Matchstick Man, Colin Jones, Steve Robinson, Robbie Regan and Joe Calzaghe – all these Welsh boxers have captivated me over the years and I've enjoyed meeting and chatting about the sport at functions with people like Jim Watt and John Conteh. They've all been great company.

Just as Welsh boxers have given me so much pride and pleas-ure over the years, so have Welsh cricketers. My love of cricket began as a young kid when my uncle would take me to St Helen's in Swansea to watch Glamorgan. I was hooked straight away by the skill of the players and the ease with which they handled all aspects of the game. They made it look effort-less. As my rugby career developed in the seventies I became friendly with two Glamorgan players, the brothers Alan and Eifion Jones. Alan scored over 1,000 runs a season for 23 consecutive years, and scored 52 first-class centuries, and yet incredibly he was never capped by England. It was the same with one of Glamorgan's greatest-ever bowlers, Don Shepherd. Those two were a match for any cricketer at county level, and yet they were continually ignored when it came to Test selection. Their absence confirmed to me what I had always sus-pected; cricket at the highest level is riddled with snobbery and prejudice. The Jones brothers were Welsh and simply beyond the pale for the England selectors, who probably thought their inclusion might lower the tone. Of course, Tony Lewis broke the mould and actually captained England, but he had to become part of the establishment – through his Cambridge education – in order to be accepted by it. He then had to prove he was a good enough cricketer.

For others, though, the unfashionability of Glamorgan counted against them. Matthew Maynard should have played many more times for England. So should Steve Watkin. The prejudice has, I think, lessened in more recent years, and Robert Croft has become Glamorgan's most-capped England player. Simon Jones, I'm sure, will go on to play many matches for England. But I've always had the feeling that Welsh boys have suffered because they had no international outlet of their own. I know Crofty considers England in cricket terms to be like playing for Great Britain, but they're still called England and there's a great deal of historical baggage to be moved aside before Welsh boys get their fair turn.

I missed Glamorgan's trip to Lord's for the Gillette Cup Final in 1977 because of rugby commitments, and I vowed then that I'd never go to Lord's until Glamorgan went back. I had to wait 23 years but finally made it for the Benson and Hedges Cup Final against Gloucestershire. I went with my two grown-up sons, Steven and James – both cricket fanatics – and it really was one of the proudest days of my life. When Matthew Maynard scored a hundred and the Glamorgan supporters broke into full voice there were tears in my eyes. And there were more tears when we eventually lost the match to Gloucestershire.

County cricketers remind me so much of rugby players from my own generation. They play hard, but they make time to socialise and enjoy talking about the game over a pint as much as playing it. That has always been part of the fun of rugby for me: the warm friendships earned and kept over time. I still try and keep in touch with many of the people I played with and against – the likes of David Duckham, Willie John McBride and Fran Cotton. Luckily for me, the success Wales, the Lions and the Barbarians enjoyed during my time means there are plenty of reunion events, dinners and get-togethers to attend. Together with occasional invitations to speak at various rugby clubs around the country, I manage to stay in touch. All this, as you can imagine, means a fair bit of travel, but the journey that sticks in my mind was, ironically, just yards from my home. It was on the eve of the Millennium and it very nearly cost me my life.

New Year's Eve has always been one of my favourite times of the year. It's a time for getting together with the family and close friends, and counting your blessings. On December 31 1999, Pat, Steven, James and I had spent the evening with close friends and family. It was not long after Pat's mother had died and I was overjoyed that the boys, both young men in their early twenties, had made the effort to attend a family gathering instead of going out with their mates. We enjoyed a wonderful meal and saw the New Year in with a few drinks, all except for Pat who was driving. At about 3 a.m. we left for the short journey home and it wasn't long before I nodded off, with Pat driving and the boys in the back. The next thing I knew there was a terrific bump, a screeching sound, and all I could feel was a nasty burning sensation on the side of my face and head. I could hear screams and sensed there was panic around me and yet I felt strangely removed from it all, as if I was in a dream.

The tyre on our BMW had suffered a blowout and Pat had been unable to prevent the car from coming off the road. We had hit the pavement and clipped a hedge, and the car had finished sliding along the road on its side with the passenger door trapped against the road. As the car had overturned the wing mirror had folded in, smashing the side window, with the result that my head had been scraped along the tarmac as we skidded to a halt. Pat and the boys somehow managed to climb out and I was vaguely aware of Steven cradling my head and talking to me. That and a fair bit of blood.

Some late-night revellers stopped their cars and in the general panic our car was flipped back off its side, something no ambulanceman would have recommended because of the danger of neck injuries. It could have been very dangerous because I was bounced around like a rag doll, but thankfully I had suffered nothing too serious. The police had been given a 'code black', meaning they were expecting fatalities, and so they had closed the road, but within a few minutes we were all on our way to Prince Philip Hospital, Llanelli, in the back of two ambulances, thankfully still breathing. There were a lot of concerned faces, and Pat was convinced I'd been killed, but once I'd been patched up I came round properly and it dawned on me just how lucky I'd been. Having been dragged along with my head hanging out of the side window, all I had suffered were a few cuts and bruises. I was still groggy, but also still merry from a fair few glasses of wine. The conclusion to a bizarre evening came when I recognised the doctor who stitched my face. He was the same medic who had put stitches in my foot just days before my final appearance for Llanelli 18 years earlier. Pat and the boys were fine, although very shaken. Once they realised I was going to be okay, however, the sight of me lying in bed with bandages wrapped around my head didn't look quite so alarming. I cannot overstate my gratitude for everything the doctors, nurses and emergency services did for me then, or my admiration for all they do.

God was on my side that night. When I saw the state of the car afterwards it made my blood run cold. It was a crumpled heap. One or all of us could easily have been killed. As it was, I was back home within a day or so. It's fair to say that my experience that night changed my life. I'm far more relaxed about things that don't really matter and spend more time thinking about things that do. It sounds trite to say that it put everything into perspective, but that is exactly what happened. It made me aware that my family comes first and everything else – work, rugby, everything – is a very distant second. Pat has always been so strong and supportive through the good times and the bad times and she means everything to me. I played rugby for 16 years and she backed me every step of the way. I must have spent 10 summers away from home during those years, but Pat coped with everything and has never resented the sacrifices she made. I know that I'm a very lucky man to have met her and to have enjoyed such a happy, contented family life with her and my two sons, James and Steven. So many times over the years people have asked me why I haven't moved to Cardiff or somewhere nearer London, but the truth is that I'm blissfully happy where I am – within a mile or so of where I grew up in Felinfoel. I look out of my windows across the two beautiful Swiss Valley reservoirs and when I go for a walk I follow the same paths and cross the same fields as when I was a kid. My best pals – John Lloyd, Geoff 'The Barber' Sherlock and Dai Dunn – live nearby and these are the same blokes I want to share a pint and chat rugby with whether we are in Llanelli or in Brisbane. Good friends mean so much to me and the help that Pat and I have received over the years from Huw and Carol Owen, Wynford and Pat Thomas, and others I could mention, has been wonderful.

CHAPTER 17

A Final Plea

My biggest fear for Welsh rugby is that the future will continue to be dwarfed by the past. In the 20 years since I stopped playing there has been a steady decline, the smooth line of the graph only occasionally ruffled by an upward blip. Looking back into the past has become a national bad habit – a bit like smoking, indulged in for the comfort it brings because you feel unable to face the here and now. We know we ought to quit the habit, but we need something positive to focus on in order to stop the craving.

Our younger-age-group rugby is a continual source of encouragement for me. Wales so often beat England and France at U21 or U19 level and even prove a match for the likes of New Zealand, South Africa and Australia. But somehow the promise is stubbed out, and at senior level we seem to be losing touch with those same opponents. Even more worrying for me than our results at national level are the falling numbers of young players keen to play the game. So many youth sides are struggling for players, so many village teams are teetering on the brink of collapse, and yet the appetite for the game among the Welsh public, and the yearning for success at international level, seems to me as strong as ever.

It is obvious to anyone with even the smallest trace of financial expertise that there is a cash crisis in the game in Wales. There has been since the game went pro in 1995, but now it has reached critical proportions at both the top and bottom ends of the game. Clubs that should be offering merely social rugby and a fun route into the game for kids are paying weekly wages to players who don't deserve a bean. I'm not saying that as a bitter old player who performed in the amateur era; my days have long gone, but it's crazy that clubs are too broke to afford decent pitches and training facilities for kids because they are paying out anything from £25 to £400 a week each to players who aren't worth a cent. It happens in my own village club of Felinfoel and it's a curse we seem unable to do anything about. Like a few other clubs in our area, we are having to take drastic measures in order to survive. For us this means selling our clubhouse, but some clubs have gone even farther and sold their grounds. Village teams that have existed for over a hundred years are having to sell their biggest assets in order to pay players of extremely limited ability. It's madness and it has to stop. Every village club should offer players stimulating rugby and the best facilities they can manage, but they should not be offering money. It requires a collective will throughout the lower divisions to get their priorities sorted out.

At the other end of the scale some of our biggest clubs are struggling to keep their heads above water. Swansea would have ceased to exist as a top-rank professional rugby club in the summer of 2002 had not a couple of businessmen changed their minds about cutting off the funding. Peter Thomas, the millionaire chairman of Cardiff, has slashed the budget. Ebbw Vale were forced to make players redundant this year or else go under and every other club in the premier division is living beyond its means. If it were not for the indulgence and loyalty of a handful of wealthy individuals, plus the faith shown by BBC Wales, then professional club rugby in Wales would have gone bankrupt long ago. There are just a few supports keeping the whole thing upright, and if any of them were kicked away then the rugby industry in Wales would fall flat on its face.

Crazy as it sounds, both tiers of the game – top and bottom – seem to have a mutual death wish, each blaming the other for all the ills in the game. The big clubs demand greater spoils, the small club wants a 'democracy' where they continue to have final say over the running of the professional game. It's completely ridiculous. Don't these little clubs realise that they are out of their depth and that the marketing, promotion and administration of the pro game must be left to the professionals? Don't the big clubs realise that without grass roots, no fresh talent will emerge and the game will die? The situation needs real leadership from the Welsh Rugby Union, but they have shown none. The general committee members on that body seem more concerned with clinging on to power, whatever it takes. That much was made obvious by the way they muddied the waters after the Sir Tasker Watkins Report, which addressed many of the problems I've mentioned.

With the club game in crisis it's no wonder Wales cannot build a successful Test team. On the international front, France and England have moved miles ahead of the rest in the Six Nations and it's only Ireland that seem to have clung on to their coat tails. This is very, very bleak news indeed for the future of Welsh rugby. My doomsday scenario is that Wales continue to be thrashed by England on a regular basis until even the most sadistic England fan becomes bored by the whole business. Once they get fed up and can't be bothered to sell out Twickenham, once the advertisers and sponsors think the public are losing interest in a wholly predictable fixture, then England will simply cut and run; and perhaps they will take France with them.

Are the BBC really going to stump up cash for a tournament involving Wales, Scotland, Ireland and Italy? I don't think so. Look at the way soccer's home internationals bit the dust once England felt they had outgrown them. They used to provide the climax to the football season and matches would be played in front of full houses. It gave the Welsh FA a regular meal ticket and provided Scottish football with their biggest day of the season, but once England pulled out it was starvation rations all round. What was great about the England–Scotland soccer internationals was that they were tense and unpredictable. But the decline of Scottish football since the demise of that fixture has been catastrophic. A team that once used to frighten, and often beat, England at Wembley now cannot beat the Faroe Islands.

I used to think the Five Nations – or Six Nations as it now is – would go on forever, but now it's in real danger. Unless the Celtic nations can improve their challenge then every economic and commercial pressure will be applied to make England and France seek new avenues. So far the Tri-Nations countries – Australia, New Zealand and South Africa – have resisted approaches from eager beavers within the RFU. But the more Wales, Scotland and Ireland lose matches and credibility, then

287

the greater will be the pressure to force change. There are already murmurings of discontent from the South that the Tri Nations needs spicing up, that fans are getting bored by only three teams. What better way of spicing it up than by introducing two new forces from the north – England and France? We are entering crunch time. Unless the old championship regains some of its lustre over the next year or so, then I reckon the game's up. It'll be a dead duck.

My two sons, Steven and James, enjoy their trips to Murrayfield and Lansdowne Road to watch Wales play. It's an event, a weekend outing. But if the tournament becomes badly devalued by the absence of England and France, would they still want to go to watch a second-class tournament? Would they even want to watch the home games? If the fans stopped going then the income coming into Welsh rugby would vanish. So, too, would any hope of ever rebuilding our national game to get back among the elite.

England are miles ahead of Wales at the moment; in terms of fitness, preparation, organisation and even flair they have gone way beyond us. When the English players came off the park after the 2002 fixture against us they looked as if they hadn't even had to break sweat. They have a depth to their domestic game which would make them favourites to beat Wales at Twickenham even if they put out their third team. That is the size of the challenge for Wales and it's one that we all have to respond to now before it's too late. It requires the clubs, both big and small, to put aside their differences and work together for the good of the national team and the national game. Most of all, it requires vision and direction from the senior figures within the WRU such as Glanmor Griffiths, David Pickering, Dennis Gethin and Terry Cobner.

The early evidence from the 2002–03 season at club level is that our clubs in Wales are simply not good enough. We need to improve, urgently, and everyone in the game is aware of that. Poor results have again sparked debate about the structure of the game in Wales and there is much talk of cutting the numbers of clubs, or even of mergers. I have come round to the view that we do need to reduce the number of top clubs, but this is such an emotional issue it has to be handled sensibly and sensitively. Five top clubs in Wales would be ideal, but we need to know the intentions of the Irish provinces and the Scottish districts. A full-blown Celtic Super 12 tournament – along the lines of the Super 12 in New Zealand, Australia and South Africa – would be a big step forward towards the recovery of our game. A reduction to five select teams in Wales – some have dubbed them 'Superclubs' – would concentrate the better players at those clubs and offer some stability for the future, as everyone would know which teams would be competing in Europe. Those that don't make Superclub status would concentrate on purely domestic rugby and leave Europe and the Celtic League to the big five. But the Scots and the Irish have to be on board. There is no point in a reduction if those five teams end up playing only against each other.

We also have to stick with clubs, not provincial or regional sides. Club rugby is in our blood and is part of our culture. You cannot just impose provinces from out of thin air and expect the fans to take to them. I know of so many people, fans of different clubs, who say they would simply stop going to rugby if their club was swallowed up by a region or district with which they felt no sense of identity. I also think there cannot be too much wrong with some aspects of our club game

289

if Llanelli can be involved in three epic matches against the European champions Leicester, as we saw last season.

The big question, then, is who should be in the top five. I don't pretend to know the answer to that. All I know is that it's going to be a painful outcome for some. There are many considerations, but the overriding one has to be to provide a successful national team. If Wales are strong, then so many other areas of the game can flourish. For the fans of Newport, the most important thing is that they beat Cardiff. For Swansea fans it's that they beat Llanelli. But all fans have to realise that nothing is more important in the long run than giving Wales a chance of beating England. That is what will spark a national revival in our game as opposed to a resurgence of one or two clubs.

Traditionally, there have been four big clubs in Wales and it seems to me that those four have to be included. Cardiff is the capital and the biggest city in Wales. Swansea also boasts a major population area in the western part of South Wales and the same goes for Newport in the east. Historically, Llanelli have always matched the performances of those three even if they cannot lay claim to the same population base. But Llanelli's support extends much farther than just the town, having come to serve the whole of West Wales beyond Swansea. So that leaves one more place for either Neath, Pontypridd, Bridgend, Ebbw Vale or Caerphilly. Ebbw Vale have a proud history but they are struggling nowadays both on and off the field. Caerphilly have done brilliantly to rise from obscurity, but they have no significant support base. Neath, Pontypridd and Bridgend all have very strong claims and I hear constantly from their fans that Llanelli have only survived in recent years because my club was bailed out by the WRU some years ago.

They're right. But it happened and you cannot turn back the clock.

So who should be the fifth club? I honestly couldn't say and I'm glad it's not my decision. I just hope they set out the criteria for all the clubs and that they're fair: that means based on population, support base and finance, together with past and present performance. Everyone has to accept the ground rules and then someone needs to decide who measures up. But my final plea is that for those outside the selected five there has to be a way back. These places cannot be stuck in stone and if any club proves its worth, on and off the field, then there has to be scope for a rethink.

It perhaps says much about the men in charge of the WRU that when Steve Hansen tried to enter this debate on BBC Wales he was quickly rapped on the knuckles and told to keep his mouth shut. The Wales coach, it seems, is not allowed to have his say on the future of Welsh rugby. Instead of acting like fourth-rate officers of the KGB, the WRU should realise that the national coach has to be at the centre of such a debate because he's the one who ultimately carries the can. If Wales fail then Hansen will pay for failure with his job.

History suggests that Hansen will fail unless there is genuine and radical change within Welsh rugby, of the kind we haven't seen for thirty years. But from what I have seen of the bloke so far, I have to say I've been reasonably impressed. I wasn't in favour of another New Zealander being given the job following the resignation of Graham Henry. I felt a Welshman would move us forward more quickly because he would have a better understanding of what needed to be done. Henry had moved us away from narrow insularity but I felt it was time to build on that with some local knowledge. But Hansen has brought

291

something back into Welsh rugby which went missing in the last days under Henry – honesty. Hansen has none of the personal charm and charisma of Henry. In fact, he sometimes looks every inch the dour New Zealand police sergeant from the provinces that he was in a previous existence. But he gives it to you straight and he works hard. I believe he also gives it to the players straight and expects them to work as hard as he does. That's not a bad starting point.

I watched Hansen closely on the Wales tour to South Africa in the summer of 2002. He gave responsibility to senior players such as Colin Charvis and they responded. The players seem to respect him and they have given committed, whole-hearted performances for their country. You cannot claim the results have been spectacular because they haven't. That is obviously the next stage for Hansen, perhaps his biggest challenge. He must turn honest endeavour into victories. If he doesn't, then a collective lack of confidence will undermine whatever progress has been made and the momentum of defeats will carry their own inevitable consequences.

In South Africa it was noticeable that players arrived on time, looked smart and eager, and behaved themselves impeccably. They were disciplined and hardworking. They lost both Tests, but should have won the second, and they generally showed they had the makings of a decent side, coached by a decent man. Hansen isn't interested in all the trappings, as Henry was. Where Henry would be out making documentaries and writing newspaper columns, I get the impression Hansen would be perfectly happy if he was the most anonymous man in Wales. He just wants to coach and that's it.

It's good to see that some of that attitude is rubbing off on his players. Ben Evans, the Swansea prop, went through a stage

when he behaved as though he was some celebrity actor from a
TV soap. He was always pictured in the newspapers hugging
people or kissing babies – sometimes even after he had been
substituted – or else he was on TV or radio telling everyone
how much it hurt when people criticised the Welsh players.
I don't want that from a prop forward! I want him to be
hard-edged and mean. I don't want to hear him bleating about
how nasty the critics are. I expect him to go out there and
murder the English front row and then turn around and stick
two fingers up at the people who doubted him. Happily, Ben
has changed and he got down to some hard graft in South
Africa, which resulted in some of the best rugby he's played
for years. Ben has got the ability to be one of the best props
in Europe and it looks as though he's finally determined to
seize his opportunity. If only Darren Morris, his Swansea
team-mate, could knuckle down and get his fitness levels sorted
out then we would have two outstanding players in the Welsh
front row. The same goes for Craig Quinnell. Instead of
complaining about what a hard time they are given by the
Welsh public, these boys should all get out there and prove
they are top professional athletes ready to do a job for their
country.

The challenge for Hansen is to get the very best out of all
these players as we head towards the 2003 World Cup.
Hopefully, those in charge of the game will give him the environment he needs in which to succeed. If he improves fitness,
skill levels, attitude and all those other things that mean the
difference between success and failure then he will have gone
a long way in the right direction. If he doesn't, then he will
recognise as much and I'm sure he won't hang around. I, for
one, have had enough of losing matches by 30 or 40 points to

England or whoever else, and enough of national coaches telling me how 'positive' certain aspects of the performance were. It's all about winning and it's time Wales started winning again.

If the best foundations were laid, then I'm convinced Wales can emerge as a major rugby force once again. We saw evidence for that during the ten-match winning streak of 1999. Our schools and youth teams continue to deliver up players of huge potential. Gavin Henson, the young Swansea fly-half, was voted International Young Player of the Year last season and there are many others with big futures ahead of them. I was very impressed with a whole crop of young talented boys who went on that Wales tour to South Africa: Craig Morgan, Rhys Williams, Dwayne Peel, Michael Owen and Richard Parks. Hansen can build a formidable team around players like these. With a few victories under its belt, a young Welsh team would grow in confidence and we could all be confident for the future.

But time is running out. A sustained revival has to start happening very soon. Some ex-players, ex-coaches and officials have already lost faith and the big danger must be that the Welsh public will lose faith too such that we end up playing in front of a half-empty Millennium Stadium.

It still means everything to me that Wales are strong again. Rugby was my passion and my obsession as a young kid and it still is today. The game gave me self-confidence as a young man, respect, some wonderful lifelong friendships, and hours and hours of fun. I know I was extremely lucky to play for Wales in an era when everything came together, and the past 20 years have left me more frustrated than I could ever have imagined. There are friends of mine who tell me that I'll never see another Welsh Grand Slam; that 1978 was my last and Wales' last. I don't believe them. I suppose I'm an optimist as well as an obsessive.

PHIL BENNETT

Career Statistics

FOR LLANELLI	Games	T	C	PG	DG	Pts
Debut: 12 Nov 66	412	132	523	292	42	2532
Last game: 18 Apr 81						

SUMMARY	Games	T	C	PG	DG	Pts
Wales Tests	29	4	18	36	2	166
Lions Tests	8	1	2	10	2	44
Wales XV	9	5	27	10	0	104
Lions XV	19	3	30	40	2	192
Barbarians	20	6	47	18	3	181
Llanelli	412	132	523	292	42	2532
TOTALS	**497**	**151**	**647**	**406**	**51**	**3219**

KEY
T= Tries
C = Conversions
PG = Penalty Goal
DG = Drop Goal

KEY

FNC = Five Nations Championship
WRU Cup = Welsh Rugby Union Cup

TESTNO = Wales's match number since they began in 1881
MIN = Total minutes on the field of play

CAP	DATE	TEST NO	VENUE	OPPONENTS
WALES TEST MATCHES				
1	22 Mar 69	279	Stade Colombes – Paris	France
	12 Apr 69	280	National Stadium – Cardiff	England
2	24 Jan 70	284	National Stadium – Cardiff	South Africa
3	7 Feb 70	285	National Stadium – Cardiff	Scotland
	28 Feb 70	286	Twickenham	England
4	4 Apr 70	288	National Stadium – Cardiff	France
	16 Jan 71	289	National Stadium – Cardiff	England
	6 Feb 71	290	Murrayfield	Scotland
	15 Jan 72	293	Twickenham	England
5	5 Feb 72	294	National Stadium – Cardiff	Scotland
	25 Mar 72	295	National Stadium – Cardiff	France
6	2 Dec 72	296	National Stadium – Cardiff	New Zealand
7	20 Jan 73	297	National Stadium – Cardiff	England
8	3 Feb 73	298	Murrayfield	Scotland
9	10 Mar 73	299	National Stadium – Cardiff	Ireland
10	24 Mar 73	300	Parc des Princes – Paris	France
11	10 Nov 73	301	National Stadium – Cardiff	Australia
12	19 Jan 74	302	National Stadium – Cardiff	Scotland
13	2 Feb 74	303	Lansdowne Road	Ireland
14	16 Feb 74	304	National Stadium – Cardiff	France
15	16 Mar 74	305	Twickenham	England
	15 Feb 75	307	National Stadium – Cardiff	England
16	1 Mar 75	308	Murrayfield	Scotland
17	15 Mar 75	309	National Stadium – Cardiff	Ireland
18	17 Jan 76	311	Twickenham	England

	RESULT	SHIRT NO	NOTES	POINTS	MIN
FNC	Drew 8–8	16	repl Gerald Davies 79'		1
FNC	Won 30–9	–			
	Drew 6–6	14			80
FNC	Won 18–9	12			80
FNC	Won 17–13	–			
FNC	Won 11–6	10			80
FNC	Won 22–6	–			
FNC	Won 19–18	–			
FNC	Won 12–3	–			
FNC	Won 35–12	16	repl JPR Williams 25'		55
FNC	Won 20–6	–			
	Lost 16–19	10		12 (4p)	80
FNC	Won 25–9	10		2 (c)	80
FNC	Lost 9–10	10		6 (2p)	80
FNC	Won 16–12	10		8 (c,2p)	80
FNC	Lost 3–12	10		3 (d)	80
	Won 24–0	10		12 (4p)	80
FNC	Won 6–0	10		2 (c)	80
FNC	Drew 9–9	10		5 (c,p)	80
FNC	Drew 16–16	10		9 (3p)	80
FNC	Lost 12–16	10		8 (c,2p)	80
FNC	Won 20–4	–			
FNC	Lost 10–12	16	Repl John Bevan 26'		54
FNC	Won 32–4	10		12 (3c,2p)	80
FNC	Won 21–9	10			80

CAP	DATE	TEST NO	VENUE	OPPONENTS
19	7 Feb 76	312	National Stadium – Cardiff	Scotland
20	21 Feb 76	313	Lansdowne Road	Ireland
21	6 Mar 76	314	National Stadium – Cardiff	France
22	15 Jan 77	315	National Stadium – Cardiff	Ireland
23	5 Feb 77	316	Parc des Princes – Paris	France
24	5 Mar 77	317	National Stadium – Cardiff	England
25	19 Mar 77	318	Murrayfield	Scotland
26	4 Feb 78	319	Twickenham	England
27	18 Feb 78	320	National Stadium – Cardiff	Scotland
28	4 Mar 78	321	Lansdowne Road	Ireland
29	18 Mar 78	322	National Stadium – Cardiff	France

BRITISH & IRISH LIONS TEST MATCHES

1	8 Jun 74	35	Cape Town	South Africa
2	22 Jun 74	36	Pretoria	South Africa
3	13 Jul 74	37	Port Elizabeth	South Africa
4	27 Jul 74	38	Johannesburg	South Africa
5	18 Jun 77	39	Wellington	New Zealand
6	9 Jul 77	40	Christchurch	New Zealand
7	30 Jul 77	41	Dunedin	New Zealand
8	13 Aug 77	42	Auckland	New Zealand

	RESULT	SHIRT NO	NOTES	POINTS	MIN
FNC	Won 28–6	10		13 (2c,3p)	80
FNC	Won 34–9	10		19 (t,3c,3p)	80
FNC	Won 19–13	10		6 (2p)	80
FNC	Won 25–9	10	Capt	10 (2c,2p)	80
FNC	Lost 9–16	10	Capt		80
FNC	Won 14–9	10	Capt		80
FNC	Won 18–9	10	Capt	14 (t,2c,2p)	80
FNC	Won 9–6	10	Capt	9 (3p)	80
FNC	Won 22–14	10	Capt	6 (d,p)	80
FNC	Won 20–16	10	Capt		80
FNC	Won 16–7	10	Capt	10 (2t,c)	80

TOTAL 2190

	RESULT	SHIRT NO	NOTES	POINTS	MIN
	Won 12–3	10		9 (3p)	80
	Won 28–9	10		9 (t,c,p)	80
	Won 26–9	10		6 (2d)	80
	Drew 13–13	10		2 (c)	80
	Lost 12–16	10	Capt	9 (3p)	80
	Won 13–9	10	Capt	9 (3p)	80
	Lost 7–19	10	Capt		80
	Lost 9–10	10	Capt		80

CAP	DATE	TEST NO	VENUE	OPPONENTS
WALES XV				
1	14 Sep 68		Buenos Aires	Argentina
2	27 May 69		New Plymouth	Taranaki
3	25 Jun 69		Suva	Fiji
4	6 Oct 73		National Stadium – Cardiff	Japan
5	27 Nov 74		National Stadium – Cardiff	New Zealand XV
6	10 Sep 75		Hong Kong	Hong Kong
7	18 Sep 75		Tokyo	Japan B
8	24 Sep 75		Olympic Stadium – Tokyo	Japan
9	16 Oct 76		National Stadium – Cardiff	Argentina
BRITISH & IRISH LIONS TOUR MATCHES				
1	15 May 74		Potchefstroom	Western Transvaal
2	25 May 74		Port Elizabeth	Eastern Province
3	1 Jun 74		Cape Town	Western Province
4	11 Jun 74		Cape Town	Western Province Univs.
5	15 Jun 74		Johannesburg	Transvaal
6	9 Jul 74		East London	SA African XV
7	20 Jul 74		Durban	Natal
8	18 May 77		Masterton	Wairapapa-Bush
9	28 May 77		New Plymouth	Taranaki
10	1 Jun 77		Taumarunui	King Country/Wanganui
11	8 Jun 77		Dunedin	Otago
12	11 Jun 77		Invercargill	Southland
13	2 Jul 77		Wellington	Wellington
14	16 Jul 77		Hamilton	Waikato
15	23 Jul 77		Auckland	Auckland
16	6 Aug 77		Whangarei	North Auckland
17	9 Aug 77		Rotorua	Bay of Plenty
18	16 Aug 77		Suva	Fiji
19	10 Sep 77		Twickenham	Barbarians

RESULT	SHIRT NO	NOTES	POINTS	MIN
Lost 5–9	10			
Drew 9–9	10		3 (p)	
Won 31–11	10			
Won 62–14	10		26 (2t,9c)	
Lost 3–12	10		3 (p)	
Won 57–3	10		21 (t,7c,p)	
Won 34–7	10		5 (c,p)	
Won 82–6	10		34 (2t,10c,2p)	
Won 20–19	10		12 (4p)	

RESULT	SHIRT NO	NOTES	POINTS	MIN
Won 59–13	10		23 (7c,3p)	
Won 28–14	10		16 (2c,4p)	
Won 17–8	10		9 (3p)	
Won 26–4	10			
Won 23–15	10		11 (c,3p)	
Won 56–10	10			
Won 34–6	10		18 (3c,4p)	
Won 41–13	10	Capt	9 (3c,p)	
Won 21–13	10	Capt	5 (c,p)	
Won 60–9	10	Capt	20 (t,8c)	
Won 12–7	10	Capt	12 (4c)	
Won 20–12	10	Capt		
Won 13–6	10	Capt	9 (3p)	
Won 18–13	10	Capt	6 (2p)	
Won 34–15	10	Capt	4 (t)	
Won 18–7	10	Capt	14 (c,4p)	
Won 23–16	14	Capt	15 (5p)	
Lost 21–25	10	Capt	13 (7,3c,p)	
Won 23–14	10	Capt	8 (c,2p)	

CAP	DATE	TEST NO	VENUE	OPPONENTS
BARBARIANS				
1	28 Mar 70		Cardiff Arms Park	Cardiff
2	29 Mar 70		St Helens – Swansea	Swansea
3	9 May 70		Murrayfield	Scotland XV
4	26 Sep 70		Lansdowne Road	Dublin Wanderers
5	24 Oct 70		Gosforth	Fiji
6	27 Jan 73		National Stadium – Cardiff	New Zealand XV
7	27 Dec 75		Welford Road – Leicester	Leicester
8	24 Jan 76		National Stadium – Cardiff	Australia XV
9	16 Apr 76		Recreation Ground – Penarth	Penarth
10	29 May 76		Boston	New England
11	2 Jun 76		Vancouver	British Colombia
12	5 Jun 76		Edmonton	Alberta
13	12 Jun 76		Toronto	All Canada
14	17 Jun 76		Halifax, Nova Scotia	Atlantic All Stars
15	4 Oct 76		The Greenyards	Melrose
16	24 Feb 77		Franklin's Gardens – Northampton	East Midlands
17	24 Mar 78		Recreation Ground – Penarth	Penarth
18	16 Dec 78		National Stadium – Cardiff	New Zealand XV
19	4 Apr 80		Recreation Ground – Penarth	Penarth
20	8 Apr 80		Rodney Parade – Newport	Newport

	DATE		VENUE	OPPONENTS
CUP FINALS				
	6 May 72		National Stadium – Cardiff	Neath
	28 Apr 73		National Stadium – Cardiff	Cardiff
	26 Apr 75		National Stadium – Cardiff	Aberavon
	24 Apr 76		National Stadium – Cardiff	Swansea

	RESULT	SHIRT NO	NOTES	POINTS	MIN
	Won 30–28	10		3 (d)	
	Won 24–8	10		6 (2d)	
	Won 33–17	10			
	Won 30–9	10			
	Lost 9–29	10			
	Won 23–11	10		7 (2c,p)	
	Won 20–11	10		4 (2c)	
	Won 19–7	10		11 (t,2c,p)	
	Lost 30–36	10			
	Won 40–12	10		12 (6c)	
	Won 34–15	10		18 (3c,4p)	
	Won 56–4	10		12 (6c)	
	Won 29–4	10		14 (c,4p)	
	Won 76–0	10		16 (2t,4c)	
	Won 47–17	10		16 (5c,2p)	
	Won 57–7	10		23 (3t,4c,p)	
	Won 84–12	10		20 (10c)	
	Lost 16–18	10		8 (c,2p)	
	Lost 22–29	10		2 (c)	
	Won 13–8	10		9 (3p)	

	RESULT	SHIRT NO	NOTES	POINTS	MIN
WRU Cup	Lost 9–15	10	Capt		
WRU Cup	Won 30–7	10		18 (3c,4p)	
WRU Cup	Won 15–6	10	Capt	4 (t)	
WRU Cup	Won 16–4	10	Capt	12 (4p)	

Index

Ackford, Paul 98, 162
Adidas 75–6
Andrew, Rob 89, 97, 98, 99, 222, 232
Andrews, Mark 264
Argentina 223–4
Australia 144, 217–19, 255, 257, 260, 264
  1991: 18, 46, 96–7, 99–100
  1999: 102
  2001: 144–55

Back, Neil 124, 161, 265, 266
Barbarians 240
Barnes, Stuart 226
Barnwell, Keith 189
Bassey, Shirley 100
Bastiat, Jean-Pierre 1, 5
Bateman, Allan 16
Bath 167
Batty, Grant 131
Beaumont, Bill 112, 246
Bedford 169–70
Bedford, Tommy 120

Benazzi, Abdel 89
Bennett, James 196, 275, 279, 280, 281, 288
Bennett, Pat 5, 39, 92, 95, 121, 128, 136, 152, 180, 183, 275, 280, 281, 282
Bennett, Phil
  Argentina 1968: 32
  Australia 1969: 145
  car accident 280–2
  Distel 74
  family life 39, 78, 127–8, 275, 282
  fitness 13–14, 177
  football 173, 175–6
  France 1970: 36
  Gullivers tours 88, 121, 145
  homesickness 136, 138
  injuries 38, 118
  Lions captain 2, 39, 126–43, 247–8
  media work 42, 191, 269–73
  New Zealand 1977: 39

retirement decision 1–8
rugby league 76–7
sales rep 274–5
self-doubt 129
sports development officer 275–6
sports shop 275
steelworks 274
teenage years 174–6
travel 73–4
Wales 1968: 31
Wales captain 1, 39, 239
West Wales 1967: 32
see also Llanelli; Wales
Bennett, Steven 5, 127, 128, 153, 196, 275, 279, 280, 282, 288
Bennett, Stuart 127
Bentley, John 124
Bergiers, Roy 181, 205
Bernat-Salles, Philippe 104
Best, George 157, 158, 213
Bevan, Derek 89
Bevan, John 39, 41
Blanco, Serge 254
Boobyer, Neil 201

Booth, Steve 166, 167
Botica, Frano 189–90
Bowen, Bleddyn 15–16, 42, 43
Bowring, Kevin 11, 51, 52–5, 228
boxing 277–8
Boyce, Max 101
Brace, Onllwyn 270
Bridgend 290
Bristow, Eric 68, 69
Brive 167
Brooke, Zinzan 265, 266
Brown, Gordon 117, 123, 130, 185, 249
Brown, Tony 24
Bunce, Frank 96, 259
Burrell, Dodd 139
Burrell, George 130
Burton, Mike 246
Busby, Sir Matt 157

Caerphilly 290
Calder, Finlay 266
Califano, Christian 262–3
Callard, Jon 167
Calzaghe, Joe 278
Campbell, Ollie 223
Campese, David (Campo) 97, 98, 218, 254–5
Canada 49
Cardiff 21, 50, 159, 167, 173, 210, 228, 286, 290
Carling, Bill 92
Carling, Will 90, 98, 99, 256
Castaignede, Thomas 10, 59
Catt, Mike 232, 240
Celtic countries 27
Charles, Prince 2
Charlton, Bobby 157
Charvis, Colin 59, 80–1, 101, 232, 292
Cholley, Gerard 164
Clement, Bill 71–3
clubs 16–17, 23, 25, 285–7, 289–91
coaching 29–51, 185, 186, 272

Cobner, Terry 2, 4, 14, 15, 41, 56, 135–6, 141, 288
Codey, David 105
Connor, Shaun 62
Conteh, John 278
corporate hospitality 161
Cotton, Fran 117, 120, 245–9, 262, 280
cricket 278–9
criticism 133, 273
Croft, Robert 279
Curvis, Brian 278

Dalglish, Kenny 249
Dallaglio, Lawrence 266, 267, 268
darts 68–70
David, Tommy 179
Davies, Adrian 92
Davies, Alan 47–50, 95
Davies, Ash 180
Davies, Gareth 8, 15
Davies, Gerald 3, 5, 8, 14, 20, 22, 23, 37, 240
Davies, Howard (Ash) 174
Davies, Jonathan 16, 42, 43, 224–9, 259, 268
Davies, Leigh 53
Davies, Mel 188, 189, 190
Davies, Mervyn 39, 117, 126, 133, 139
Davies, Nigel 186, 201, 202
Davies, Phil 186, 201
Davies, Terry 107
Dawes, John 31, 35–40
1978: 5
Bennett 127
character 34
Lions 129, 130, 132, 136, 139, 143
London Welsh 179
Dawson, Matt 140, 148–9, 232
Delaney, Lawrence 177, 202
der Beer, Jannie 102–3
Devereux, John 16
Distel, Sacha 74
Dominici, Christophe 104

Dooley, Wade 98, 268
du Plesis, Morne 117
du Randt, Os 263
Duckham, David 280
Duggan, Willie 137, 142
Dunn, Dai 282
Dunvant 22, 24

Eales, John 96, 263–4
Ebbw Vale 57, 286, 290
Edwards, Gareth 39
1973: 133
1977: 74
1978: 3, 6, 7
1999: 19
Bennett 214
character 236–41
Lions 117, 118, 119, 125
mentoring 63
professionalism 75, 83
retirement 2, 8, 14
tennis 242
Ella, Mark 154, 218–19, 259, 260
England 220–2, 248, 286, 288
1991: 97–100
1995: 89–92
1999: 102
2002: 26–7
clubs 25
coaches 55
Europe 160–1
professionalism 82–3
winning 25–7
Eriksson, Sven Goran 29
Erskine, Joe 278
Europe 156–71
European Cup see Heineken Cup
Evans, Alan 68
Evans, Alex 49–50, 87–8
Evans, Ben 63, 292–3
Evans, Denis 19
Evans, Gareth 5
Evans, Geoff 87
Evans, Ieuan 16, 42, 62, 87–8, 121, 167, 186, 201, 254, 255, 268
Evans, Peter 210

Evans, Stuart 16
Evans, Trevor 131

FA Cup Finals 21
fans 161–3, 193
  Australian 144
  English 26–7, 91
  European 165
  expectations 4
  Lions 110, 115, 116,
    120, 146, 147
  Llanelli 202, 274
  Neath 270
  New Zealand 104
  Pontypool 270
  Scottish 103
  South African 93
  Welsh 4, 7, 9–10, 11, 34,
    52, 104, 288, 289–90
Farr-Jones, Nick 154, 260
Faulkner, Charlie 14, 81,
  262
Felinfoel 143, 285
Felinfoel Youth 176
Fenwick, Steve 7, 14, 75,
  141, 205, 258
fitness 177
Fitzpatrick, Sean 87, 95,
  263
Five Nations 49, 59
football 156–8, 287
Ford, Steve 188
forwards 261–2
Fouroux, Jacques 258
France 26, 254, 258, 262,
  286
  1970: 36
  1977: 74
  1978: 5–7
  1988: 42
  1998: 9–10, 52
  1999: 59, 103–4
  Europe 160
Fraser, Liz 69
friendships 280, 282–3

Gale, Norman 72
Gallacher, Stuart 188,
  189
Gallion, Jerome 5, 6
Galthie, Fabien 10

Garbajosa, Xavier 10
George, Eddie 121
Gethin, Dennis 288
Gibbs, Scott 16, 60, 101,
  121–2, 259, 268
Gibson, Mike 3
Giggs, Ryan 79
Glamorgan 278, 279
Glas, Stephane 10
Going, Sid 137
Goodall, Ken 214
Grainger, Keith 25
Grand Slam 1, 5, 7
Gravell, Ray (Grav) 2, 14,
  42, 132–3, 179, 202–7
Gray, Tony 41–2, 43
great players 232
Greenwood, Will 232
Gregan, George 260
Grewcock, Danny 82
Griffiths, Dewi 271
Griffiths, Glanmor 20, 21,
  22, 67, 288
Griffiths, Ron 270
Guscott, Jeremy 98, 122,
  228, 259, 268

Haden, Andy 137
Hadley, Adrian 16, 42
Hain, Peter 121
Halifax 76–7
Hall, Mike 88
Hamer, Malcolm 68
Hamilton, Gordon 97
Hansen, Steve 27, 200,
  291–3
Harris, Des 116
Harrison, Justin 152
Hastings, Gavin 254, 268
Hayward, Byron 65
Healey, Austin 140,
  148–9, 150, 160, 161,
  166
Heath, Ted 121
Heineken Cup 158–63,
  170
Henry, Graham 30, 53,
  55–67
  1998: 57–8
  1999 : 18, 59–60, 64–6,
    100, 101

2001: 37, 66, 67, 148,
  149, 150, 151, 152,
  180
2002: 27, 66
former internationals
  61–4
mentoring 63–4
Henson, Gavin 294
Herbert, Peter 189, 195
Hill, Andy 181
Holmes, Terry 8, 15, 260,
  268
Hopkins, Chico 179
Horan, Tim 99, 105,
  257–8
Howarth, Shane 24, 65,
  101
Howley, Rob 53, 54, 63,
  66, 101, 121, 260
Hudson, Tom 177
Humphreys, David 169
Humphreys, Jonathan 88,
  92

Imbernon, Jean-François
  164
international players,
  former 61–4
International Rugby Board
  18
Ireland 2, 3–4, 26, 66, 160
Irvine, Andy 117, 138,
  249–51
Italy 26

Jackson, Peter 38
James, Carwyn
  Bennett 174–5
  Llanelli 169, 173, 178,
    179, 180, 181, 182–5
  media 133, 139
  rugby's future 17, 34–5
  Wales 49
James, Dafydd 147
Jenkins, Albert 172–3
Jenkins, Gareth (Gypo) 48,
  49, 101, 184, 185,
  186–7, 200
Jenkins, Neil 6, 10, 59, 62,
  63, 101, 121, 122,
  229–31, 232

John, Alan 212
John, Barry 36, 133, 139,
    176, 195, 211–15, 238
John, Clive 212
John, Dennis 58
Johnson, Martin (Jonno)
    criticism 139–40
    England 82, 161, 232,
        267, 268
    Henry 149
    Lions 37, 122, 123, 124,
        231
    professionalism 79, 82
Jones, Alan 278
Jones, Colin 278
Jones, David Parry 271
Jones, Derwyn 88, 92
Jones, DK 174
Jones, Eifion 278
Jones, Gwyn 20, 201
Jones, Ian 264
Jones, Ivor 173
Jones, Jeff 154
Jones, Ken 107
Jones, Leigh 62
Jones, Lewis 173
Jones, Lyn 186
Jones, Mark 16
Jones, Michael 265, 266
Jones, Robert 45, 260
Jones, Simon 154, 276,
    279
Jones, Stephen 63,
    199–200

Kafer, Rod 166
Kay, Ben 82
Keane, Roy 161
Kennedy, Ken 114
Kinnock, Neil 108
Kirk, David 105
Kirwan, John 255
Knight, Lawrie 141
Kronfeld, Josh 166, 266
Kyle, Jackie 209

Lam, Pat 96
Lamaison, Christophe 10,
    104
Laporte, Bernard 160
Laws, Brian 189

Lazarenko, Cliff 69–70
Leicester 160, 161, 166–7
Leonard, Jason 98, 263,
    268
Lewis, Allan 186, 225
Lewis, Emyr 186, 201
Lewis, Tony 279
Lievremont, Thomas 10
Lima, Brian 96
Lions 107–8, 152, 246
    99 call 119, 120
    1971: 237
    1974: 108–10, 113–20,
        182, 246–7
    1977: 2, 39, 126–43,
        247–8, 250
    1997: 121, 150–1, 231
    2001: 67, 144–55
Little, Jason 99
Little, Walter 259
Llanelli 13–14, 172–5,
    176–92
    Bedford 169–70
    captain 129
    Europe 159–60, 165, 168
    James 17, 34–5
    Leicester 166
    New Zealand 178, 181
    players 163, 193–207
    support 290
    Welsh Cup 169, 241
    Welsh team 48
Lloyd, John 40–1, 68, 282
Lloyd, Leon 166
Lomu, Jonah 87, 89–90,
    94, 104, 240, 256–7
London Scottish 79
Lowe, John 68, 69
Lynagh, Michael 97,
    217–18, 259

MacLean, John 206
Mallett, Nick 58
Manchester United 156–7,
    276–7
Mandela, Nelson 86, 93–4,
    110–11
Marshall, Pat 131
Martin, Allan 6, 14, 42
Matthews, Cerys 100
May, Phil 177, 202

Maynard, Matthew 279
McBride, Willie John
    Bennett 280
    captain 113, 124
    character 233–6
    Lions 109, 110, 113,
        115, 118, 119, 120
    team talk 122–3, 180
McBryde, Robin 82, 201
McCoist, Ally 249
McDowell, Steve 262
McGeechan, Ian 117, 126,
    150–1, 189, 222
McLauchlan, Ian (Mighty
    Mouse) 117, 246, 249
McRae, Duncan 145
Meads, Colin 235, 243
media 131, 133, 135, 139,
    140
Mehrtens, Andrew 55
mentoring 63–4
midweek players 150–1
Millar, Syd 114, 118, 151
Millennium Stadium 20,
    21, 100
Miller, Eric 124
Moon, Rupert 177, 201–2
Moore, Brian 98
Morgan, Cliff 173, 209–11
Morgan, Craig 294
Morgan, Doug 137, 141
Moriarty, Paul 16
Morris, Darren 63, 293
Morris, Trevor 175
Mourie, Graham 141
Munster 161
Murphy, Geordan 166
Murray, Ed 168

Nash, David 30, 31
Neary, Tony 246
Neath 45, 46, 79, 129,
    225–6, 270, 290
New Zealand 262, 263,
    264, 265–6
    1969: 243
    1971: 243–4
    1972: 178, 181
    1977: 2, 39, 129–43,
        247–8, 250
    1987: 105

1988: 42
1995: 89–90, 256
1997: 54–5
1999: 103–4
Newcastle 221–2
Newport 22, 24–5, 191, 216, 290
No. 10 position 208
Norster, Bob 16, 49, 95
Northampton 167, 189
Ntamack, Emile 165

O'Connor, Terry 131
O'Driscoll, Brian 79, 147–8, 259
O'Gara, Ronan 145
opinions 133, 252, 269, 272
Orange Free State 118
Orr, Phil 130
Osborne, Billy 137, 141
Owen, Huw and Carol 283
Owen, Johnny 278
Owen, Michael 294

Paparemborde, Robert 5, 164
Parker Pen Shield 170
Parks, Richard 294
Peel, Bert 198–9
Peel, Dwayne 198, 199, 294
Perpignan 163, 165
Phillips, Rowland 16
Pickering, David 64, 288
Pienaar, François 86
Poidevan, Simon 154, 265
Pontypridd 23, 167–8, 230, 290
Pooler 270
Porta, Hugo 223–4
press conferences 44
Price, Graham 63, 81, 131, 262
Price, Terry 174
Probyn, Jeff 98
Proctor, Wayne 186, 201
professionalism 13, 19, 21, 70–83, 188, 273
Pugh, Vernon 18–19, 20, 78

Quinnell, Craig 59, 293
Quinnell, Derek 2, 14, 41, 43, 141, 194–5, 198
Quinnell, Scott 16, 59, 79, 101, 147, 148, 191, 194, 195–8, 268

Ramsey, Sir Alf 30
Rees, Leighton 68, 69
Rees, Peter 177
referees 120
Regan, Robbie 278
RFU (Rugby Football Union) 22, 248
Richards, David 8
Richards, Dean 166
Richmond 79
Ring, Mark 42, 95–6
Rives, Jean-Pierre 5, 7, 74
Robertson, Bruce 137
Robinson, Jason 79, 147, 221, 267
Robinson, Steve 278
Rogers, Peter 101
Rowlands, Clive 31–4
Ruddock, Mike 48, 56
Rugby Football Union (RFU) 22, 248
rugby league, players move to 16, 43, 44, 76, 196, 216, 226–7, 259
rugby union
league players return 228
payment 70
Welsh decline 12–28, 286
Rutherford, John 222–3
Ryan, John 44

Sadourny, Luc 10
Scotland 15, 26, 27–8, 160, 222–3, 250, 251
Sella, Philippe 257, 258–9
Shelford, Wayne (Buck) 265
Shepherd, Don 278
Sherlock, Geoff 282
Sinkinson, Brett 65, 101
Six Nations 26, 27–8, 66, 85, 162, 287
Skinner, Mick 98
Skrela, Jean-Claude 5, 6, 7

Slattery, Fergus 117
Smith, Ollie 167
Smith, Tom 121
Sole, David 268
South Africa 11, 86, 107–25, 260
1974: 237–8
1998: 58
1999: 102
2002: 83, 292
Soweto 111
sponsorship 75–6
St Helens 77
Stander, Rompy 112
Stein, Jock 173
Stransky, Joel 94
superclubs 289–91
Swansea 163–4, 270, 285–6, 290
Swansea Town 175

Taylor, Hemi 88
Taylor, Mark 101
Teague, Mike 98, 267
team talks 32–3, 122–3
Teichmann, Gary 24
Telfer, Jim 121
tennis 242
Terfel, Bryn 101
Thomas, Alun 114, 118
Thomas, Arwel 53
Thomas, Brian 129
Thomas, Delme 72, 177, 181, 204, 235
Thomas, Eddie 278
Thomas, Iestyn 63
Thomas, JBG 131
Thomas, Peter 159, 286
Thomas, Roy 82
Thomas, Wynford and Pat 283
Thorburn, Paul 105
Tobias, Errol 112
Top Cat see Rowlands, Clive
Tournaire, Franck 165
Townsend, Gregor 222–3
training 34, 37
Tri-Nations countries 27, 287–8
Triple Crown 2, 3, 16, 39

Trueman, Fred 69
Tuilagi, Freddie 167

Ulster 168–9
Underwood, Rory 98, 268
Underwood, Tony 89
Uttley, Roger 117, 126, 246

Van der Westhuizen, Joost 260–1
Visser, Chute 112, 118

Waldron, Ron 45–6
Wales
  1970s 40, 126
  1980s 40–4
  1990s 44–51, 52–65
  1999: 18, 294
  2001: 66
  2002: 66, 292
  cash crisis 285–7
  coaches 30–51
  decline 12–28, 286
  future 284–95
  Grand Slam 1, 5, 7
  losing matches 15, 18, 45, 46
  selectors 17, 31, 34, 38
  team 8, 14, 15–16, 42, 101
  Triple Crown 2, 3, 16
  World Cup 85
  younger players 284, 294
  see also WRU (Welsh Rugby Union)
Wallace, Paul 121

Walters, Ian 189, 190
Watkin, Steven 279
Watkins, David 61, 215–17
Watkins, Sir Tasker 22
Watt, Jim 278
Wells, John 166
Welsh qualification 65
Welsh Rugby Union see WRU
Wembley 9
West Wales 1967: 32
Western Samoa 95, 96, 101
Wheel, Geoff 14, 164
Wheeler, Peter 141, 246
Wilkinson, Jonny 79, 148, 149, 200, 220–2, 267
Williams, Brynmor 137
Williams, Chester 111
Williams, JJ 2, 14, 62
  1977: 74
  1978: 3–4, 6
  Gravell 205–6
  Jenkins 231, 269–70
  Lions 110, 117, 118, 136, 141
  Llanelli 183
  training 37
Williams, JPR 2, 8, 14, 62
  1977: 74
  1978: 3
  character 241–5
  Edwards 239–40
  Lions 114–15, 117, 120
  London Welsh 179
  professionalism 75
  training 37

Williams, Ray 17, 36
Williams, RH 107, 174
Williams, Rhys 294
Wilson, David 265
Windsor, Bobby 2, 4, 14, 72–3, 75, 81, 82, 262
  Lions 1974: 115, 117, 119, 246
Winstone, Howard 277
Winterbottom, Peter 98, 265, 266, 268
Winterbottom, Walter 30
Wood, Keith 121, 263, 268
Woodward, Clive 55, 82, 84–5, 90, 152, 161, 222
World XV Invitational matches 112
World Cup 85, 106
  1987: 105
  1991: 47–8, 95–100
  1995: 50, 86–95, 256
  1999: 65–6, 100–6
WRU (Welsh Rugby Union)
  chairmen 19, 20
  coaches 30–51, 291
  management 21–3, 288
  professionalism 70–2
  Working Party report 2001: 20, 22–3
  see also Wales

Young, Dai 16, 101, 232
Young, David 263
young people 25, 276, 284–5